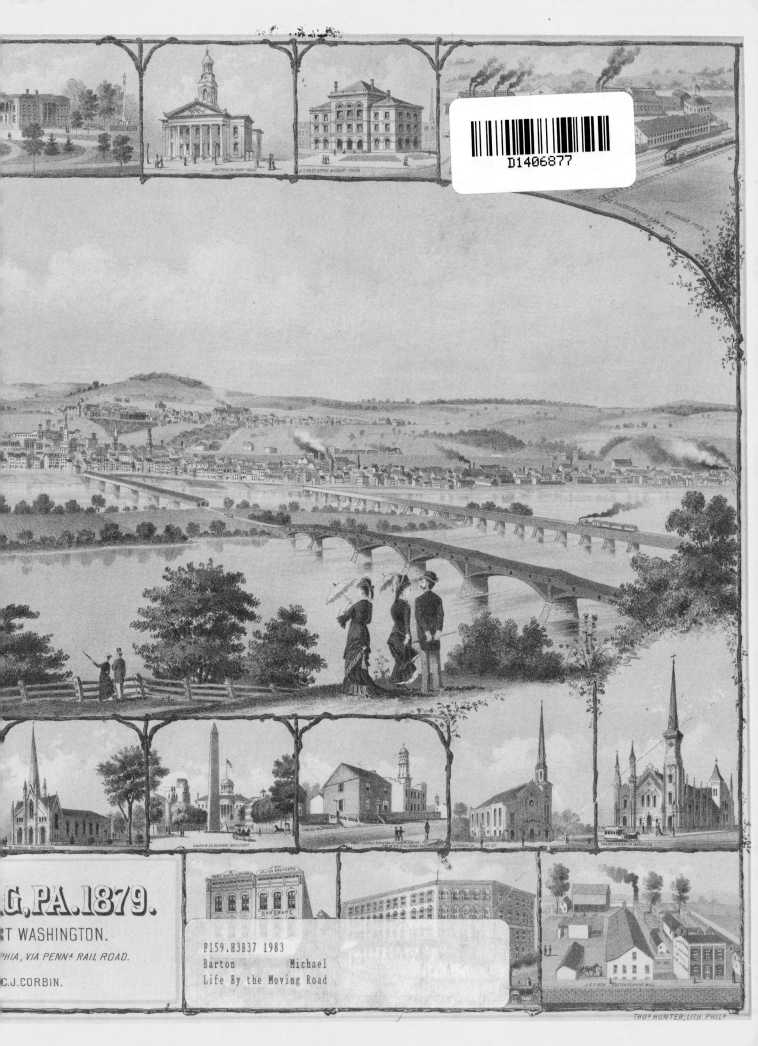

...G, PA. 1879.

...RT WASHINGTON.

...PHIA, VIA PENNᴬ RAIL ROAD.

...C. J. CORBIN.

THOˢ HUNTER, LITH. PHILᴬ

LIFE BY THE MOVING ROAD

The dome of the current capitol has crowned Harrisburg since the building was dedicated in 1906.

LIFE BY THE MOVING ROAD

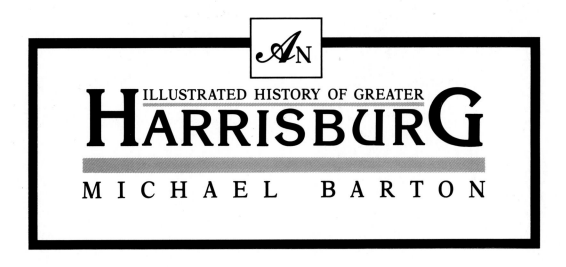

AN ILLUSTRATED HISTORY OF GREATER

HARRISBURG

MICHAEL BARTON

PICTORIAL RESEARCH BY IRWIN RICHMAN AND JOHN BECK

"PARTNERS IN PROGRESS" BY MARK H. DORFMAN

PRODUCED IN COOPERATION WITH
THE CHAMBER OF COMMERCE—GREATER HARRISBURG AREA
WINDSOR PUBLICATIONS, WOODLAND HILLS, CALIFORNIA

Windsor Publications, Inc.
History Book Division

Publisher: John M. Phillips
Editorial Director: Lissa Sanders
Production Supervisor: Katherine Cooper
Senior Picture Editor: Teri Davis Greenberg
Senior Corporate History Editor: Karen Story
Corporate History Editor: Phyllis Gray
Marketing Director: Ellen Kettenbeil
Production Manager: James Burke
Design Director: Alex D'Anca
Art Production Manager: Dee Cooper
Typesetting Manager: E. Beryl Myers
Proofreading Manager: Doris R. Malkin

Staff for *Life By The Moving Road*
Senior Editor: F. Jill Charboneau
Picture Editor: Jim Mather
Copy Editor: Leslie King
Editorial Assistants: Susan Block, Judith Hunter,
    Patricia Morris
Sales Managers: Ernie Fredette, William Koons
Sales Representative: Evelyn Burian
Proofreaders: Henriette Henderson, Jeff Leckrone,
    Kaylene Ohman
Production Artists: Beth Bowman, Julie Sloto
Typographers: Barbara Neiman, Cynthia Pinter
Designer: Alex D'Anca
Layout Artist: Melinda Wade

Library of Congress Cataloging in Publication Data

Barton, Michael.
    Life by the moving road.

    Bibliography: p.
    Includes index.
        1. Harrisburg (Pa.)—History. 2. Harrisburg (Pa.)—
Description. 3. Harrisburg (Pa.)—Industries.
4. Harrisburg Region (Pa.)—History. 5. Harrisburg
Region (Pa.)—Description and travel. 6. Harrisburg
Region (Pa.)—Industries. I. Dorfman, Mark.
II. Title.
F159.H3B37   1983   974.8'18   83-14839
ISBN 0-89781-064-3

DEDICATION

For Jane, Jonathan, and Effie,
although they wanted me instead

Ralph Trembly derived this hand-colored lithograph of the burning of John Harris from the late-19th-century painting by Benjamin F. Reeder, who borrowed heavily from Benjamin West's famous 1771 painting "Penn's Treaty with the Indians" for the composition. Courtesy, Historical Society of Dauphin County (HSDC)

CONTENTS

Acknowledgments   *12*

Introduction   *13*

Epigraph   *15*

I

Prologue: The Moving Road That Used To Be   *17*

II

1733: The Attempted History of John Harris' Burning   *25*

III

October 3, 1794: George Washington and the Start of Stopping By   *35*

IV

January 14, 1836: The First Crusades   *41*

V

February 25, 1858: Seven Women Healing   *47*

VI

June 20-July 4, 1863: The Lesser Battles of Greater Harrisburg   *57*

VII

April 29, 1877: The Funeral of Harry Cook in the Old "Ate" Ward   *67*

VIII

September 14, 1885: Children's Day at the Dauphin County Centennial Celebration   *75*

IX
January 1, 1904: Harrisbrag   83

X
1911: Aliens in Israel   91

XI
1917: Cub's Ragtime   99

XII
March 31, 1928: The Bottom Line   111

XIII
July 14, 1939: Two Tales of a City   115

XIV
May 3, 1946-June 4, 1981: Harve Taylor's Secret Diary   121

XV
Epilogue: The Moving Road That Might Be   128

XVI
Greater Harrisburg's Neighbors by Mark Dorfman   145

XVII
Partners in Progress   151

Patrons   216
Bibliography   217
Index   220

Mechanics Bank   Dauphin Bank   Harris Mansion & Grave   Penns

VIEW OF

This "View of Harrisburg, Penn." dates from 1855 and was "Drawn on Stone from Nature and The Daguerreotype by J.T. Williams, York, Pa." During the pre-Civil War period many American cities received the "bird's eye" treatment by American artists and publishers. Vignettes around the borders of this large format (35" x 23") graphic show notable buildings, most of which are now destroyed or altered beyond recognition. (HSDC)

ACKNOWLEDGMENTS

Life By the Moving Road is a series of essays about what I think are meaning-filled events in the history of Greater Harrisburg. You might call the essays written snapshots. Some are taken of important people and famous events, such as John Harris' capture and George Washington's visit, but most record lesser beings on unknown days, such as Harry Cook's funeral and "Cub" Huston's boyhood.

I tried to write about fresh subjects, such as the State Lunatic Hospital, or else subjects I thought still needed writing about, such as the 1885 Centennial. I decided not to write about those subjects I thought we are lucky to know enough about for now, such as the Paxton Boys, the Whig Convention, the Capitol Graft, the life of Milton Hershey, or just about anything Paul Beers has covered well already. (I look forward to his "City Contented/City Discontented" newspaper columns being turned into a book.) I tried to use evidence which had not been employed before, such as the diaries of R.I. Young and Sallie Simonton, and I also tried to broadcast wider some new and excellent scholarship, such as Professor William Wilson's research on the "City Beautiful" movement and John Bodnar's work on the social history of Steelton.

All this amounts to saying that this somewhat unusual and surely incomplete history represents my fallible judgments to a large extent and the reliable industry of other historians to an even greater extent. My purpose throughout has been to help readers "feel" as well as know Greater Harrisburg's past daily life.

I am specifically indebted to my partners, Irwin Richman and Mark Dorfman, for their expert work on the illustrations and business histories. The three of us are beholden to the staff and members of the Historical Society of Dauphin County, who let us rifle their files and roam loose in their shop. Not once did they betray their panic. Indeed, very much of the evidence in this book comes straight from their collections.

I appreciate the many people who, when they found out I was working on this history, invited me to use their memories and their private material in my research. I promised some of them I'd try to use them, but I wasn't able to, and I apologize for that. I boldly invited myself in on other friends and colleagues to ask for help. I say thank you again.

The Greater Harrisburg Chamber of Commerce and the book's Advisory Board sponsored and promoted this project. I must certainly acknowledge their patronage and their trust.

I owe much to Windsor Publications and my delightful senior editor, Jill Charboneau, who gave me nearly complete freedom and wholly intelligent advice, from the day I proposed a different sort of book to the day I sent in the overdue manuscript, (which my copy editor, Leslie King, then expertly tinkered with.)

Finally, I am grateful to the past of Greater Harrisburg for being such a grand story.

INTRODUCTION

When Dr. Michael Barton began his assignment of writing *Life By the Moving Road*, he said he wanted to achieve "a feeling for place." He added that indeed there is a certain quality—not just random peculiarities, but deeply felt convictions and characteristics—to this place along the Susquehanna River that has been a community now for 265 years.

Harrisburg and Dauphin County both will celebrate their bicentennials in 1985. Two hundred years is a long time, and such a community evolves traditions, ways of thinking and traits that give it an identity. It would be strange if such a community, with its human warmth and occasional wraths, weren't a bit distinct with a heritage like that. As its citizens well know, their hometown isn't just another banana in the bunch of American regions.

It is one of life's fulfilling experiences for the transient, as well as the native-born, Harrisburgher to grow to be a part of this community's advantages, enthusiasms and even disappointments. The challenge to any Harrisburg writer is to delve beneath the surface, sort out the local varieties and vagations, and with receptive insight carefully distill the essence of such a proud and free people.

Dr. Barton has done the job with finesse. Devising an original, creative format to trace the epochs and with a lively style, he is able, like the best of the storytellers, to relate the joys and sorrows of *Life By the Moving Road*. Newcomers and old-timers, readers of all persuasion, should be delighted by this splendid volume, for it has the seriousness, the craftsmanship and charm, not just of another historical chronicle or series of essays, but of art.

Paul B. Beers,
associate editor,
Patriot-News

Troops from Harrisburg gathered at Camp Boas before seeing action during the Civil War. (HSDC)

This Taufshein, a birth and baptismal certificate, is a fine example of the Fraktur used by the Pennsylvania German population in the 18th and 19th centuries.

EPIGRAPH

"I beg your pardon," said the Mole, pulling himself together with an effort. "You must think me very rude, but all this is so new to me. So—this—is—a—River!"

"*The* River," corrected the Rat.

"And you really live by the river? What a jolly life!"

"By it and with it and on it and in it," said the Rat. "It's brother and sister to me, and aunts, and company, and food and drink, and (naturally) washing. It's my world, and I don't want any other. What it hasn't got is not worth having, and what it doesn't know is not worth knowing. Lord! the times we've had together!"

Kenneth Grahame
The Wind in the Willows

By the early 1840s, when this lithograph was made,
Harrisburg had become a thriving river port. It was the capital
of the Commonwealth of Pennsylvania; it boasted that great
engineering marvel of its day, the Camelback Bridge; and it
had already become an important rail center. (HSDC)

Right: Barges carried coal for Harrisburg down the
Susquehanna from nearby mines to be unloaded at Front
Street, shown here. Much coal was lost overboard along the
way, and, until the 1960s, barges salvaging coal from the
river bottom were a common sight. (HSDC)

I
THE MOVING ROAD
THAT USED TO BE

Gertrude Stein's charge against Oakland—"There's no there there"—cannot be put to Greater Harrisburg. There's a here here, a feeling for place come from custom and geography. The literal core of our history and sense of "here" is the Susquehanna River, and so it is important to know how the city's river was used in the past. But it is even more important to know that this is still the river's city.

The Great Valley of the Appalachian Mountains runs up from Alabama and across to Newfoundland. The narrow valley of the Susquehanna River goes down from New York to Chesapeake Bay. In southeastern Pennsylvania these valleys cross paths, and there is Greater Harrisburg, on the shores of the Susquehanna River, where the Cumberland part of the Great Valley from the west meets the Lebanon part of the Great Valley from the east. Trains, boats, ferries, canals, bridges, roads, and people all wind up knotted here, where the elder John Harris, without a bird's eye view, simply found a good spot to ford the river and sell some lots.

There is only one drawback to this convenient geography. The Susquehanna drains all the central part of Pennsylvania. Because this central part is hilly, the river receives all the rain water quickly and melting snow eventually. When the river freezes in the Winter, ice floes can also jam it in the Spring. It would be difficult to find a river more likely to overflow, and, since Harrisburg lies below its major feeding branches, a city more likely to flood.

The first recorded major flood was in 1744, the second in 1758, then 1772, 1784, 1786 (when the overflow left pumpkins from upstream all over), 1800, 1814, 1817, 1846 (when Camelback Bridge was half destroyed), 1865, 1889 (the first well-documented disaster), 1894, 1902 (when Camelback Bridge was finally destroyed), 1904, 1921, 1936 (the second worst), 1972 (the very worst), and 1975. Actually, these are only the floods mentioned most often. There have been more than 40 in the last 200 years.

We can tell from reading the diary of Mrs. Sallie Simonton that when you have felt one flood, you have felt them all. Her description seems close to what we ourselves might describe:

March 16th, 17th, 18th, 1865. Never since we became friends, and that is a long time ago, even so far back as I can remember, for I was born and raised on its banks, have I seen our usually placid river rise in such bold and defiant might as during the three days above named. The spring freshet . . . came upon us in all its devastating power. The bank was daily thronged with people, who with no little interest watched and waited to see if the old railroad bridge would give way before the mighty current of swollen waters as they lashed against its side. Almost contrary to our most sanguine expectations, with the aid of ropes and iron stays, it passed safely through the crisis, its battered sides bearing witness to the severity of the contest. Good for you old bridge. . . . Meanwhile, the waters

The flood of 1889 left the Camelback Bridge only somewhat intact, as can be seen in this photograph taken from the Cumberland County end of the bridge, on the west shore opposite Harrisburg. (HSDC)

Above: *The second worst flood to hit Harrisburg was that of March 1936. Shipoke is to the right, beyond the Reading Railroad Bridge. The photographer's boat was evidently stationed directly in front of the John Harris mansion. (HSDC)*

Left: *The Camelback Bridge endured for so many years and survived so much abuse because it was an elaborate and craftily engineered wooden structure. The beams, joists, and supports were all made big to withstand shock, and assembled so that individual members could easily be replaced when they began to decay. (HSDC)*

The Kelso Ferry House, on the West Shore near the Cumberland Valley Railroad Bridge, was built in 1734 and was used by ferry masters in the pre-bridge era. (HSDC)

began to creep stealthily over our nice green ward, laying waste trees, fences, etc., coming nearer and nearer even into our very abodes, taking lordly possession and shoving out the lawful owners. What was once terra firma became a waste of waters navigable by small craft. Here and there were to be seen some half dozen heads peering out of the top-most story of a dwelling while beneath was a little barge unloading its contents of bread and food for the hungry inmates. . . . At this juncture of affairs, river, canal, and creek united in forming one vast sea of water; . . . For three days we lived on an island, holding no communication with the outer world around us, every avenue of ingress and egress being closed. No

water, no gas, the works for the time being submerged, we were in fact transported to primitive times and made to realize the difference between the convenience of the present and the inconveniences of the past.

Otherwise, life on the moving road is not what is used to be. The river used to carry cargo. An early historian, J.P. Keller, wrote that in Spring, 1827, exactly 1,631 rafts, 1,370 arks, and about 300 keelboats ("broadhorns") passed Harrisburg. The rafts were trees lashed together, bound for lumber yards; the arks and broadhorns carried coal, flour, whiskey, and wheat. Another historian, the Reverend Silas

Swallow, writing in 1915, said one time he saw 20 lumber rafts on the river while he stood in one spot. The great rafts were 150 or 300 feet long, made of trees 25 to 80 feet long. The rafts were not more than 25 feet wide, in order to pass through the channels and rapids. Later, cargo used to be gotten from the river itself, as coal dredgers would scrape "black diamonds" from the bottom.

Steamboats used to be on the river. In 1825 three docked at Harrisburg on their way north. In 1826 one of them, the *Susquehanna*, exploded, and steamboating fizzled. Only the Millersburg ferry remains to remind us of the riverine travel.

The river used to be a place for grand fun. Hundreds of children would swim in it every summer day off City Island. Scores of rowboats and canoes used to be launched from private moorings or boat clubs along both banks. A large and popular dance floor used to be anchored in the river where a fellow, if he had a striped blazer and a straw skim-

mer, would take his gal and her chaperone for a date. There his corseted sweetheart could admire him for winning the single sculls race that afternoon, or for captaining the first-place crew.

They used to tell some good stories about the river. Reverend Swallow told two of them to the Historical Society of Dauphin County. They were about the men who worked the river.

The raftsmen were jolly crews not always mindful of others' rights, and by no means sticklers for the golden rule. . . . four jolly but hungry raftsmen asked a good house wife to sell them bread and pastry. She browbeat them as thieves, and they, intent on being what she trusted them to be, put two fence rails under her clay-formed garden oven and carried it and its half baked bread, pies and cakes to the raft, and then floated; meanwhile watching the contents of the oven that they might not get too well done. They feasted for two or three days. In their tramp return, two

As late as 1901, log rafts continued to float past the city. Within a few years, they too would be gone, and the Susquehanna would become an almost functionless presence in the life of the city. (HSDC)

A low river level, as in this photo from about 1900, was certainly less destructive than a flood, but it still created many problems for Harrisburg residents. (HSDC)

The Pennsylvania Canal and towpath, pictured here at the Dauphin Narrows about 1900, was then a major artery of transportation. The common mode of transportation has changed, however, and this site today is paved over to accomodate trucks and automobiles on Route 22. (HSDC)

The statewide canal system was an engineering wonder of 19th-century Pennsylvania. The canals carried both travelers and commercial goods until the 1920s. Traces of the canal bed and the towpath are still visible around Harrisburg. (HSDC)

weeks afterward, toward their home a hundred miles further north, they stopped and paid the good lady for the oven and its contents, and then tramped on northward. Ever after, it is said, she spoke well of the river men.

All the raftsmen of that period knew a pilot known as "Uncle Ben." Some of his descendants live in the vicinity of Harrisburg now. He was a logician of the practical type. A fellow worker steered the raft on which they were floating within a foot of a rock, and when Uncle Ben, the pilot, chided him for so close a call, he excused himself by saying, "a miss is as good as a mile." Uncle Ben dissented and they came near to blows in the hour's argument that followed. Next morning when the steersman awoke, laying on the raft with only a horse blanket for a bed, he was in a rage because someone while he slept had placed a putrid fish within an inch of his nose and he had been smelling the odor all night. Uncle Ben condoled with him, but this time chided him for ill temper, since "a miss is as good as a mile," and the fish had not touched his nose. Thereafter that particular raft was steered as far as possible from danger.

Today the old gritty uses of the river are dried up, the stories have stopped, and there is less playing in it. Since the city built a retaining wall of steps and the Dock Street dam down by Shipoke, it looks different—no more puddles and sand bars in the summer, or muddy, littered shorelines in the Spring. The water is now mainly a place for some bass fishing, power boating, and man drowning. While the river used to be, literally, part of our ancestors (they drank it until the city found a new source for water), and our ancestors used to be, literally, part of the river (it took all the city's sewage), now our sodality is only aesthetic. The ornamental Susquehanna lolls by, and we look at it, or jog along it. But each year we fear that Sallie's friend may still astonish.

Sinclair's lithograph of the attempted burning of John Harris certainly does not suggest that his assailants were intoxicated. In fact, the Indians appear quite soberly purposeful. Nor does the picture give any hint that Harris will shortly be dramatically rescued. (HSDC)

II
THE ATTEMPTED HISTORY OF JOHN HARRIS' BURNING

In 1733 America was a land of little villages. Of its nearly half million citizens, only 12,000 lived in Boston, 10,000 in Philadelphia, and 7,000 in New York (a city then merely twice the size of Charleston, South Carolina and Newport, Rhode Island). The rest of the world was larger in every way: in 1720, when six patients in Boston died from smallpox innoculations, 60,000 in Marseilles died from Bubonic plague, and 300,000 in Calcutta would soon die in an earthquake and wind storm.

By 1733 the elder John Harris had settled on the east shore of the Susquehanna River in south central Pennsylvania. Like other emigrants, he expected to escape those immense miseries of the Old World, and he also prefigured his ferry landing might become another peaceful and prosperous American village. So like earlier pioneers, such as New York's Peter Minuit and Philadelphia's William Penn, John Harris began to palaver and trade with the Indians. But in doing so, a particularly New World misery befell him—he was accosted by his customers. Their attempt to burn him is the first famous story of Greater Harrisburg's history. Many other white captives left written narratives of their adventure and internment, but Harris didn't, so his biographers and illustrators were able to retell and redraw the story, depending on the lessons they wanted to learn and then teach. Their search for a usable past is as interesting as what they thought they found.

1733:

One could call the elder John Harris a chicaning, gambling, slave-holding brewer. Or one could call him an inventive, foresighted, masterly pioneer. Call him both kinds of men at once or somebody in between them, but Harrisburg wants a history of its first settler, John Harris, and especially of his attempted burning by the Indians, and has had to settle for a story.

The story is a myth beyond the facts—"a belief embodying a visionary ideal"—since the mysterious establisher did not leave a detailed account of his actions or even his looks.

There has been no controversy about the ordinary facts of John Harris' life, so let us move right along to the most extraordinary "event" of his days at the ferry, paying close attention to the several versions of the story written by Harrisburg historians. The first version, in I. Daniel Rupp's *History of Dauphin County*, published in 1846, noted that the story of the attempted burning had "excited considerable interest" and had been the object of "much inquiry." Rupp's description of the event quotes from an account by George W. Harris, the first John Harris' great-grandson:

On one occasion, a band of Indians, who had been down the river, or as is said, to the East, on a trading excursion, came to his house. Some, or most of them, were intoxicated. They asked for lum, *meaning West India rum, as the modern whiskey was not then manufactured in Pennsylvania. Seeing they were already intoxicated, he feared mischief, if he gave them more; and he refused. They became enraged and seized him and tied him to the mulberry tree to burn him. Whilst they were proceeding to execute*

their purpose, he was released, after a struggle, by other Indians of the neighborhood, who generally came across the river. How the alarm was given to them, whether by firing a gun or otherwise, or by whom, is not now certainly known. In remembrance of this event, he afterwards directed that on his death he should be buried under the mulberry tree, which had been the scene of this adventure. Part of the trunk of this tree is still standing. It is ten feet up to the lowest limb, and the stump is eleven feet, six inches in circumference. The writer (G.W. Harris) of this has eaten mulberries from this tree, which was one of the largest of its species.

The second version of the assault, in George Morgan's *Annals of Harrisburg*, published 12 years later in 1858, shows plagiarism of Rupp:

. . . it happened one day that a number of Indians of the Mahanoy, Mahotongo or Shawanese tribe, (most probably the latter,) who had been down the river either on a predatory or trading expediton, stopped at the house of Mr. Harris on their return northward. Most, or all of them, were under the influence of liquor, and demanded of Mr. Harris an additional supply of lum, meaning West India rum, as the modern whiskey was not then manufactured in the Province. Perceiving that they were already intoxicated, and fearing mischief, Mr. Harris refused to grant the demand; whereupon they became greatly exasperated and dragged him to an adjoining mulberry tree, to which they firmly bound him.

And then Morgan worked on embellishment, adding much fuel to Harris' fire:

Here they declared their intention to

Left: *Relicwood was dearly loved by the 19th century. The root and slab are supposed to be pieces of the Mulberry Tree to which John Harris was tied. The gavel's silver band announces that it, too, was carved from the same sacred wood. Photo by Mark Dorfman (HSDC)*

Above: *This steel engraving from Dr. William H. Egle's History of the County of Dauphin (1883) is a curiosity in that it is identical with the anonymous watercolor shown on the back cover, except that Harris and all of the Indians (except for the innocuous group in the canoe) have been removed. Possibly the artist (or Dr. Egle) wanted to show a scene less frantic than the attempted burning and used the other picture as a source. (HSDC)*

G. Gilbert

torture and burn him alive, and bade him prepare for instant death. Dry wood was gathered and piled around his feet, and torches held in readiness to kindle it; the yells of the enraged savages echoed along the river shore and through the surrounding forest, while with demoniac gestures they danced around their victim. Death in its most cruel form was before him; and, bereft of hope, he gave himself up for lost. In vain he supplicated for mercy, and offered to give up everything in exchange for life; but the savages were deaf to his entreaties, and declared he should die. The flaming torch was advanced toward the pile, and about being applied, when a band of friendly Indians, supposed to have belonged to the Paxton tribe ... burst suddenly upon the scene and set him at liberty.

The one new feature of Morgan's version is his introduction of a new character in the drama:

These Indians were led on by a negro man named "Hercules," a slave belonging to Mr. Harris, who at the first alarm ran to the neighboring tribe to beg for succor, and now brought it to his master's relief. The deliverance was well-timed. A moment's delay would have been fatal. The presence of mind, the decision, the speed of this negro alone saved Mr. Harris; and so sensible was he of the great service rendered to him by this poor slave that he instantly emancipated him, and some of the descendants of the worthy Hercules resided in the borough for a number of years, enjoying their freedom, so nobly won.

The rescue, wrote Morgan, was "a signal deliverance; it was a manifest evidence of God's merciful interposition," and Harris' grave by the mulberry tree was likewise "a momento at once of savage ebriety, domestic fidelity, and above all, of the watchfullness of Him 'who alone can inflict or withold the stroke of death'." These "facts" had been gathered from an account of the incident published in 1828 by the legislator Samuel Breck, who had heard them from Robert Harris, the grandson of the elder John Harris. Robert "had received them as part of the traditional history of his family." Morgan's argument for trusting the tale asked his readers, in effect, to believe any idea that could not be disproved:

As there has never been any documentary evidence to substantiate this exciting episode in the life of Mr. Harris, there are some disposed to consider it a myth; yet we might very properly ask, has there been anything adduced to disprove it? Tradition may err; but it strikes us that if it does in this case, it would not have remained over one hundred and thirty years without being discovered.

The distinctive feature of Morgan's account is that he has inserted Hercules into the rescue; Rupp, you will recall, had George Harris saying that no one knew for certain who had given the alarm. Morgan believed that Robert Harris' memory was accurate when he included Hercules in the story he told to Samuel Breck in 1828, but that Robert's memory "had become impaired by old age" when he later left Hercules out of the story he told to William S. Reeder in 1839. But Morgan's effort to patch this problem does not explain why Robert and George Harris' accounts seem to disagree on so vital a point as Her-

Opposite: *G. Gilbert, whoever he may have been, captured the essential elements of the Harris burning with greater fidelity (although with even less skill) than Sinclair in this woodcut for the cover of a German-language almanac from the 1840s. The bad Indians are still passing the jug as they tipsily set out to accomplish their fell purpose, as the rescue party—complete with Hercules in the vanguard—rushes out of the woods. (HSDC)*

cules.

The third version of the story, in Dr. William Egle's *History of the County of Dauphin,* published in 1883, supplied as much corroborating evidence as Egle could still find. He began by admitting that there were "all sorts of versions" of the incident "and even doubts of its truthfulness." But Egle asserted that "It was no myth, this attempt to burn John Harris, and although the pen and pencil have joined in making there from a romance and heightened it with many a gaudy coloring, yet accurate resources have furnished us with the details here given." Egle revised Morgan's estimate that the "Shawanese" had assaulted Harris; in fact, Egle called them Harris' best allies and said they saved him from the raiding party, possibly of "Onondagoes." Egle's account of the event is otherwise brisk and not exceptional. His effort at substantiation took up more space than the re-telling of the attempted burning, and he even cited his own grandmother's testimony. Egle did add one new anecdote, however:

Mr. Maclay also furnished a statement, which he had heard from his mother, to the effect that some friends endeavored to dissuade the old gentleman, Mr. Harris, from his determination to be buried under the mulberry tree, alleging that the river bank was being washed away and the grave might be exposed and perhaps washed away, and that he ought to be buried in the Paxtang church graveyard, but that he silenced all argument by saying that if you bury me out in Paxtang, I'll get up and come back.

The fourth version, published in 1907, is hardly a variant. Luther

Reily Kelker wrote in the three-volume *History of Dauphin County,* that for "many of the facts herein given" about the attempted burning of Harris, he was "indebted to the late Dr. Egle." But Kelker understated his debt—every word of his four-page description comes straight from Egle's *History of the County of Dauphin,* excepting the last paragraph which Kelker wrote.

The fifth version first appeared in Marian Inglewood's "Then and Now in Harrisburg" column in the *Patriot;* it reappeared in her book of the same title published several months later, in 1925. The first "modern" cumulative version of the event, Inglewood's prose style is just efficiently plain, not ornately romantic. Here the Indians are dispossessed Native Americans, not passionate savages (they are not even "intoxicated"):

The Indians who lived here were in the main friends of Mr. Harris and the other settlers, although a band occasionally happened along who resented the intrusion of the white man and tried to make things unpleasant for him. Upon one such occasion a number of Indians whom Mr. Harris had unintentionally made angry by refusing to sell them "fire water," dragged the pioneer to a mulberry tree near the bank of the river, bound him hand and foot, and declared they were going to burn him alive.

Here Hercules is simply a timely rescuer, not a perfectly loyal and brave slave:

But just as the torch was about to be applied, a different kind of war whoop resounded through the forest, and a band of friendly Indians rushed forward, scattered the would-be torturers,

and set John Harris free.

Hercules, a negro slave who belonged to the Harris family, had hurried to a tribe on the western side of the river as soon as he saw the plight his master was in, and succeeded in bringing help just in the nick of time. A few minutes' longer delay would have been fatal.

It was almost a miraculous deliverance. Hercules was given his freedom at once as a reward for the part he played in the rescue. And as a reminder to every one how God had saved him that day, Mr. Harris said that when he died he wanted to be buried under the mulberry tree where he came very nearly being tortured to death. His family tried to dissuade him from his purpose, and suggested the cemetery at the old Paxtang church as being far more fitting, but he told them bluntly if they buried him there he'd get up and walk back.

In short, Inglewood and her audience were not Victorians. They did not have the same needs as Rupp, Morgan, Egle-Kelker, and

Tinian, *built about 1760 in present day Highspire, was the home of Colonel James Burd (1726-1798), one of Dauphin County's most influential citizens and a veteran of both the French and Indian, and the Revolutionary wars. Tinian, seen in this 1930 photo with the original stone partly exposed, is now much altered and covered with aluminum siding. (HSDC)*

Before the Revolution, John Harris built his mansion about 100 yards further from the riverbank than the site of his father's cabin and grave. Somewhat enlarged and Victorianized by Simon Cameron, the mansion is otherwise unchanged. The grave of John Harris sits surrounded by a small iron fence and shaded by a mulberry (but not the original mulberry, which perished of flood, Pennsylvania winters, and old age some years ago). (HSDC) From Art Work of Harrisburg *(Chicago: W.H. Parish Publishing Co., 1892)*

their readers. She treated the story as being entirely credible, and was happy to spice it with color and drama. But in her final analysis it is only "almost miraculous."

The sixth version, in Dr. George P. Donehoo's *Harrisburg, The City Beautiful, Romantic, and Historic,* published in 1927, is most striking for its insistence on the usefulness, if not the truthfulness, of the event. There are no new details in his version and no new documents cited; Donehoo confesses that he has "hunted in vain for some reference to this incident in the letters and other documents of the period, but has been unable to find any mention of it. The story, therefore . . . must rest entirely upon tradition." Then comes his final appeal to the jury:

. . . we "critical historians" sometimes do more harm than good when we do away with all of our interesting and beautiful traditions because we can find no documentary evidence to support them. . . . What good does it do to get rid of them? They may be but "traditions," but these traditions have through years or through the centuries become historic traditions, worthy of perpetuation because of the romance they contain and because of the lessons which they teach.

And these were the lessons Donehoo thought the tradition taught.

The story shows that John Harris was a man of conviction, that he did not love his trade more than he did what was right, even when so doing endangered his life; it also reveals the devotion of a colored slave to his master, who must have treated him kindly, or he would not have sought to release him, and it also reveals the oft-time forgotten fact that Indians, when friends of the white man, protected their white friends even against the members of their own race.

Let us, therefore, as Harrisburgers keep the "tradition" of John Harris and his mulberry tree, just as we, as Americans, keep the "tradition" of George Washington and his cherry tree. . . .

Perhaps Donehoo did not want the facts to get in the way of his "good story," for he might risk losing a pluperfectly glorious past, present, and purpose.

As if all the old descriptions and discussions had become too snarled, the seventh and eighth versions of the attempted history told Harris' story on its own terms quickly, and then looked for perspective and irony, two crucial parts of our own generation's historical sensibility. In Paul Beers' *Profiles from the Susquehanna Valley,* published in 1973, we find the suggestion that if Harris had not built his first house so near the river, then the railroad would have laid its tracks right where Riverfront Park is now. Then in Richard Steinmetz, Sr. and Robert Hoffsommer's *This Was Harrisburg,* published in 1976, we find the observation that "Harrisburg owes its existence to the faithful devotion of a black slave."

The point in retelling these versions of the Harris legend is to demonstrate that each generation retells its history to find a usable past. What one generation accepts, the next questions, and then the next one insists upon, and back and forth until the latest generation can only shrug. One wishes Hercules had left a version. The legend is that he was buried unceremoniously where Harrisburg Hospital now stands, or else near John Harris, or else. . . .

A visit by George Washington is long remembered by the cities that can claim such a distinction. His trip through Harrisburg in 1794 is etched in the memories of local historians. From Cirker, Dictionary of American Portraits *(Dover: 1967)*

III
GEORGE WASHINGTON AND THE START OF STOPPING BY

In the generation after independence was secured and the republic was established, American and European observers began to take a more analytical than astonished look at this country. Their purpose was to explain to themselves and their readers just exactly what kind of place, and idea, had just been invented in America. The observers' own invention was the travelogue—the visitor's commentary, the trip diary, the letter home—a new type of literature for a new civilization. The best ones are American classics: Alexis de Tocqueville's Democracy in America *(1835), Frances Trollope's* Domestic Manners of the Americans *(1832), Lewis and Clark's* Journals *(1814), Francis Grund's* Aristocracy in America *(1839), and Harriet Martineau's* Society in America *(1837). The hundreds of lesser ones are at least informative. In all these travel accounts the facts that townspeople might take for granted were revealing details for the travelers.*

Harrisburg was mentioned often in such accounts. Indeed, it had to be, because it was almost impossible to traverse Pennsylvania without travelling through Harrisburg. Nature funneled the westward movement this way, into the Great Valley and across the river, so that tens of millions of Americans can say, "Oh yes, I've been to Harrisburg. I was on my way to...."

October 3, 1794:

George Washington was almost more itinerant than President. It is almost embarrassing to say he stayed here overnight too. The President arrived in Harrisburg late the afternoon of October 3, 1794. He was on his way to Carlisle to take command of the troops who would quench the Whiskey Rebellion in western Pennsylvania. A. Boyd Hamilton, former President of the Historical Society of Dauphin County, wrote that Washington uncovered his head and stood up in his carriage while it rolled up Second from Paxton Street. The Burgesses met him at the southeast corner of Market Square. They spoke a "very carefully worded" greeting to him (they pledged their moral support toward stopping the rebellion, but said "our sphere of action is too limited to produce any important effects"), and Washington's reply "smoothed over many political differences," according to Hamilton (the President said the inhabitants of Harrisburg were "virtuous and enlightened men" and that he

appreciated their support of the Constitution and their "zealous and efficient exercise" in "defense of the laws"). Neither side was full of candor—Hamilton guessed there were only five Federalists in a town of 875 residents to support the President.

Washington stood on a stone horse block to deliver his speech. His name and the date of his visit were later inscribed on it, and the block now serves the John Harris Mansion as a stepping stone to the porch. Hamilton said there were few details but much debate on where the President ate and slept that night (probably at the Jones House on the southeast corner of Market Square) and whether he drove his own coach across the Susquehanna or rode on Harris' ferry (in his diary Washington simply wrote, "forded the Susquehanna").

The 200th anniversary of Washington's birth, celebrated in 1932, was the occasion for local newspapers to reprint the story of his visit in all its glory, including the President's remark that he judged

While the claim to be the "oldest in the country" might be questioned, the Independence Island Rope Ferry, seen in this early 20th century postcard, was a survivor of a common 18th-century ferry type. Courtesy, Pennsylvania Historical and Museum Commission (PHMC)

Harrisburg "considerable" after he had dined and "walked through and around the town." When he departed on October 4, there was, according to Captain Samuel Dewees' diary, "great weeping and mourning," purportedly by the "women and children" who "covered" the "banks of the river on the town side," though it may have been the innkeeper Dewees heard in distress, since there is no record of Washington ever paying his bill.

What did other visitors say after stopping by Harrisburg in its early years? J.P. Keller, in a speech to the Historical Society of Dauphin County at the turn of the century, retrieved many reminiscences. The Reverend Manasseh Cutler, travelling through in 1787, said Harrisburg was "a beautiful town" containing about "one hundred houses" and "a great number of taverns" but "no churches yet." The people "appear well dressed, some gay," he wrote.

John Penn, a grandson of William Penn, said, in 1788, that the town's "situation," meaning its location, "is one of the finest I ever saw," but "Lebanon is infinitely larger."

About 1795 the Duke de la Rochefoucauld, touring America, said Harrisburg was more "compact" than Reading and had "a better appearance." Its "Germans and Irishmen" were "sensible and industrious," despite the "thirty-eight inns" compacted in town, a "number out of all proportion to that of Europe."

Miss Margaret Dwight, travelling from Connecticut to Ohio, stayed overnight in Harrisburg in 1810. She was not favorably impressed by the cockfight which took place at the tavern where she and her party

slept. Neither was she pleased by the many "drunken, swearing wretches" she met: "A great many of the best young men of the town became so intoxicated that they could not get home unassisted," she testified. "Harrisburg is a very dissipated place I am sure," she concluded.

The 1819 diary of Ludwig Gall, offered recently in the *Pennsylvania Magazine of History and Biography* by Frederick Trautmann, tells a marvelous story about early Harrisburg. On August 30 Gall, trying to persuade other Germans to emigrate to America, wrote that "Harrisburg is one of those wonders that rise out of the wilderness and astonish Europeans . . . I know of no region of similar size, even along the Rhine, that surpasses the region around Harrisburg in extent, variety, and perfection of natural beauty." Such descriptions of the landscape and characterizations of the New World become repetitious in travellers' journals. But Gall's account of the contagious spirit of freedom in Harrisburg is unique. His bound ser-

A visitor to Harrisburg in the late 18th or early 19th century might have stayed at the Golden Sheaf, which was built on the northwest corner of Front and Market streets by John and Andrew Krause in 1791. Early hotels tended to be primitive at best, and cautious travelers often arranged to stop in private houses. By 1900, the Harrisburg Club House Building stood on the site of the Golden Sheaf. (HSDC)

Artists of all types and presidents are the best-remembered Harrisburg visitors. Shown here are: pianist Louis Moreau Gottschalk, singer Jenny Lind, and Presidents Lincoln, McKinley, Grant, and Roosevelt. From Cirker, Dictionary of American Portraits *(Dover: 1967)*

vant, whose passage to America Gall had paid, was becoming "coarser and more impudent" as he kowtowed to his master each day:

One morning, eight days after we arrived, he came half-drunk to me and, his hat on, spoke with unwonted familiarity. He knew the law in America, he said, and I had better realize he was my equal. If I didn't give him a seat at my table and a suit of Sunday clothes as good as mine, he was obliged to stay with me not an hour more. In fact he stayed less than an hour: I reprimanded him and he left and did not return. Although it had been in vain when my other servants had run away, I offered in English- and German-language newspapers a reward of $10 for the capture and return of this fellow, Peter Wissel by name. Next day he was delivered to me in the home of Justice of the Peace Mayer, in Harrisburg, by a neighborhood farmer.... Wissel repeated his assertion that he would return to me only on the condition that he eat at my table, as was the custom in this country. I had no choice therefore but to request that he be jailed until he promised to improve ... Six weeks later the rascal wrote me that he would return to my service for two years if I would pay him $60 a year and cancel his debt to me, and if I expected him to return on any other terms, I must have no idea of life in an American jail. This message prompted me to inspect the jail. He was right: I had no idea of life in an American jail. I found him and eight of his ilk, in clean and decent clothes, sitting at a table in a big, airy, well-lighted room. On the table were newspapers, a bottle of whiskey, and of all things, playing cards—when gambling outside was against the law.... Methodists with a misplaced love of humanity supplied him and his fellows with an abundance

of food and drink. "You see for yourself," he said. "I want for nothing here. I have no reason to wish to live elsewhere."... In the end I had to let the fellow go....

But Gall also found out later that Harrisburg was not all liberty and license in 1819:

Yet, the touted freedom of conscience notwithstanding, the prohibition on Sunday of work, hunting, dancing, and other amusements, and even music is strictly enforced. Indeed, I've been told, a Dutch physician, on the complaint of a neighbor, had to pay a fine of $4 because, ignorant of the law, he didn't stop on Sunday the musical clock he brought from Europe ... I paid $4 because I worked a few minutes in my flower beds. My Neighbor was paid $2, in reward for his pious zeal...

That was what you found in Harrisburg if you stopped by in the early days—beauty, liberty, and propriety, or the land's, the man's, and the law's differing dignities. You found America.

A half-century after the Lochiel's heyday, the Commonwealth Hotel was the most luxurious place to stay in Harrisburg. The building was most likely erected in three stages by three different architects who felt that continuing the exact design of their predecessor would have shown a terrible lack of imagination. (HSDC) From Art Work of Harrisburg

"General" Mitchell (whose proper first name has been forgotten—if indeed he ever had another) was born into slavery in 1845, presumably not in Pennsylvania, which was a free state. He resided in Harrisburg from some time in the mid-19th century until his death early in the 1900s. He was regarded with respect and affection by all who knew him. (HSDC)

IV
THE FIRST CRUSADES

America's first age of reform came in the 1830s, after the Founding Fathers were gone and their progeny began striving to live up to them (Presidents John Adams and Thomas Jefferson brought that fact home when they both died on July 4, 1826). Andrew Jackson was President now, and provided the image, if not entirely the reality, that this would be the "era of the common man." The American Society for the Promotion of Temperance was organized in 1826. William Lloyd Garrison published the first issue of his abolitionist newspaper The Liberator *in 1831, and the American Anti-Slavery Society was founded in 1833 (nearly 200,000 Americans had joined anti-slavery societies by 1850). Oberlin College in Ohio, established in 1833, became the first college to admit both women and men, both white and black. McGuffey's* Readers, *thoroughly moralistic schoolbooks, were first published in 1836, the same year Massachusetts required children to attend school for at least three months a year, and the same year the Transcendental Club was formed in Boston. Its most prominent member, Ralph Waldo Emerson, announced, "What is man born for, but to be a reformer?" Ironically, neither Emerson nor his soul-mate, Henry David Thoreau, was ever very active in any reform movement.*

Greater Harrisburg's reformers were better organized. They worked against profanity, slavery, and whiskey, or at least promised they would.

January 14, 1836:

Two weeks after New Year's, 1836, the Harrisburg Anti-Slavery Society was founded by about a hundred men and women. The Reverend Nathan Stem, Rector of St. Stephen's Episcopal Church, was elected President. Dr. William Rutherford, 31, physician and raccoon hunter, and Mordecai McKinney, 40, lawyer and defender of fugitive slaves, were Vice-Presidents. The Society's Corresponding Secretary was Samuel Cross, an Irish schoolteacher who "had faith in the efficacy of the two R's—Rattan and Ruler—to enforce the rules." (According to one anonymous historian, the schoolboys used to sing, "Cross by name and Cross by nature and Cross jumped out of an Irish potater.")

The founding was no convenient moral gesture practiced a comfortable distance from slavers. Harrisburg was a station on the Underground Railroad from Maryland to Canada, and the citizens had seen runaway slaves and abolitionists roughed up in town. On April 25, 1825, wrote one reporter: "a large crowd of colored men and boys made a desperate effort to take a poor fugitive slave from his owner and the officers of the law. They came streaming in hot haste . . . a tumultuous crowd." However, "they were unsuccessful in releasing the fugitive, and sixteen of the mob were arrested." Twelve were convicted, and 11 of those (one escaped) "went to the treadmill." In 1847 Frederick Douglass, the most famous ex-slave, and William Lloyd Garrison, the most famous abolitionist, held an anti-slavery rally at the Dauphin County Court House in Harrisburg. Both were abused by the crowd.

A safer crusade was the local temperance movement. But it is also more difficult to understand, for compared to the Constitution of the Harrisburg Anti-Slavery Society (the Preamble said, "our national existence is based on this principle, as recognized in the Declaration of Independence, that 'all mankind are created equal'"), what are we to make of the principles of Mr. C.

William Lloyd Garrison and Frederick Douglass came to Harrisburg in 1847 to hold an antislavery rally at the Dauphin County Courthouse. They were undaunted by the hostile reaction they received from much of the crowd. From Cirker, Dictionary of American Portraits *(Dover: 1967)*

Lewis, temperance lecturer at the Lochiel Church, who in 1869 urged:

Let our prating about social and political equalities have an end, and by our love for humanity, for ourselves and posterity, show that the first, highest and noblest equality within the reach of man's highest aspirations is—That all men should live soberly.

The Young Men's and Young Ladies'

Total Abstinence Society of Harrisburg was already active in 1840 when William R. Dewitt lectured in an unidentified local Presbyterian Church on "Profanity and Intemperance, Prevailing Evils." From his long "discourse," as he called it, we may read the following lines:

You often hear individuals exclaim . . . "Oh heavens! What a mistake!" "My Goodness! How you frighten me!" This is profanity.

There is no object in the Universe so disgusting as a female inebriate.

The pure cold water system is the republican system.

In 1844 the Central Division of the Sons of Temperance was also organized in Harrisburg by over 200 men (who must not have imagined their acronym—SOT), including Simon Cameron (whose cider jug was recently discovered in a clandestine cupboard at the Historical Society of Dauphin County). Their constitution was a model amalgam of common sense, morality, and good manners. They pledged themselves to practice temperance,

The first steam locomotive pulled the first passenger train into Harrisburg on September 16, 1839. The city soon became and long remained a major rail center. (HSDC)

Simon Cameron, a man of considerable wealth, acquired the Harris mansion from the heirs of John Harris, enlarged and Victorianized it, and dwelt there for the better part of half a century. He was perpetually active in the affairs of Harrisburg— including the temperance movement. In this, he showed a bit of harmless hypocrisy—his cider jug was recently found, hidden away behind a cupboard in his house. (HSDC)

fellowship, and mutual aid, to avoid "ungenerous remarks and sarcastic language" at meetings, and to attend one another's funerals, "unless the brother died of some contagious or infectious disease." A man would not be admitted to the Sons if he were "incapacitated from earning a living" or if he received "five or more black balls" when the box was passed. If any brother took benefits by "feigning sickness," or if he "divulged the private affairs of the Order," or if he brought up for discussion a subject "of a sectarian or political character," or if he failed to purchase his own "regalia" when an officer, or if he broke his pledge not to "make, buy, sell, or use, as a beverage, any spiritous or malt liquors, wine, or cider," then he would be expelled from the brotherhood and his name "erased from the book." The boys spent most of their time preaching to the converted, in

costume and comradeship.

Out in the countryside of Harrisburg, the temperance movement was more subtle, and possibly more effective. William Simonton's unpublished memoir *Notes on My Recollections of Country Life in West Hanover Township, Dauphin County, Pennsylvania* from the late 1830s shows how clever farmers scheduled sobriety without breaking up bottles and bars with an ax:

The custom of setting out the decanter and sugar bowl when friends made a social call, and of taking the bottle into the harvest field had been so long and generally in force, that working men claimed it as their right, no less than their privilege to have some stimulant "to keep them cool in summer, and warm and comfortable in winter!" Gradually however, by the substitution of "ginger small beer at 10 o'clock piece," and a dram of something

The farmers in this scene of haying (to say nothing of their mules) appear to be models of sobriety. It is nevertheless true that until the temperance movement achieved momentum in the 1830s and 1840s, the practice of lubricating the day's chores with alcohol was widespread. (HSDC)

Though it has been extensively altered, the John Elder house, built in 1740, is probably the oldest in Dauphin County. (HSDC)

stronger at regular meal time, the bottle was kept out of sight, and the opportunity for drinking to excess limited. In the course of a few years, the drinking usages thus curtailed were generally, though not wholly, abandoned, and the practice of having the decanter and glasses at hand on every social occasion, ceased to prevail among the more influential families. . .

If we have a little fun now reading the immensities of temperance reformers, we should be informed that public drunkenness and alcoholism were huge problems in the 19th century. Recent research shows that their fear and anger had substance and purpose. For example, in Spofford's *1843 Harrisburg Directory* we read that city brewers produced 465,000 gallons of beer and ale that year for 7,800 citizens. If just half of that amount was consumed in the city, and if half the city's population was male, and if half those males were between the ages of 20 and 70, and if half those adult males drank beer, then each of those 975 quaffed about two-thirds of a gallon of beer a day, accounting for five million bottles of beer in 1843.

Considering the immediate effects of Harrisburg's anti-slavery and temperance movements, it seems ironical that what the reformers boldly denounced, they did not immediately deter, and what they quietly detoured, they eventually got less of.

The Reverend Henry Boehm (1775-1877) linked 19th century Harrisburg to its colonial past. Until his death at the age of 102, he preached at the Locust Street Methodist Episcopal Church, which had grown from a log structure to an imposing masonry edifice. (HSDC)

The main building of the State Lunatic Hospital boasted this Lombardic tower. The atmosphere of the hospital was (and remains) more like that of an exclusive private school than that of an insane asylum. (HSDC) From Art Work of Harrisburg

V
SEVEN WOMEN
HEALING

By the 1850s America was becoming a land of institutions, organizations, and associations. Alexis de Tocqueville had foreseen this development and wrote in the 1830s, "Americans of all ages, all conditions, and all dispositions constantly form associations. . . . The Americans make associations to give entertainments, to found seminaries, to build inns, to construct churches, to diffuse books, to send missionaries to the antipodes. In this manner they found hospitals, prisons, and schools."

One of the largest such institutions in Harrisburg was the State Lunatic Hospital. Founded in 1851, it was one of 38 state hospitals for the insane in existence by 1860. By 1901 another 100 had been built in the United States. Many of these institutions, including Harrisburg's, followed the ideal design which Dr. Thomas Kirkbride had first conceived in 1847, the same year the American Medical Association was formed and three years after the Association of Medical Superintendents of American Institutions for the Insane was established.

But if medicine was becoming well-organized by mid-century, it was still far from being well-practiced by modern standards. With all due respect, medical treatment in the past was nearly as much to be avoided as sickness itself. Anesthesia and antisepsis were undeveloped, and vaccination was not ubiquitous. Regular physicians, quacks, or homeopaths, they were quickly trained in a few months of coursework and apprenticeship. There was not very much to learn, in any case, so the black-coated, cane-carrying, horse-riding doctors were mainly admired for their character. They concocted their own medicines and tried to devise ways to make sure they were paid for their work. Dr. William Henry Egle, reflecting on the practice of medicine in Harrisburg, said, "Ah, me. I shudder when I think of it!"

The case records of patients at the Lunatic Hospital in Harrisburg show how "psychological medicine" was malpracticed there before the Civil War, and also how society in general thought about mind and body in those days.

February 25, 1858:

The most obvious but unknown institution in Harrisburg has always been the "state hospital," as we call it now. The Pennsylvania State Lunatic Hospital opened on October 6, 1851, under the management of 30-year-old Dr. John Curwen. It was located about a mile-and-a-half north of Harrisburg on 130 acres of farmland. It consisted of a central building with adjacent wings, so constructed that all would be "light and cheerful" with much "free natural ventilation" in keeping with the Victorian concern for "airy" surroundings. It had four floors, "a large Tuscan portico with a flight of twenty steps to the main entrance," a dome, and a view.

There were no accommodations at first for the "most violent and noisy class of patients" in the main building, so additional cottages were constructed for them on the grounds. These are the only original buildings still standing. The State Lunatic Hospital, in sum, looked like other asylums of its time—an architectural monument in a bucolic environment, both the building and the setting designed to relieve the mentally diseased.

The hospital stated its principles as inoffensively as possible in its *First Annual Report:*

There are those who believed, and many still continue to entertain the belief, that insanity is to be attributed to supernatural agency; that it is either a direct punishment from the Almighty, "by the visitation of God," for sins committed, or that it is through the agency of the Prince of Darkness.

That such might be the fact is not denied, but it is much more in accordance with true religion and sound philosophy to refer it to natural causes, which are known to be effective in its production. We know that the mind is influenced in different degrees by different and varying conditions of the bodily organization, even in health; and it is but one step farther, and a very natural one, in the chain of causes, to refer disordered manifestations of the

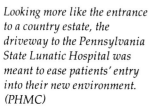

Looking more like the entrance to a country estate, the driveway to the Pennsylvania State Lunatic Hospital was meant to ease patients' entry into their new environment. (PHMC)

Far left: *Dr. John Curwen, first superintendent of the Pennsylvania State Lunatic Hospital, served in that capacity for 30 years. With a century's hindsight it is easy to find Curwen's diagnoses naive and his treatments extreme. At a time, however, when mental illness was thought to indicate the wrath of God, a failure of character, or the intervention of the moon, his methods were quite progressive. Courtesy, Harrisburg State Hospital*

Left: *Dorothea Dix was a leader in the movement to improve treatment of the mentally ill. Her work brought about the founding of many hosptials, including the Harrisburg State Hospital. From Cirker,* Dictionary of American Portraits *(Dover: 1967)*

mind to diseased conditions of the bodily organs.

But if they thought insanity was certainly a medical problem, and probably not a religious one, the psychiatrists of the time ("alienists") believed it was nevertheless a moral problem, since insanity could influence one's "moral faculties." Thus, the hospital had to be morally as well as medically influential on its patients—it had a chapel, and the first gift donated was a "handsome Bible," arranged through the good offices of Miss Dorothea Dix, who had been influential herself in urging the state legislature to build the hospital. The staff was told to have "zeal" and "devotion," especially the assistant physician, who should visit all the patients every evening and "exert over them all the moral influence in his power." He would be assisted by the steward, who "shall observe the conduct of the inmates at the religious meetings." No drinkers would be hired, and there would be no smoking on the grounds. This ethos went by the official name of "moral treatment," meaning give the patients rest, recreation, sympathy, and morality. This treatment came at a price: the hospital would supplement its state appropriation by charging patients two dollars per week for room and board, if they were supported by the public, and three to 10 dollars per week, if they were private, depending on the "trouble" they were and their "ability to pay." ("Higher prices are paid by a special agreement with the superintendent for extra attention and accommodations.")

In 1858, 151 patients were admitted and 134 were discharged, either restored, improved, stationary, or dead, leaving 267 resident at the end of the year (119 were private patients, 148 public charges; 150

The pastoral setting of the Harrisburg State Hospital belies the often misguided, though well-intentioned, treatment once given to patients diagnosed as mentally ill. (PHMC)

were male, 117 female.) There was room for 300. The main disorders presented by the patients were acute and chronic "mania," "melancholy," and "dementia." There were also "imbeciles" and "epileptics." The causes of their disorders were undetermined in about half the cases, but otherwise 30 suspected causes were listed, including, at the top of the list, "domestic trouble" and "ill health." The most curious etiologies listed were "spiritual rappings," "female troubles," "politics," "religious excitement," "failure in business," "novel reading," "mortified pride," "exposure to the sun," and "excessive study."

Indeed, Dr. Curwen had more to say about the dangers of "excessive study" in the 1858 *Annual Report:*

The great tendency of the period is to over-exertion and stimulation in every department—the haste to be accounted learned, as well as the haste to be rich . . . As a general thing children are sent to school too young . . . they are encouraged and urged forward to a degree their powers are unable to bear . . . under ten years of age very little mental effort should be required of children, and they should be allowed a large amount of exercise, bodily health and strength being more necessary and desirable than any learning at that age . . . an incalculable amount of injury is done to those who have passed the age of ten . . . youth of both sexes, between the age of ten and twenty, are expected to perform duties much beyond what should ever be required of them. . . .

Curwen was evidently wrong-headed in his worries. (Perhaps the young doctor's complaints were mainly disguising the troubles of his own scholastic, and mental, career—he entered Yale at 15.) Nearly all his male patients were farmers, laborers, merchants, craftsmen, and jobless men, and nearly all his female patients were the wives of such men. In eight years after the opening of the hospital, out of more than 1,000 patients treated, only 30 formally educated (and therefore possibly over-exercised) minds were admitted for a rest in this asylum.

In any case, those excerpts taken from the hospital's annual reports only hint at the nature of normal life in the institution—the features of its public face. We get a more intimate description of everyday reality by reading the superintendent's casebooks, especially the brief records of seven of the female patients who arrived in 1858.

Clara was admitted on February 25, 1858. She was single, age 20, and lived in Franklin County. Her attack was caused by "parental influence with an engagement." She would sit in a corner and cover her face with her hands. She was given "the usual purge" and pulverized

The laundry of the State Hospital was thoroughly modern. The women in uniform were undoubtedly members of the staff; but it is probable that the men, who are not in uniform, were patients assigned to work in the laundry as part of their therapy. Courtesy, Harrisburg State Hospital

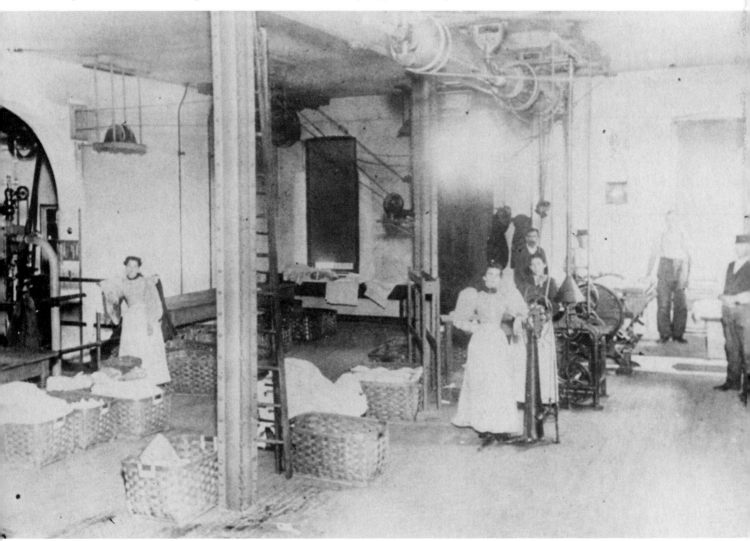

opium on admission. During her stay she was reported "careless in dress, often immodest." She was discharged after 6 months on August 21, 1858, her condition "improved."

Sarah was also admitted on February 25, 1858. She was born in Ireland and lived in Venango County. She was 33 and the wife of a store clerk. A week prior to admission she had received a "revelation of calamity for her friends and relatives," but also the assurance that "all will die happy." They purged her and administered liquid opium. They described her as "cheerful during good health, kind and benevolent, but has strong passions and deep prejudices." While riding in a carriage on the grounds she tried to escape. She was discharged after four months on June 20, 1858, her condition "without material change though at times improved and again becomes worse."

Leah was admitted on June 3, 1858. She was a "colored woman," age 40, and lived in Tioga. A week prior to admission she had become destructive. During 20 months preceeding confinement she had "lost seven children, which occasioned a great deal of anxiety." They purged her and gave her opium. They described her as "naturally kind and affectionate; though easily excited, is readily calmed." On June 20 she refused to wear clothing and was destructive. On September 2 a "fly plaster was put on her abdomen," and "after dressing with a poultice, granulated morphine was sprinkled on the surface." She died the same day.

Elizabeth was admitted on August 9, 1858. She was 41, the wife of a laborer, and lived in Schuykill County. Twelve days prior to admission she had become incoherent and evinced "a great fear of harmless objects and dogs; a slight interference with her plans would bring on an attack against others." She used tobacco, they noted. Her attack was caused, they said, by the death of her child 6 weeks ago and the loss of 4 others over a short time. She suffered from "hysterical and rheumatic affections; had forbodings of evil during all pregnancies." They let one quart of blood from her. She was purged and given opium. She was discharged after four months, on December 8, 1858, her condition "restored."

Jane was admitted on October 23, 1858. She was married, age 34, and lived in York County. A week prior to admission she had been incoherent and tore her clothes; this was caused by her "being threatened with divorce by her husband for some irregularities in her conduct." She was purged and given powdered opium. On February 14, 1859, about four months after admission, she died.

Catharine was admitted on November 18, 1858. She was married, age 45, and lived in Lebanon County. She had been "liable to hysterical troubles" since August, partly owing to the fact that even though she was a good church member, she "thinks she is lost forever by the idea that her profession of religion was that of a hypocrite." She was administered pulverized opium on admission, along with a purgative. When they interviewed her again in February 1859, they found that she was afraid to answer questions "for fear of error." In early June she said that

Opposite: *Treatment at the State Hospital emphasized light, air, activity, and medication. The presence of the female attendants tells us that this is the ladies' wing of the hospital. One can imagine Dr. Curwen's female patients recovering (or failing to recover) just beyond those open doors. Courtesy, Harrisburg State Hospital*

her children didn't belong to her and that she had no home. She was discharged and sent home on June 30, 1859, though she believed her husband now lived in the hospital and that she still had no home. Her condition after seven months was regarded as "improved."

Esther was admitted three days after Christmas in 1858. She was single, 21, and lived in Lancaster County. Two months prior to admission she began feeling that she was "good for nothing," because, she said, "her mother had neglected her upbringing," and thus, she was "different" from the other girls. The immediate reason for her admission, however, was her attempts to destroy herself by "holding her face under water and throwing herself off chairs." They purged her and gave her opium. She busied herself sewing and knitting. In early 1859 she made "abortive attempts now and then to hang herself," and "she spoke of starving herself." She was discharged after nine months on September 2, 1859, her condition "restored."

Notice the consistent qualities of these diagnoses. They suggest that women were perceived as being constitutionally unstable—they could be driven insane, supposedly, by body functions, interference in their love affairs, too religious devotion, the threat of divorce, the loss of children, and inattention by their own mothers. In effect, whenever a woman's fundamental feminine identity was disturbed (as Victorian culture defined both femininity and disturbance) it was guessed that she might go over the brink. And some of them probably did.

Notice the consistent, even monotonous, qualities of the therapies. They tried to keep the women busy, of course, but what is more revealing is the astonishing pharmacopia of chemicals administered. However important "moral treatment" was in antebellum asylums, these records show us that "medical" therapy was given to all patients. In fact, a tally of medication notes on all female patients' records in the 1850s shows that there were more than 90 different purgatives, emetics, sedatives, tonics, and other remedies the doctors could choose from. Most patients received four or five different medications on a sporadic schedule. These included "the usual purge," quinine, castor oil, ipecac, opium, morphine, calomel, powdered rhubarb, eggnog, and ice water injections (one suspects that patients improved in order that treatment might be stopped). All this was going on while the annual reports made it seem that recreation was the main activity—carriage rides, magic lantern shows, bowling, reading, and planting Simon Cameron's gift of vegetable seeds.

While she was doing research for me, Caroline Liebman found a tombstone on the grounds of the State Hospital. It marks the grave of Hannah Weber, age 34, who died there on September 26, 1866. Hannah was the only patient who left a "case record" in her own words:

Weep not my friends, why should I
[unclear] Or linger longer here
I now am freed from every woe
Relieved from every fear

She had finally found healing, despite everything the doctors could do for her.

Opposite: *Toward the end of the 19th century, many photographs of the State Hospital were taken, but they tend to concentrate far more on the facilities and the staff than upon the patients. No studies of female patients seem to have survived, but there is this picture of a dapperly dressed male patient and his dog. Courtesy, Harrisburg State Hospital*

Although Camp Curtin prepared men for bloody war, most of what occurred there was quite peaceable. For the care of the sick and wounded, the camp maintained a large, clean military hospital. (HSDC)

VI
THE LESSER BATTLES OF GREATER HARRISBURG

The Civil War was the most fundamental contest of American life. The North fought for the future—the necessity of nationhood, the first inklings of full equality, the whole might of industrial civilization organized against a moral and economic anachronism. The South fought for a "way of life"—the hard fact of slavery, a confederacy of agrarian communities, the dreams of manly and womanly honor.

Most of the war took place below the Mason-Dixon line, Pennsylvania's southern border—except one battle, when General Robert E. Lee brought 70,000 troops into the Commonwealth on the way to Harrisburg and Washington, D.C. He was intercepted by General George Meade and 93,000 men near Gettysburg, Pennsylvania on July 1, 1863. When they limped away from one another a few days later, more than 43,000 men were left behind on the ground, either killed or wounded. Meade was the "winner," inasmuch as Lee retreated. Union troops took Vicksburg, Mississippi, on July 4, and the Civil War began to end. Gettysburg was the greatest battle in the history of the Western Hemisphere (and one of America's most symbolic events), and Harrisburg was one of the largest targets that was never hit.

Here are some personal accounts from Camp Hill, the capital city, and Middletown about preparations for the invasion. They document the miss and its myth, as some Harrisburghers would claim more glory than the War Department would ever crown.

June 20 – July 4, 1863:

If wars are too important to be left to the generals, then perhaps they should be run by travel agents. They could look beyond the battle, and beyond the peace, to the eventual victory of trinket shops, highway markers, and historic inns. They would have told Custer, for example, to make his last stand within a short drive from Denver instead of Lodge Grass, Montana—in real estate and battlefield tourism, location is everything. Thus, if only a capital city tour guide had been at Cemetery Ridge to tell Meade to let Lee march a few miles farther in early July 1863, the Union still could have stopped the Rebels at the river and every child would have to memorize the Harrisburg Address and admire the stirring painting of "Pickett's Wade Across the Susquehanna." As it is, Gettysburg gets the glory.

Still, greater Harrisburg's preparations for war were important in its own history, and we are fortunate to have several private accounts of them. First, we have the brief narratives collected at the turn of the century by A.M. Bowman and submitted by Casper Dull to the Historical Society of Dauphin County in 1936. These give the view from the West Shore of the invasion. Dull's point was to prove that the Confederates got as far as Camp Hill just before the Battle of Gettysburg; to be specific, that they got to 32nd and Market streets, known then as Oyster's Point. Transcribed, typed, and bound like legal depositions, these testimonies from West Shore citizens remind us that it was great sport in those days to conjecture about what regiments marched how many yards in which direction, in preference to a discussion of what

the war, and the victory, were all about. The unexpected characteristics of these memoirs are the rancor they display against allies instead of the enemy and their Yankee drollery.

Mr. Martin Brinton testified that "We were between the Rebel pickets and the advance New York pickets. We were asked where we belonged.... One of our party said, 'We came out here to see how things looked.' The New Yorkers asked us if we saw any Rebels. Mr. Bates said, 'I had three or four for breakfast' ... the New York men had been taking fish, apple-butter, meat, blankets, bed clothing, etc. They had also taken old Mrs. Oyster's linen." Brinton then told of another coy conversation between Charles Flemming, a Union "spy" from Mechanicsburg, and some Confederate pickets. Flemming was sitting on a fence on the road between New Cumberland and White Hill. Several Rebels approached him on horseback and asked, "Have you seen any Rebels?" He said, "No Sir." They said, "Do we look like Rebels?" He said, "I don't know, you are all strangers to me."

Mr. Z. Bowman also thought ill of the New York troops stationed on the West Shore. He swore that "New Yorkers turned out to be our worst enemies. They killed our hogs, chickens, and so on." He saw them wearing the "great high hats" they'd stolen from Mrs. Oyster. "Nice mark to shoot at," he said.

Mr. Samuel Shopp repeated many of the previous themes in his testimony. He swore that "The raid was in July. I forget just what year." On the matter of bombardment, he said, "I guess I picked up about fifteen shells that were not exploded,

On April 23, 1865, Zion Lutheran Church held a memorial service for the assassinated President Lincoln. Conducting the service was the Reverend Charles A. Hay, pictured here. (HSDC)

and I gave them nearly all to parties who wanted them as relics—some in Philadelphia, New York City, and other places." On the matter of Rebels and New Yorkers: "I only talked to a few of the Rebels. They were not very sociable. I heard one of them say they 'got into Pennsyl-

vania, but they didn't know how the devil to get out."

John Mater mentioned a close call he had with a mysterious stranger:

He wore black clothes, a splendid black frock coat, and was about five feet ten inches in height, and slightly built. A

Fort Washington was built in 1863 when the Union feared the Confederate army would not be stopped at Gettysburg. The earthworks were still visible, though overgrown, by the time of this 1930 photo. (HSDC)

Opposite: *General Joseph F. Knipe, a native of Harrisburg, was in charge of the city's defenses when Lee's army invaded Pennsylvania. At some point in the hostilities, he paused long enough to sit in full battle dress for an unknown photographer. (HSDC)*

fine looking man. He had a straight knife on his belt . . . It hung below his coat two or three inches. I asked him if he was going out to our fellows. He said, "No, the dumb devils would just as soon shoot their friends as their enemies. . . ." He was a spy. We knew he was a Rebel. . . .

Mater closed with the speculation that "The Rebels could have easily gone into Harrisburg, if it wasn't for the Battle of Gettysburg. We had a bad set of men—those New Yorkers."

The view from Harrisburg of the invasion is presented in a full narrative by Henry Demming. This was written at Casper Dull's request in 1900. Demming was in a good position to be a thorough observer; though less than 21, he had already served three enlistments in the Union army by July 1863, and while

recuperating in Harrisburg from two wounds he was the City Editor of the *Daily Telegraph*. He began,

Refugees began coming in considerable numbers as early as the 20th of June, and sometimes the old Harrisburg bridge was choked up with farmers and others fleeing from a threatening foe. There was a constant flow through Harrisburg, from west to east, of all sorts of vehicles, as well as droves of cattle, horses, sheep and swine. The people of Harrisburg who remained in the city wondered where all the fleeing people came from, as the flow was so continuous and large.

The first sound of war that Harrisburg heard was on Tuesday evening, June 30, when Confederate forces were met in Camp Hill by General Joseph Knipe's troops. After this engagment, units were raised to

defend the city. They dug in by Harris' grave. They had reason to anticipate the worst, since everyone had seen the glare given by the burning of the Columbia bridge and the Carlisle barracks on the night of June 28.

But the only assault they stopped was a spy's mission about four o'clock in the morning of July 2. First Corporal Demming himself caught the man, who was dressed as a cavalry captain and hiding on a raft in the river. He was locked up for a while, but for some reason was released, then captured again. This would seem to be a fairly mundane encounter, but Demming made a good deal of it in his memoir. First, he quoted from a story he had written for the *Telegraph* on July 2:

. . . a flat boat was discovered coming down stream, containing what was supposed to be a man. The guard ordered the person who was on board to stop the craft, but the order not being obeyed he fired. This had the effect of causing the occupant of the boat (which, by the way, had just struck a rock and remained fast), to dodge down and secrete himself in the inside. He was warned to get up and run his boat in to the shore where the guard was, but not complying a second shot was fired at the boat. This had no effect, and the corporal of the guard, accompanied by Sergeant Gratz, of the same company, took possession of another boat, lying along the shore, and pulled out to the flat. On nearing it, it presented a deserted appearance; but when the craft came alongside, lo, and behold, a man with the uniform of a cavalry officer, and wearing a captain's straps, was discovered cramped up in one corner of the flat boat.

He was arrested and ordered to leave the flat and get into the boat alongside.

This he did, but not without remonstrating sometime with his captors, protesting against being arrested in this ungentlemanly manner, as he termed it, and rudely compelled by subalterns to leave his own boat. When the party reached the shore, the officer was searched and a loaded four shooter (Sharp's), and a new hatchet taken from him.

When they took the uniform off the man, who gave his name as J.H.M. Weitbrecht, they found a map of the Susquehanna on which fords had been marked.

The capstone of Demming's memoir to Dull was this testimony:

Fully twenty years after the close of the Rebellion a former captain of General Stuart's Black Horse cavalry called to see me at Harrisburg, and stated that if the Confederate captain had not been captured at Harris Park the night of July 1-2, 1863, that a portion of Stuart's command would have crossed the Susquehanna at the ford opposite Camp Curtin that morning, burned all the public buildings, levied from the citizens $500,000 in cash, besides provisions, and carried off a number of the most prominent residents as hostages. He also stated that the supposed Rebel captain was an officer of another rank, the "dare devil" of the Confederate army; that when captured he gave an assumed name, and had a number of confederates in Harrisburg at the time; that he escaped from Fort Delaware, rejoined the Confederate army. . . .

Demming did nothing to temper the hyperbole in his memoir to Casper Dull. On the very first of the 14 pages, he wrote:

Several Confederate officers told me

afterwards that their belief was if the capital city of the second state of the Union could be captured, the capital lying so far north of Washington, they would be recognized as a confederacy, or at least as belligerents, by the nations of Europe; that this would lead to the opening of the ports of the South; and, with the ports not blockaded, they could secure all the munitions of war desired, and ultimately their independence.

If Harrisburg could not boast about a battle, at least it could be proud to imagine what it had prevented (nothing less than the collapse of Western civilization, apparently), for if Henry Demming, able catcher of spies, had not done his duty, one could guess that the South might have won the war and left the house divided.

Of course, Demming was not lying—he was only inflating, as did other memorialists of the Civil War, many of them finding warrant for saying that they and their comrades had been the proverbial blacksmiths who had kept the nail from falling out of the horse's shoe, thus saving the shoe, the horse, the rider, the message, the battle, the war, and the nation.

Lastly, we read the view of the invasion seen from the interior of the East Shore, available in the diary of R.I. Young of Middletown. Young first tried to get into the war on Wednesday, June 24, when he went to Harrisburg. The next day he tried "to get Eby to go in a cavelry with me but he would not go so I came home at half past one." He had his chance in Middletown by Saturday the 27th: "In the evening their was a meeting in the square for the purpos of starting a company." Young and his comrades were formally

organized the next day: "At nine oclock we had a meeting and all that signed their names to the company fell in rank and Rover marched us around town and then we adjourned to meet at seven in the evening." They hadn't been able to convince everyone in town, however, that the danger was sufficient: "Some others would not go becaus they would not go out of town," he wrote.

But with the help of his father ("Father told me he would take me to Harrisburg if I would go over the river in the trenches"), Young got up a crowd and went to Camp Curtin. They drew rations for 18 men and then went into the city to draw arms, but the armory was closed.

The next day, June 29, they started back to Middletown with 240 guns and 9,000 rounds of ammunition. "We got home about seven and some of the boys had a fite," he wrote, but Young and a friend were able to organize another company of 40 men in less than three hours. Eight of them, including the diarist, guarded a ford until four in the morning.

The next day, June 30, they mustered the new company and

Copied from a daguerreotype, circa 1860, this photograph of a horse and carriage is considered the oldest surviving photographic image of Harrisburg. (HSDC)

elected officers. Young became 3rd Sergeant. They drilled again in the evening, and went on picket again all night. And they drilled again the next day—if the Rebels invaded, Middletown's defenders would be orderly.

Late at night on July 3, there was a commotion:

The foundry bell rang and all the companies came out for it was an alarm but when they looked to see who rang the bell they could not be found so D. Cambell went in the shop and up in the garret we fount two of the boys and two down stairs we took them to the [squire's] office and he charged them two dollars a peace.

That was as much alarm as Middletown would have to bear. On the 4th of July Young's company "marched all over town" again. It was time for Young's father to spur him again: "father told me he would equip me if I would go so I went to Harrisburg." In the city he per-suaded Donald Cameron (Simon Cameron's son) "to go to the captin and see if he would take me." Young was not able to find out until Sunday if a company would take him. In any case, he never informed his diary; on Sunday, July 5, he only wrote "I was in Harrisburg all day." That was his last entry. Did he become a soldier, abandon his civilian diary, and start a war journal? There is no record of any R.I. Young becoming a member of a Pennsylvania unit during the Civil War. Perhaps he simply retired his diary and went back to Middletown when he saw that there would be no invasion.

These Civil War narratives from Camp Hill, Harrisburg, and Middletown are not quite as momentous as the chronicles of Gettysburg or even Carlisle, which was actually shelled and occupied. But the plain quality of Greater Harrisburg's days of war is worth knowing, for it shows the ennui that was the enemy of most men most of the time.

Despite the city's preparations (and perhaps some keen anticipation in certain quarters) Harrisburg sat untouched as the Civil War passed it by. Nearby Carlisle, as shown in Thomas Nast's drawing, was shelled by rebel troops and subsequently occupied. Courtesy, Cumberland County Historical Society

"Pappy" Boyer was a leader of the drive to clean up the Eighth
Ward, considered to be Harrisburg's moral low spot. When he
was not busy with such crusades or with his job as Poor
Director, Boyer entertained the youngsters of Harrisburg
with, first, this "kiddy tram," and, later, an
automobile. (HSDC)

VII
THE FUNERAL OF HARRY COOK IN THE OLD "ATE" WARD

By 1877 the Reconstruction of the South was over. Northern troops had been withdrawn from the conquered province, and both sides were free to concentrate on the material matters at hand—the completion of the industrial revolution. Rutherford B. Hayes, having just been elected President even though 250,000 more citizens had voted for Samuel J. Tilden, started Easter egg hunts on the Capitol lawn. Party politics and public architecture both became Byzantine in their complexity. In Pennsylvania, Senator Simon Cameron directed the former while the brilliant Frank Furness designed the latter. Also in Pennsylvania, according to Otto Bettman, "The railroad companies drew the map of the urban age. Altoona was a child of the Pennsylvania. The Lackawanna turned Slocum's Hole into Scranton." The railroads drew their way right into town—in Philadelphia the tracks came to the doorsteps of City Hall, the biggest building in America before the Pentagon. In Harrisburg the tracks cut the city in half, from top to bottom, but John Harris' and William Maclay's early planning had denied them the riverfront. There was a Grand Opera House built at Third and Walnut, and a high obelisk erected at Second and State to honor Civil War soldiers. Horses instead of men were now pulling the fire trucks around the city from blaze to blaze.

*Mark Twain and Charles Dudley Warner would name a novel after these years—*The Gilded Age, *a time when the surface of life was shiny and expensive, hiding whatever base metal was beneath it. By watching the funeral of Harry Cook in Harrisburg, one can scratch this city's bright surface and see the rowdy life below it.*

One day in 1912, as the demolition began in the Eighth Ward just east of the Capitol, an anonymous historian, looking at the leveling from one of the Capitol's windows, spoke his remembrance of the locale. We are drawn to it especially for his account of the funeral of Morris Henry Cook, who, with his wife Hattie, had owned the Ward's Lafayette Hall, famous in the past as a gambling den and rum mill.

I'll never forget the funeral of Harry Cook. [When] he died his wife determined that he should have a gorgeous funeral, with brass band accompaniment. Fancy that. On the day of the funeral the remains lay in state in the barroom, surrounded by floral tributes galore from the loving wife. Deceased was attired in his best suit, lavender trousers, black velvet coat, with rose in the lapel, low cut vest, open front starched shirt containing a diamond pin as big as the end of your thumb, low collar with wide-flowing white scarf, side-whiskers and moustache waxed to needle points. And that casket was solid rosewood with a plethora of silver ornaments and a large silver plate containing name, age and date of death of deceased. From early morn to the time set for the funeral, there was a constant stream of people going and coming to look upon the face of Harry. And the funeral procession was one never to be forgotten. First came the brass band playing the Dead March, followed by the minister and pallbearers, and then the hearse decorated with floral emblems. Then came the widow in deep mourning in a carriage all by herself, followed by at least fifty carriages containing the dead man's intimates and denizens of the underworld. Before the casket was closed the big diamond stud was taken from the dead man's shirt front, and his diamond rings, three in number, removed from his fingers. Hundreds followed the procession, and altogether it was such a funeral as is described by Mark Twain in telling of the burial of Buck Fanshaw. So, too, events in the Eighth ward were dated from Harry Cook's funeral.

The event has remarkable lessons to teach us about everyday life in the old "Ate" Ward. Like the funerals of Chicago mobsters in the 1920s, the last rites of Harry Cook reveal something of the relationship between underworld and overworld.

The popularity and panache of the funeral suggest that the saloon keeper had countless customers wanting every kind of miscreant's recreation, and so often that Harry and Hattie became a singularly wealthy partnership. But their prosperity was probably not able to purchase them official respectability, so they took advantage of the right occasion both to copy and to mock the propriety of those who had gotten rich correctly.

Suit Harry like a Sultan, follow him like a Pharaoh, inter him like the Inca. Buy the blessing of the priest and the bonhomie of the police. Choose the choicest coffin for the corpse, afford the finest fragrance from the florist. Gather a group that nears the size of the lamenting for Lincoln. And afterwards with every bottle and bet, the Eighth will elevate him more than all the mayors.

Harry Cook, "tall, well-proportioned, handsome, of commanding appearance, a ready and effective conversationalist," was dead at 40. He was, according to his remembrancer, the Eighth Ward's most "typical and representative"

citizen. His constituents included many recently emigrated Russian Jews and even more blacks, who had been ensconced in the Eighth Ward long before (some were escapees from slavery). They lined the streets at his funeral, and "many a dusky eye shed tears," for Cook was said to have had "a heart readily touched by tales of woe. He had given money lavishly to the poor and the needy. He had helped bury the dead of these poor folk when men who would have considered Harry Cook's touch contamination had turned coldly away."

But if Harry was "typical," his Lafayette Hall was hardly common. It was described as being like "certain pretentious resorts of the day in New York." The basement was a restaurant, the first floor an ornate barroom, and the next floor "a free-and-easy dance hall where most anything would go." Even the Hall's

This cigar store Indian has a long history of ownership in Dauphin County. It is now in the collection of the Historical Society of Dauphin County. Photo, Mark H. Dorfman

Although the tobacco shop at the left can scarcely be taken as a sign of depravity, this is an aspect of the Eighth Ward by day. This view of West Alley from North Street shows a neighborhood going to seed and eventually to be obliterated. (HSDC)

stalls for horses had mirrors. The Lafayette was connected to other buildings in the neighborhood that were managed by Hattie Cook.

The low life collecting in Lafayette Hall had three sources. First, there were the canal boat men ("the men who followed the tow path . . . were not generally the men who sought out a prayer meeting when they tied up for the night"). Then there were the Up-River Yankees ("For months they wrought laboriously amidst primeval solitudes . . . with the Spring freshets, they would take their rafts to the lower Susquehanna . . . many of them made Harrisburg their objective point for a seance with the various phases of

Harrisburg's letter carriers sat for this group portrait in 1879. The city's first letter carrier, Jonas K. Rudy, is in the middle of the front row. President James K. Polk appointed Rudy in 1847. (HSDC)

sin prior to their departure for another long era of cutting and logging"). And finally there were the Civil War Yankees—about 300,000 en toto lolled around Camp Curtin in the northern part of Harrisburg during the 1860s.

The soldiers at Camp Curtin had "money to burn and a burning desire to spend it," and in Harrisburg there were "maids of the town, and matrons too, whose husbands were at the front, who were willing to assist in the depletion of plethoric pocketbooks." The camp's "wild young blades, freed from the shackles of home restraint," rushed to the Eighth Ward, where, on Sundays especially, the "drink flowed in maddening swirls," and "brutal fights commenced." For many years thereafter, wrote one reporter, the city was jammed with "flotsam and jetsam, storm-tossed wreckage on life's sea, that dated from Camp Curtin days."

After the Civil War there was a fourth source of low life in the Eighth Ward, the State Street Bridge Gang. In 1873 a bridge was completed on State Street over the Pennsylvania Railroad tracks. It protected pedestrians from one danger but exposed them to another as the bridge became a hangout for the Eighth Ward "toughs," who were reputed to be even rougher than the "Sixteen Bleeders." They bullied and robbed citizens bottlenecked at the bridge until an even tougher judge put one of them in jail for two years for stealing a dime.

All the while the Eighth was rugged, some efforts were made to damp the debauch. In the 1870s a moral crusade was begun by businessmen, the evangelist Samuel Sayford, and Poor Director Charles

The second Rockville Bridge replaced its wooden predecessor in 1877. The famed stone arch bridge would in turn replace this steel structure crossing the Susquehanna River and the Pennsylvania Canal. (HSDC)

Dauphin County Court judges John Snyder, John Pearson, and Isaac Mumma posed in the courtroom in front of a trompe l'oeil painting of Justice for this 1870s photo. (HSDC)

The beaux arts-style Harrisburg Post Office is shown under construction in 1880. A building with a distinguished air, it was razed in the 1960s to make way for the black cube Federal Building. (HSDC)

Boyer. They got Harry Cook's liquor license rescinded, and Harrisburg's "last glorious palace of sin" was emptied after Cook's death. About 20 years later, John W. Brown turned the Hall into a Rescue Mission. He left the decor more or less the same: the marble bar stayed, and behind it all the cobwebbed bottles, "but the walls that once re-echoed to bald blasphemy and obscene jests were now the scene of earnest prayer and melodious songs of praise."

The rest of the Eighth Ward was born again in 1912, when the plans for the Capitol Park Extension were completed. Demolition was vigorous until 1919, then measured until the project was finished in 1940. Now Harry Cook's old neighborhood is lawn and state office buildings. Between Walnut and North streets and Fourth Street and the Pennsylvania Railroad tracks, the wreckers removed 527 buildings, including hundreds of residences, a brewery, market house,

shoe company, coach works, iron foundry, several hotels, fire houses, churches, and schools.

The *Harrisburg Telegraph* seemed a little sad about the wrecking as it began in 1912, but covered it mainly as "progress" since the old Ward had been the city's biggest pen for black sheep—"crimes beyond number have been committed in the Eighth Ward ... some of the most sensational murders on the police records of the city have had the Eighth Ward for a stage setting." Also in 1912, J. Howard Wert, a moralist who seemed delighted to write about immorality, began publishing a series of three dozen articles on "The Passing of the Old Eighth"; these essays, quoted often here, remain our best sources on its everyday history.

The Eighth was a classic example of the fleshpots that existed around industrial entrepots in late Victorian America. The Ward was allegedly notorious around the state, but it could not have been much worse in its time than Philadelphia's and Pittsburgh's worst neighborhoods. But it was probably more decadent, in its own way, than anything we would dream to demolish in Harrisburg in our time. If you believe in clean, uncrowded streets, legal products and merchants, and fairly gentle nights—all civilized virtues, certainly—then you will likely view the evacuation and pacification of the Eighth Ward as a "reform." Yet, it is clear that the Ward served certain human needs, for how could it have prospered otherwise? It was the scene for the expression of particular types of manhood and womanhood, and the only "community" many deviates and minorities could find.

The Eighth Ward in its heyday and Harry Cook both seem to have passed into history undocumented by any surviving photographs. The pictures that do survive give only a hint of the rough-and-tumble life of the streets. Here is the West Side of Filbert Street looking north from Walnut in 1910. (HSDC)

The Bolton Hotel, now known as the Warner, has been a landmark on Market Square since the mid-19th century. In this early 20th-century postcard, the Bolton proudly displays a mansardic roof that was probably added in the 1870s. (PHMC)

The members of the Harrisburg Wheel Club proudly display their "ordinaries," the high-wheeled bicycles that added adventure to the new sport. (HSDC)

VIII
CHILDREN'S DAY AT THE DAUPHIN COUNTY CENTENNIAL CELEBRATION

The late 19th century was a time for celebrations in America. There were hundreds of hundredth birthday parties in towns, counties, states, and the nation itself. The Centennial Exposition in Philadelphia in 1876 saluted the signing of the Declaration of Independence. The party was set up in Fairmount Park inside 180 buildings, including the largest wooden building ever nailed together in America. President Grant and Emperor Dom Pedro of Brazil turned on a giant steam engine that powered the whole affair.

Other similarly symbolic and national displays abounded. Yellowstone National Park had opened in 1872, a tribute to nature. The National Baseball League was organized in 1876, saluting sport (the first All-American football team would be announced in 1889). The first national Labor Day was held in New York in 1882, a recognition of human energy. Buffalo Bill Cody brought out his national Wild West Show in 1883, a paean to the frontier past. The Brooklyn Bridge, symbol of greatest engineering, was completed in 1883, and the Washington Monument, shrine to the greatest patriot, was capstoned in 1884. The Statue of Liberty, come-on to the world, was done in 1886.

Dauphin County's Centennial Celebration of 1885 was the local example of this national spirit that hoped to bring the country together, toast it, and then move it forward. The details of Children's Day on September 14, however, suggest the house was still divided against itself.

September 14, 1885:

Harrisburg's Centennial was sensational. The celebration lasted four days, from Monday, September 14, 1885, to Thursday the 17th, and brought 100,000 people into town. The first day was Children's Day, the second, Military and Civic Day, the third, Industrial Display Day, and the fourth, Firemen's Day.

An antiquarian display ran throughout the celebration, and it was the city's biggest flea market ever. Though no antiques were sold, only shown, it included anything imaginably historical, from the founder John Harris' silver knee buckles to a wooden cup made from the tree to which his father was tied; from Captain Eli Daugherty's embattled pocket Bible and gold watch ("A Confederate bullet struck the watch . . . and then penetrated the Bible, stopping about half way") to W. Wallace Geety's leftover grapeshot ("entered Mr. Geety's head at the base of the nose"); from D.S. Early's wooden cuckoo clock ("Very old") to John B. Cox's blunderbuss ("No history"). It sounds just like the sort of artifactual sideshow the old Historical Society of Dauphin County would have sponsored. It was "conceded on all sides the most unique, as it was the most successful, exhibition of the kind ever held in this or any other country."

The volume documenting the celebration, *Centenary Memorial of the Erection of the County of Dauphin and the Founding of the City of Harrisburg* was edited by the famous local historian Dr. William Henry Egle and published a year later. Setting aside the pieces of the true mulberry tree, *Centennial* is probably the city's most ubiquitous memorabilia; boxes of them can still be

bought. Like so many salutes from the past, it is full of lists of committees, names, numbers, things, and all the words of all the speeches their leaders gave.

Between the lines of all this propriety, and oftentimes right in them, we can find unofficial insights into Harrisburg's social life a hundred years ago. This is especially the case with Finley Thomas' recounting of the details of the parade on Children's Day; he was an eyewitness because he was the Chief Marshal.

Harrisburg, wrote Thomas, brought in the first day of the Centennial celebration with "whoop and hurrah, and ding dong, and boom and whizz." A cannon shot started it all, then church bells chimed. Trains and wagons came in full of "country cousins" from everywhere, "all bent on having a good time." The city was festooned with flags, bunting, and gaudy calico, "But like Harrisburg, it never awakened to the fact that it *ought to decorate* until the last hour . . . It

Dr. William Henry Egle (1831-1901), when not engaged in the practice of medicine, became the principal historian of Harrisburg and Dauphin County in the 19th century. This daguerreotype shows him in his early twenties, obviously keen to begin his twofold career. (HSDC)

This late 19th century postcard celebrates one of Harrisburg's firehouses and its up-to-date equipment. (PHMC)

The Rockville Bridge, north of Harrisburg, is justly acclaimed as the longest stone arch bridge in the world. (PHMC)

seemed as if they realized for the first time that Harrisburg was really going to have a Centennial celebration to amount to something."

"The school children took possession of Harrisburg on Monday," he continued. They collected in their classrooms around town by 8:15 that morning, ready for the invasion of Harris Park, along the river. Perhaps with forethought of the chaos to come, "many teachers absented themselves and refused to take part in the proceedings."

Thomas thought he saw ethnic groups mingled. The children "were of all sorts, sizes, and conditions and colors. There were children of all nationalities—from the fresh-looking, sturdy thoroughbred American through the gamut of English, French, Swede, Irish, Italian, German and every other country." He also thought he saw classes mingled. "The boy whose father can count his money by the thousands marched linked arms with the lad whose father works for ninety cents

The Harris Park School as it appeared around 1890 gives an idea of the solid structures the city was providing for the education of its children. Here the 4,542 youngsters assembled to march to John Harris's nearby grave. (HSDC) From Art Work of Harrisburg

a day as a laborer." Those two classes were at truce together on account of their similar sentiment for their country's sign: "They both wore the American flag on their bosoms." He thought that sign even allowed the races to mingle: "The little colored boy bore aloft his flag and marched with the same saucy, independent step as his whiter school-fellow." But the schools were segregated, and so was the march. According to the text, the children would proceed in the following order:

Verbeke street school, estimated 525 children in charge of supervisory principal and teacher.
Lincoln school (colored), North Street, W. H. Layton, principal, 60 scholars.

Calder street school (colored) marshaled by Mr. Scott, 50 scholars.
Paxtang school, Miss Kate Miller, principal, 70 scholars.

When there was drill order, Thomas credits that to the difference between boys and girls. "The girls, as a rule, marched better than the boys, although the Harris Park boys made a pretty appearance sixteen abreast."

While the children rendezvoused at Harris Park around the grave of John Harris the elder, "a livelier crowd was never seen." The girls, again, were generally "quiet and well-behaved," but the "true boys," again, "held high carnival." Possibly forgetting the code of concord, they took time for a "few fights":

Links with the past are seen in the above faces of two female centenarians, and a dignified legislative doorkeeper, all recorded in late 19th-century photographs. (HSDC)

Dr. Eysler looks on while young pharmacist Harry O. Millen compounds a prescription in Eysler's Drug Store, circa 1885. (HSDC)

A newspaper reporter separated two boys who were at it hammer and tongs to the great delight of their school-fellows. Two boys banged each other over the head with flag sticks, and were parted; but it was all in fun, and so then and there over the grounds the lads had little battles, which lasted a few minutes, and then the participants were good friends again.

When they arrived at the obelisk at Second and State streets, the children sang "My Country 'Tis of Thee," and prepared to be issued their souvenir, a card about seven by nine inches depicting an earlier tribe of spirited Americans sportive in their own way (a picture of "An Attempt to Burn John Harris at the Present Site of Harrisburg, in the

Year 1720"). Each youth was to receive a card after countermarching by the monument. Scanning the 4,542 pairs of hands (the official count, at least), the organizing committee "determined to carry out the programme and the band was ordered to play. It did so with a will and the countermarch began." Each child got his momento, if "amid much shouting and jostling."

Later that evening the Court House was filled with an "intelligent" audience ready for an "intellectual treat," a speech by Judge John Bayard McPherson. Besides the cerebral sort in the crowd, "also many ladies graced the occasion with their smiling, beauteous and benign presence."

General Simon Cameron, the Centennial's organizer, introduced their orator. The Judge had much to insist. Harrisburg's history was the struggle of free men against nature and savage, he said, until "man touched the shoulder of his fellow-man and set himself to establish social order." They had done that today, he claimed:

Our race knows well the power of an ordered state, yields easily to wise restraint, will bear, nay, will command, that rule be strong on fit occasion; . . . through every form it does demand the substance of control. In the main this principle has not been shaken, and today it is the base on which our massive strength finds rest.

Jos. Claster's clothing and notion store was housed in an old building at the southeast corner of Second and Chestnut streets. The unpaved streets and the trolley tracks were typical of 1890s Harrisburg. (HSDC)

Although the centennial celebration of 1885 was an extravagant civic wingding, few photographs survive to memorialize it. A great welcoming arch was built at the corner of Fifth and Market streets. It is pictured here just as the celebration was getting underway. (HSDC)

But the control and the order of that celebration day were only skin deep even when they showed. Thomas' observations inadvertently reveal a society quite taken with differences between native and immigrant, rich and poor, black and white, young and old, and male and female. He had witnessed disunity, but interpreted it as unity.

In his prayer before noon at the Court House, after the parade, the Reverend William Harris read the morning's general events more deeply and worriedly than either Judge McPherson or Chief Marshal Thomas:

Defend our liberties, preserve our unity, save us from violence, discord and confusion, from pride and arrogancy, and from every evil way. Fashion into one happy people the multitude brought hither out of many kindred and tongues.

The Old Home Week parade of 1905 included these women's groups. (HSDC)

IX
HARRISBRAG

By the time Americans saw the 20th century arriving, they also noticed the trouble the 19th century had left behind. Forty years of remarkable urban and industrial growth needed to be reconsidered, redirected, and reorganized—reformed, in short. This was the time for "progressivism" of one sort or another in government and society. Its leaders were Presidents Theodore Roosevelt and Woodrow Wilson, Governors John Altgeld, Robert M. LaFollette, and Hiram Johnson, and countless mayors, professionals, journalists, and businessmen. Their national achievements included passage of such laws as the Sherman Anti-Trust Act (1890), the Pure Food and Drug Act (1906), and the Federal Trade Commission Act (1914). At the state and municipal levels, the initiative, referendum, recall, direct primary, and short ballot reforms were most significant.

Progressivism had its aesthetic side too, which can be seen in the "City Beautiful" movements of the early 20th century. The idea was to up-date urban life, especially by building modern transportation, sanitation, and recreation systems, and even more noticeably by landscaping great parks. The supreme achievement was Frederick Law Olmsted's Central Park in New York City. The broad plazas, green spaces, and ornate monuments of the Chicago World's Fair of 1893 were also models for other cities to follow. All this required careful coordination by public and private leaders.

Harrisburg's beautification and modernization, which is still appreciated, was among the best-planned and best-looking projects in the country. We begin this story by looking at a little public relations pamphlet published by the Harrisburg Daily Telegraph *in 1904, puffery to the city's progress supposedly written by its carrier boys.*

January 1, 1904:

If you are looking for highfalutin' phrases, neatly turned sentences and Websterian ponderosity, understand right now that you will not find them here. This is going to be a plain statement of fact and facts . . . We believe in Harrisburg. . . .

The *Telegraph* carrier boys' pitch to the city might be admired for its vigor, if not its artfulness. Their 20-page New Year's card for 1904 tried to list everything the city should be famous for. "Proud? You bet," they said. "Harrisburg has outgrown the clothes of ten years ago and is beginning to put on a brand new suit of the latest style, made by experts." They wanted their readers to know that the city would take "the biggest brace in its history this year," that "the whole country" had begun "to talk of the Harrisburg idea," including "thousands of newspapers." This place, they said, "is not a bump on a log. She moves and keeps a-movin'."

In 1904 "almost all" the greater Harrisburg area's citizens "come to town to shop," they claimed, and those shoppers would soon have more paved streets to travel on. The water filtration plant on Island Park would soon be completed. "Harrisburg does not live in the dark at night"—there were 450 street lights. They counted 180 "schools" in the city! A new Masonic temple was being built, a new city hall was promised, the new state capitol would be finished by next January, and a new Reading passenger station was scheduled to open in April. "There may be some vacant houses in Harrisburg," they said, but only "for a minute," because there were

The proposed view of the new capitol closely resembles the project as completed. The elaborate statuary over the portico, however, was never finished. The plaza in front of the capitol is used for a legislative parking lot today. (HSDC)

22 building and loan associations scurrying to satisfy buyers and sellers. There were three telegraph and two telephone companies, 19 daily and weekly newspapers, and 100 passenger trains landing each day. "In this respect . . . Harrisburg is several to the good over Philadelphia." The city boasted "the finest Young Men's Christian Association building in the state, outside of Philadelphia," a "magnificent amusement hall—the Lyceum," a new steel bridge over the river, the state champion baseball team, and "the best" athletic grounds.

What did the city manufacture? Four thousand men worked in city iron and steel factories and 8,000 "on our borders" (meaning Steelton). They further listed:

picture frames	*mantels*
patent medicines	*mince meat*
pleasure carriages	*nails*
awnings	*rubber stamps*
pretzels	*sewer pipe*
band instruments	*shirts*
barber supplies	*umbrellas*
brooms	*typewriters*
coffins	*stained glass*
cigars	*silks*
sun bonnets	*leather*
revolvers	*lime*
organs	*liquor*

and many other practical products.

"Harrisburg has everything to make it the greatest inland city of Pennsylvania," they concluded, and promised "that's what it's going to be before the decade closes."

Professor William H. Wilson's history of Harrisburg's "City Beautiful" movement, published recently in *Pennsylvania History*, shows why the newsboys were so exuberant and how their town became a modern metropolis after

1900. His main points are that the movement was well-planned by prominent private citizens, and that their good plans were executed by private experts, with public money.

Mira Lloyd Dock's speech to the Board of Trade on December 20, 1900, started the spree. Her show of 100 stereoptican slides compared Harrisburg's "hideous conditions" to the good taste of Milwaukee, Boston, and European cities. She also emphasized "the cash value of cleanliness and beauty," insuring a good chance of success for her recommended reforms.

Mira Lloyd Dock, born into wealth, early on tired of music, art, and the other subjects young ladies of good family were expected to devote themselves to. She became an ardent and effective proponent of environmentalism and women's liberation (although that is not what it was called 80 years ago). Her Civic Club was instrumental in the election of Vance McCormick in 1902 and the subsequent transformation of the city. (HSDC)

The election of 1902 concentrated almost entirely on the environment and the quality of life in Harrisburg. The good guys (who won) were reformers like Vance McCormick (who became mayor) and J. Horace McFarland—with Mira Dock an acknowledged presence behind the scenes (where it was said a lady belonged). This streetcar with its banners rolled around Harrisburg on election day, clanging citizens to awareness. Courtesy, McFarland Papers (PHMC)

In April 1901, the *Telegraph* began headlining on the front page its support for city improvements and beautification. There should be "parks, pure water, paved streets, a city hall." A campaign for a bond issue was led by J. Horace McFarland, Mira Dock, and 19 other respectable burghers who were mostly mainstream Protestants, Republicans, well-educated, and relatively young—the average about 40 years of age. The coming election of Vance McCormick in 1902 would assure mayoral support. In Professor Wilson's words, "the elite would assume its class responsibility," for they never doubted that "physical improvement would elevate the urban population." True utilitarians, they would promote the greatest good for the greatest number, (or at least what the campaigners thought was good for them, as there is no record of the greatest number being asked exactly what they wanted.)

A private fund was established to retain expert advice, and the campaigners firmly buttonholed the elite for donations. Wilson quotes McFarland as saying, "men with nothing to do but run big industries"—such as John Reynders, Superintendent of Pennsylvania Steel—"came into your office and looked pleasant until you cashed up, or signed up." The campaigners then controlled this fund, and thus the planning. Engineers and architects were brought in and put to work. James Fuertes of New York took charge of the river, water, and sewage plans, M.R. Sherred of Newark handled streets, and Warren Manning of Boston, a friend of Dock and McFarland, designed parks and boulevards.

With sound plans in hand, the campaigners now called themselves the Harrisburg League for Municipal Improvement, and convinced city council to submit a $1,090,000 bond issue for approval at the next election in February 1902. The League opened an office downtown, began raising more money for publicity, and recruited ordinary citizens to join up, charging $1.00 for membership. They had public meetings, invited questions, and provided answers, because some opposition to their plans was appearing. According to Wilson, skeptics argued that this "Front Street Scheme" would raise taxes and rents as well as elevate the moral tone. The League had local youth deliver leaflets to every home in the city, broadsides that called their opponents "tight-fisted clams." The Civic Club, headquarters for the city's active women, got behind the League and more stereoptican shows were put on. The state legislature cooperated by proposing to move the capital back to Philadelphia unless Harrisburg freshened up, and nature assisted too, by overflowing Paxton Creek in

The E.G. Hoover Jewelry Store was a Harrisburg institution until it went of business recently. Its longest business interruption came when the Penn Harris Hotel next to it was demolished. By accident the hotel fell on the jewelry store. (HSDC)

A group of prosperous Harrisburg businessmen began the Poor Man's Fishing Club on the Susquehanna in the 1890s. (HSDC)

December and January, fortuitously demonstrating the need for flood control.

According to Wilson, the League also tried a little quiet manipulation of public opinion before the election:

Its members investigated how drinking water from the sewage-laden Susquehanna was affecting the incidence of typhoid, and were dismayed to learn of no dramatic increase in the disease. They did discover lax reporting among local physicians. The doctors were encouraged to bring their reports up to date in January. The result was a manufactured typhoid "epidemic" of thirty cases in one month, double the number of the previous quarter. After the successful bond issue campaign in February the reported cases dropped to nine and in March they fell to four.

The election of February 18, 1902, was a slick victory. The bond issue was passed by two out of three voters, 7,319 to 3,729. Middle class wards approved it more strongly than working class wards, but there was no denying the widespread support.

By 1915 the improvements had been installed. Parkland had increased from 46 to 958 acres. A 140-acre lake was created. The river was deepened by a dam, and concrete steps three miles long were built on the banks. Island Park, one of 11 new parks, had athletic fields and a grandstand. There was a nine-hole golf course in Reservoir Park. Seventy-four miles of roads were now paved, up from about four miles in 1902. The city had filtered water, intercepting sewers, and better flood control. Another $1,341,000 in bonds had been approved for public works. Meanwhile, the city's population had grown from 51,000 to 73,000, and working privately, McFarland and Herman Miller had developed lovely Bellevue Park.

McFarland announced that no other city in the country had done so many valuable things at once, so "harmoniously" and so reliant "upon the plans of experts." Knowing what the burghers wanted to hear, he said Harrisburg was "a made-over town with a degree of efficiency" that reminded him of "the average German city."

As a direct result of the election of 1902, citizens of Harrisburg stopped drinking and bathing directly in the water of the Susquehanna. Some of the work required to complete the civic water system is pictured here, as workers lay pipe to a filtration house. (HSDC)

Bunting decorates a Locust Street commercial building, still standing today, decorated for the dedication of the new capitol in 1906. (HSDC)

It is Professor Wilson's final judgement, however, that by 1915 Harrisburg's "City Beautiful" movement had tired as well as triumphed. J. Horace McFarland had continued to lead but was continually frustrated, being forced to "meddle" rather than manage. As a member of the Park Commission, McFarland felt surrounded by dunces, according to Wilson. McFarland told Dock, " . . . [they] didn't know a pine from a pumpkin. . . ." (At one time he had had to rescue his sacred shade trees from being toppled by the workmen laying sewers.) The President of the Park Commission let billboards be put on his own property even after McFarland offered to match the advertising revenues if the President would desist. McFarland said he "upset a scheme . . . to girdle Front Street by a trolley line," but found one of his own civic associates had been behind it. He and another park commissioner, one M. Harvey Taylor, did not get along well. McFarland considered Taylor a man whose "dignity" consisted of "running a cigar store." As their last snub, his opponents left McFarland off the new Planning Commission in 1914.

City planning would continue after 1915 in Harrisburg, but it would be headed for the "City Practical" more than the "City Beautiful." Still, the old improvers had built even better than they knew, and they showed the progressive's neatest skill: how to organize.

This truck being used by the Harrisburg Transfer Company was a "Morton Truck built in Harrisburg." Like many communities, Harrisburg had a small automotive industry at the turn of the century. (HSDC)

X
ALIENS IN ISRAEL

*In the age of American industry, Pennsylvania forged both swords
and plowshares or anything else of iron and steel, making engines,
locomotives, and rails for them to run on, electrical equipment, automobile accessories, and machines to make machines. Pittsburgh
became the largest center of metal production in the world, and the
great furnaces in Steelton, just outside Harrisburg, were rarely cool.
Great fortunes, great organizations, and great factories grew up
together, all propelled by great gangs of labor.*

*Most of the men who worked in Steelton in 1911 were not born
Americans. They were recent immigrants, taking the Statue of Liberty's calling seriously. From 1900 to 1910, nearly nine million came
to this country. Leopold Stokowski, about to be appointed Musical
Director of the Philadelphia Orchestra, was an immigrant too, but
the steel men had little in common with him, for they would be conducted by the rhythms of the mills, and stare at smokestacks instead
of batons. They changed the construction and composition of this
country forever, and became the base, eventually, of the new cities,
new politics, and new economy. They equipped us for two world
wars and won them both.*

*Ultimately they were Steelton—company town, manufacturer of
new Americans, cathedral of blood iron trade, stacked houses facing
the fires that grow bones for tall buildings, reminder that all of us
were once outsiders.*

1911:

In 1911 the United States Immigration Commission published 42 volumes of information on the effects of immigration on America, especially on industry. From a portion of the Commission's report *Immigrants in Industries, Part 2: Iron and Steel*, we discover that the commissioners believed that the nation's future would depend on the assimilation of the "new" immigrants from southern and eastern Europe, just as they believed that the nation's past had depended on the assimilation of the "old" immigrants from northern and western Europe. But the report found that the new immigrants were not assimilating, were not "melting" in the pot of public life. The Serbs, Croats, Bulgarians from Macedonia, Slovenes, Magyars, Jews, Poles, Slovaks—often just referred to in the newspapers as "Slavs" or "Austrians"—were still peasants under their workclothes.

To be sure, the commissioners

Charles M. Schwab, president of Bethlehem Steel in the early 1900s, had a vital role in the expansion of the steel industry. His decisions profoundly affected the development of Steelton and many other Pennsylvania towns. From Cirker, Dictionary of American Portraits *(Dover: 1967)*

were proud that America had received new immigrants that were "the strongest, the most enterprising, and the best of their class." They were officially happy that even the new immigrants' "racial and physical characteristics do not survive under the new social and climatic environment of America."

The good results aside, however, the Commission saw the need for a plan to exclude the new immigrants, if not eliminate them. Enough immigration was enough, the commissioners concurred. Their report pronounced that "the American people, as in the past," would continue to "welcome the oppressed" to the Promised Land, but henceforth, they recommended, immigration should be "such both in quality and quantity as not to make too difficult the process of assimilation." Future laws on the "admission of aliens should be based primarily upon economic or business considerations touching the prosperity and well-being of our people." Such laws would repeal "the natural incentive to treat the immigration movement from the standpoint of sentiment." No sentiment need be lost on the new immigrants in any case, asserted the commissioners, because they were not "oppressed":

. . . emigration from Europe is not now an absolute economic necessity, and as a rule those who emigrate to the United States are impelled by a desire for betterment rather than the necessity of escaping intolerable conditions.

The Commission thus proposed laws that would exclude "those unable to read or write in some language," exclude "unskilled laborers unaccompanied by wives

City elementary schools were seldom coeducational in the years before World War I, as attested to by this unidentified class in 1910. (HSDC)

or families,'' and increase ''the amount of money required to be in possession of the immigrant.'' Furthermore, they proposed that ''any alien who becomes a public charge within three years after his arrival should be subject to deportation.'' The commissioners had built a tight case, on paper, against the new aliens. Eventually, embodied in the Immigration Act of 1924, the commissioners' restrictive sentiments severely rationed immigration from southern and eastern Europe and stopped it altogether from the Orient.

The United States Immigration Commission report of 1911 is relevant to the history of Greater Harrisburg because its rationale came partly from the Commission's study of Steelton, contained in volume eight. The commissioners believed they saw some of the worst effects of the new immigration in that town's rugged life, a miniature of the feudal old world they knew America must never be.

Professor John Bodnar's analysis of the Commission's report, covered in his book *Immigration and Industrialization: Ethnicity in an American Mill Town, 1870-1940*, shows, for example, that Steelton's

Opposite top: *In the early 1900s cars were a rare sight in the country north of Harrisburg. A note attached to this photograph suggests that the cars belonged to historically minded Harrisburghers who were on an exploratory trip to the countryside. (HSDC)*

Opposite bottom: *Driving a coach and four was a gentleman's sport. A group of Harrisburg gentlemen visit Gettysburg in this 1910 photo. (HSDC)*

housing was precisely segregated in 1910. The native-born whites, Irish, and Germans all lived mixed together north of Front Street on the West Side. Blacks and Jews had neighborhoods of their own north of Front Street across from the steel mill. At the "Lower End," still north of Front Street, lived most of the Italians and Slovenes and the bulk of the Serbs and Croats. South of Front Street, in between the railroad tracks and the canal and just west of the mill, lived all the Bulgarians and the remainder of the Serbs and Croats— the "foreign part" of town, according to the local newspaper. This segregation had settled down on Steelton between 1880 and 1910. In 1880 no one living in Steelton had been born in southern or eastern Europe. By 1910 Italians, Slovenians, and Croatians were one-third of the town's population, and more than one-half of the steel mill's workforce.

Jobs and wages were just as precisely segregated in the mill by 1910. Where working conditions were the harshest, there one found the most foreign-born and black workers, and where conditions were less harsh, there one found the fewest ethnics. Bodnar writes,

In 1902 five "Austrians"—Jurovic, Marovoich, Gatis, Muza, and Radjanovic—were burned to death "in a horrible manner" when molten metal from the open hearth poured on them. In 1906 Anton Pijac, a boy of sixteen, fell through the top of a gas oven and was cremated. . . . The list of victims in 1907 speaks for itself: Tesak, Pajolic, Stifko, Knukle, Termer, Petruti, Pierce, Oconicke, Ukelic, Krameric, Szep, Peffer, Gross, Susic, Restoff, Trajbarico, Polanec, Turnbaugh, and Pugar.

Nearly 80 percent of all the native whites were skilled workers earning more than $1.50 per day in 1910. About 59 percent of the native blacks were in that category. Approximately 47 percent of the Slovenians, 34 percent of the Croatians, 14 percent of the Serbians, and 8 percent of the Bulgarians were skilled workers making that rate of pay. All the remainder of the eastern Europeans were unskilled workers making less than $1.50 per day. The average unskilled immigrant earned 11 cents an hour. The ore shovels were called "Hunky banjos." Of 136 foremen, 117 were Americans, Germans, or Irish. And according to Bodnar, the immigrants would not rise from rags to riches very soon: "The distinctive characteristic of Steelton's work force from 1880 to 1925 was career immobility."

The commissioners found that social segregation in Steelton was coupled with ethnic antagonism. Their report said there was "general deprecation" of the immigrants rather than "open hostility." Copying down some of the native white's stereotyping (and engaging in a little of their own), the commissioners wrote,

The Magyars are regarded as the most effective laborers on the general labor force. They drink more alcoholic liquor than the Macedonians, but less than the Slavs, and are considered more trustworthy than the latter. The South Italians . . . are active, but less industrious than the Croatians, and less able to endure high temperatures . . . [the Italians] have a poor reputation for trustworthiness. The Macedonians are conscientious plodders, willing to do the work required of them, but ineffective through awkwardness . . . The negro is

Horace McFarland, author, rosarian, and businessman, sits on a rise amidst a growth of virgin hemlock trees at Fort Hunter. McFarland was instrumental in founding the rose garden near Polyclinic Hospital. (HSDC)

dy people who came before the sixties to find a place where they might worship God according to the dictates of their own conscience, to build homes for themselves . . . but from pauper districts of Southern Europe . . . the incubators of nihilism, anarchy, disease, and crime . . .

Therefore, be it resolved that we demand enactment of such laws as will shield us from the depressing effects of unrestricted immigration, to the end that the American laborer may not only be protected against the product of foreign pauper laborer, but that we may be protected against direct competition in our own country by the incoming of the COMPETITIVE ALIEN—the foreign pauper laborers themselves.

It is Bodnar's judgement, however, that the Anglo-Saxon leadership of Steelton was ultimately more interested in controlling the new immigrants than in condemning them. He writes,

Ethnic communities could remain as long as immigrants cleaned neighborhoods, ceased particular ethnic customs such as parading, limited their drinking, learned the lessons of Protestant Christianity, memorized patriotic songs, spoke English, voted Republican, and above all, were thrifty and content.

The aliens' response to "general deprecation," was to "turn inward and occupy themselves with their own problems," says Bodnar. They organized fraternal associations and churches based on ethnicity and kinship, and waited for the day their children would inherit the earth beyond the hearth.

Now Steelton's best days are gone, the youngsters sigh, but the worst days too, the elders say.

no longer a factor in the general labor gang . . . strange to say, he is unable to endure the intense and steady heat of the open hearth . . .

"The American laborer does not care to work with the 'Hunkie'," observed the commissioners, who decided it was best to douse the flame before the lid blew off the melting pot.

American laborers' opinions of the "Hunkies" had not been kept a secret. In 1905 the Order of United American Mechanics' Steelton chapter, an organization of native white skilled workers, issued the following proclamation:

Whereas, the record of immigration shows that more than 800,000 foreign-born persons landed upon American soil during the past year—not the stur-

IRON WORKS OF THE McCORMICK ESTATE AT HARRISBURG, PA.

NEW YORK DAILY GRAPHIC - MAY 3, 1878

The iron and steel industries became important to Dauphin County before the Civil War. The post-Civil War years saw the flowering of the family-owned operations. Iron and steel strengthened the fortunes of such local families as the Camerons and the McCormicks. (HSDC)

Wistar Iron Works, shown in this late 19th century photo, stood along the Pennsylvania canal. A producer of pig iron, it was typical of the many independent iron and steel mills that developed in the Harrisburg area. (HSDC)

*Dressed for gym at the age of about ten, Cub Houston sported
a white shirt, black trousers, black stockings, and high-button
gym shoes. Courtesy, Cub Houston*

XI
CUB'S RAGTIME

When did modern times begin? Some historians say America has always been a modern society, that it never had to overthrow Old World ways. Others say old times here were forgotten after the Civil War, after Americans had faced the facts of total conflict and whole populations had fought one another, not just professional soldiers meeting on a field of honor. Still others say modern times began after World War I, after Americans had sensed that President Wilson's "war to end all wars" led mainly to their intermission, when radios and cars began to occupy so many of our hours, and shocking new forms of creativity signaled a new sensibility, when men and women ceased to wear only dark clothes and to think only the brightest thoughts.

All three dates are persuasive, but especially the last one. Examining life in 1917 specifically, one can see the last light of innocence just before the dawn of modern doubt. By 1917, 24 states had voted to prohibit alcohol, completing the ultimate Victorian reform, but Margaret Sanger had just opened America's first birth control clinic in Brooklyn, defying the ultimate Victorian taboo. Norman Rockwell had just begun to illustrate covers for the Saturday Evening Post, *creating a remarkable reservoir of images of the traditional good life, yet "Dada" artists were executing works of "meaningful nothing, where nothing has any meaning." In 1917 old-fashioned ideas dominated the new movies—"Birth of a Nation," "The Tramp," and "The Perils of Pauline" reassured everyone that romance and bravery were still reliable, but James Joyce and D.H. Lawrence were writing novels that Harriet Beecher Stowe and Sir Walter Scott would have never imagined.*

This time in between the past and the future, the maudlin and the modern, was a ragtime, and in this chapter "Cub" Huston's own marvelous snapshot of his growing up in Harrisburg before World War I shows a city in the last years of its own childhood.

1917:

Harrisburg had a ragtime before the Great War. We can know something of it—at least a child's fine time of it—because Ralph "Cub" Huston, born in 1907, raised and living in Harrisburg today, has written down his ragtime from memory. His concrete particulars of porch swings and candy counters are antiques for us now. His details bespeak a lost city that was occasionally cosmopolitan but usually a congestion of little communities, and citizens who were quite conscious of one's social class and native country but still congenial. Such facts show us how it *felt* to live then. Other boys from unluckier streets would have different memories to tell us. Still, read a little of his "No—Back and Over" as it is, full of realism, nostalgia, and humanity, and enjoy.

"Early in the 1900s row houses were built. Although they all looked alike, each had its own roofed porch separated from the next neighbor by a rail fence. These porches were wide enough to have a three or four-person swing on which cushions were used to make it more comfortable. Smaller homes and those on narrow streets did not enjoy the luxury of porches, but they did have their steps. Steps were used as gathering places for family and friends. They were the original air conditioners, libraries, school rooms, romantic nooks, and forums for discussion. They were home base for games, and a desert island if you thought so. They were privilege for good deportment, as well as prison for misbehaving.

"After supper the whole neighborhood would sit out front. First came the kids, and then, when the dishes were washed and dried, the grown-ups came out. If there were too many to squeeze comfortably in the space, chairs or benches were moved onto the sidewalks. Everyone did it. On most of the narrow streets or alleys the sidewalks were as proportionately narrow, so one could get more air by moving the chair out on the street. The street sitters faced the house and rested their feet on the curbing.

"The steps were wide enough to take care of all eight in our family. Mama and Papa, five kids, and Aunt Mira, who lived with us. Papa was the provider of all this, but he really didn't have much chance to use either the porch or the bench. He worked 16 hours a day. He did have Wednesday nights and every other Friday afternoon and Sunday nights off. Our Mothers used wood or coal ranges, and what martyrs our Mothers were. In those days everyone had to have hot meals or you would not survive. The stoves were kept going for three hots, starting with oatmeal and eggs for breakfast. Three meals a day plus making beds, washing, ironing, baking, emptying slop jars, sewing, helping with lessons, taking care of the sick and old people, and still loving. That was Mother.

"Grocers had long, hard days. They opened their stores at six or seven in the morning. Men coming from their nightshifts would stop to buy the things that had been written on a list the night before. The grocer's day continued until late at night. Neighborhood stores were seldom longer than a home living room; in fact, many were located in what would have been the parlor. Yet, in that small space you could find everything a family would need for survival.

"Strange as it now seems, not very

much was pre-packaged. Flour and sugar were delivered to the store in barrels, and you could buy as much as you wanted. Other things came to the grocer in barrels, such as cod, vinegar, pickles, and crackers. Lard came in wooden buckets, and barrels of coal oil and molasses were kept in the grocer's cellar or an adjoining shed. Molasses was no problem in warm weather, but in cold weather it was a real job to draw a pint or quart. Customers bringing oil cans to be filled would usually leave them on the sidewalk as they entered the store. This was done to make sure the order for other things would not smell of oil.

After the grocer filled an oil can, he usually plugged the spout with a potato so that the oil would not spill on the way home.

"In groceries you found out that everything was not odorless, colorless, or tasteless. Entering you could smell coffee, tea, bananas, apples, pickles, smoked meats, coal oil, peanut butter, limburger cheese, and candy.

"Although corner groceries were scattered all over the city, most every family, rich and poor alike, went to market. This was a way of life, and what an experience. In Harrisburg, the markets were open on Wednesdays and Saturdays, from

The Harrisburg Public Library had the state's first bookmobile. Painted bright red and nicknamed "the Cardinal," it went into operation in 1925. These Harrisburg students would wait in line to use it. Courtesy, Dauphin County Library System

"Going to market" meant going to the market house where the farmers and butchers brought their meat and produce. This is the West Harrisburg Market House Company, a building of sufficient grandeur to be memorialized in Art Work of Harrisburg. *The boy with the wagon just to the right of the telegraph pole is preparing to earn his spending money by hauling purchases for the customers. (HSDC)*

early in the morning until about nine at night. Uptowners generally went to Broad, Central City and Shipokers to Chestnut, and Hillers to Allison. Occasionally lines would be crossed, but not very often.

"You left home with wicker baskets. Paper bags were not plentiful, and those used had been used before and saved for the next market. Our family was a three-basket one. Baskets became heavier and heavier as you did your buying. At first you would hold them with your hand until your fingers would swell; then you used your arm until ridges would appear on your skin. You would change from one arm to

the other until it really didn't matter—they both hurt.

"Practically all the sellers were real farmers or real butchers. In season, each stall would have lettuce, endive, carrots, turnips, beets, eggs, tomatoes, potatoes, cabbage, celery, and corn. These were regular items. Then there were special seasons, including one with the most delectable, sweetest strawberries in the entire world from York County. You could look at a stall and tell which farmers were from York County by the looks of their berries. Country sounds were also heard: roosters crowing, geese honking, and ducks quacking. You

would see people leaving the market carrying one or more live chickens by their feet. Dressed chickens were displayed with the yellow fat extending from the innards. This would help the buyers know how much flavor could be expected.

"Markets also provided opportunities for boys to earn money. Those of us having wagons would park outside the entrances and bid for the chance to haul the baskets to the homes of the shoppers. You had no set rate, as you were at the mercy of the customer. You learned the tricks of the trade. You learned to tip your cap, smile at the right time, how to be careful at curbs, and how to show appreciation. You also learned which customers were generous, and which ones to avoid if you could. On good days you could earn more than a dollar. . . .

"The Gods with barrels of ambrosia were not any richer than a kid with a penny in a candy store. With a penny one had a choice of a most wonderful assortment. Perhaps the most difficult decisions we made in our lifetime were those made in front of candy counters. You would feast your eyes from left to right, from right to left, from front to back, and even diagonally. You had to decide not only on taste, but also on which items gave the

Most market houses were little more than sheds that provided shelter for the farmers' stalls. Many isolated towns in Pennsylvania have such markets to this day, and their wares are incomparably better than the prepackaged provender of supermarkets. (HSDC)

Patriotic floats were a staple of Memorial Day parades. This 1912 float recalls the War of 1812. (HSDC)

most for your money. There were four-fors, three-fors, two-fors, and the more expensive one-for. We had to choose from sour balls, orange bananas, cocoanut strips or straps, all kinds of assorted chocolates and cordials, caramels, Necco wafers, jujubes, peppermint sticks, hard cherries on wire, and cherries in chocolate. There were long, thin glass tubes, or straws filled with multi-colored beads of sugar. If you wanted something to last a long time, you usually picked sour balls or lollypops. Boys had fun buying licorice, because they could emulate their elders by pretending they were chewing tobacco.

"Private and public horse stables were located throughout Harrisburg. Many of the wealthy along Front Street had stables on their own property. Others less affluent, but still able to own one or more horses, stabled them away from their homes. Horses pulled surries, sedans, cabs, buggies, and runabouts. There were delivery wagons, carts, milk and ice wagons, hearses, brewery and huckster wagons. There were pony carts and junk wagons. There were hundreds of them. Horses were broken to the wagon, but not street broken. Street cleaners were necessary for the health and appearance of the community. I will never forget the aroma of brewery horse urine. From a health standpoint, I am glad it has disappeared with other things, but it was distinctive and more acceptable than automobile gas fumes.

Irving College, a women's college, expired earlier this century. Its buildings still stand in Mechanicsburg, but they are now apartments. (PHMC)

"Every parade worth watching had its horses. What a variety of parades. Memorial Day, Fourth of July, Labor Day, Election, Patriotic, School, Circus and Columbus Day, minstrel shows and conventions were all occasions for parades. The inauguration of the Governor brought out a whole company of mounted State Police. What steeds they had and what riders the Police were! When they passed the onlookers applauded, not only because of their appearance, but also as a gesture of appreciation for the job they did. The Police made sure citizens were protected. They were tough men, but gentlemen.

"Circus parades were fantastic. Their bands played a different kind of music. It was loud and fast. Circus horses were fascinating. Teams of matched pairs, fours, sixes, and eights pulled the wagons. Drivers had up to eight pairs of reins in their hands. Their real skill became apparent when they showed how they could manipulate turning corners. Circus wagons were perhaps the most highly decorated vehicles ever seen by man. Animals from the circus menagerie were included in parades. There were lions, tigers, bears, hyenas, and others. Camels were led by men dressed as Arabs. The last thing in a circus parade was the calliope, the only enjoyable out-of-tune instrument in the world. The notes seemed to explode in your ears, and they meant the end of the greatest free show on earth.

"Great names of the theatre world included Harrisburg in their stops. Howard Thurston, the great magician, was usually scheduled for performances at the Orpheum Theatre for the week between Christmas and New Year's. He also gave a free performance for orphans and underprivileged kids at Fahnestock Hall in the old YMCA. It was his custom to have one of the boys from the Y help in a couple of his acts. I was chosen and acted as his stooge.

"I am somewhat clumsy, and yet I appeared with the great Pavlova. A couple of my pals and I were offered fifty cents apiece to put on gunny sacks and act as peasants in one of her scenes. It was the easiest money I ever earned. All we had to do was sit in a group as this graceful lady danced around us. Someone from the cast applied make-up to our faces. I wore mine home to show my folks.

"Another popular, almost yearly, visitor to Harrisburg was Lyman Howe. He was a world traveler who took motion pictures and then narrated them as he showed them. To appreciate the impact his presentations had on us, it must be remembered that geography lessons told little of customs, people, or scenery. Howe's lectures and the *National Geographic* magazine were our only real contacts with the rest of the world.

"Father T.B. Johnson was assigned

to St. Patrick's Cathedral as the Assistant Pastor. To the neighborhood kids he was Roman Catholic, Lutheran, Methodist, Presbyterian, and Jewish. He was White and he was Black. Everyone knew him and everyone loved him. Although he was not physically large, he was a ball of fire. He played baseball and touch football with us. When there was a death, sickness, or misfortune in the neighborhood, the first person to call on the family was usually Father Johnson. When good fortune came, he was there to congratulate. To him, denominations or sects were names only. If he saw differences between religions and races, he didn't show it.

"One time a few of his parishioners thought the hat he was wearing was too shabby and not proper for a man of the cloth. They took up a collection among themselves and bought Father Johnson a new, fine-looking one. Within a day or two the Reverend was again wearing his old, shabby hat. One of the donors asked the good man about this, and he humbly replied that he had given the new hat to some poor man who didn't own one. 'You see,' said Father Johnson, 'I had two hats, but only one small head.' When this saintly man was transferred to another out-of-town

As he grew, Cub enjoyed the adventures that enlivened the days of adolescents 80 years ago. When he was about 13, he and his friend Junior Forrer captured (and presumably dispatched) a copperhead—an event sufficiently momentous to call for a photograph. Courtesy, Cub Houston

parish, something went out of our lives with him.

"James Bruner was a black butler for Mrs. Lyman D. Gilbert. I suppose I was five or six years old when we first became acquainted. Although 20 or more years passed from our first meeting to our last, he was the only one I have known who didn't change in manner or appearance. He was well-groomed, kindly, gracious in manner, polite, concerned, and he always had the warmest smile. The Governor's mansion was one block away from the Gilbert residence. It was common in those days to see a distinguished Governor walking about town. Many of them knew James and would stop and chat with him as he swept the sidewalk or trimmed the hedge. He looked like a fashion plate even while doing these chores.

"Living as close to Front Street as we did, the word 'rich' became a part of our early vocabulary. We used the word in many ways, but seldom with rancor. In reputation of character, some of the rich were paupers, but that was their business. Perhaps local residents knew of the few indiscretions, but knowing, paid little or no attention. Some of the rich were first-class snobs, but like those who were rumored to have had indiscretions, we could ignore or forget them.

"Lyman Gilbert came to our house one day and said he and Mrs. Gilbert were going on an extended trip. He wanted our family to move into their home and live there while they were gone. He said, 'You know, John, with your youngsters around and using our furniture and rugs, the moths won't get into things.' My Dad thought awhile and replied, 'That's right, Lyman, but what

would keep the moths away from ours?'

"I am sure that I knew the names of everyone in all the streets in our neighborhood before going to first grade. These people also knew me and where I lived. You learned which ones would smile, wave, or greet you. These were by far the majority. Then there were others who were born crabs and didn't change as long as they lived. You shared your neighbors' difficulties and were glad when nice things happened to them. Your walks were saddened at times by seeing crepes on some doors. These homes were hard to pass by, whether you knew the deceased or not. You just did not feel good when you saw a crepe.

"Within three blocks on our particular street were Whites, Negroes, Italians, Germans, Swedes, English, Jews, and Irish. Before anyone gets the idea that all living was peaches and cream, it should be understood that we had our fights and misunderstandings. We had teacher's pets, sissies, and roughnecks. We had religious and race differences, but all these were subject to change on short notice. We called some of the Jews we were sore at 'Christ Killers,' but these same guys invited us to their Bar Mitzvah ceremonies. One of the boys had an Uncle in the German Army. This boy and other members of his family were not warmly accepted during the War. There was nothing wrong with the boy or his family, other than their being German. It must have been lonely for them during this period.

"As kids we never knew that the whole world was not the same as Liberty Street, nor did we care. These people were our friends, our cronies, our teammates, our life."

Even as a boy of four or five, Cub Houston took to the outdoor life. Here he displays some fish he evidently caught himself. His clothing was standard for a boy of his day, including black stockings, high button shoes, and (Houston points out specifically) pants . . . not knickers. Courtesy, Cub Houston

*An ad for "The Busy Bee" shows the waiters, countermen,
and owners ready to serve food in their modern,
1920s establishment. (PHMC)*

XII
THE BOTTOM LINE

*America and Greater Harrisburg were coming of age together in the Twenties. Charles Lindbergh flew the Atlantic in 1927; Harrisburg shared its first airport with York in 1930. The first commercially sponsored radio program was broadcast from New York City in 1922; Radio Station WHP turned on in Harrisburg in 1924. Notre Dame's "Four Horsemen" upset Army in football in 1924; Harrisburg Tech claimed the national high school championship in 1919, scoring 701 points to none for its opponents. The team from John Harris High went undefeated from 1929 to 1931. The "Charleston" was the step to dance in America in 1925; George Reist's Dance Boat was the place to whirl in Harrisburg. In a sensational trial in Chicago, Nathan Leopold and Richard Loeb were convicted of the "thrill killing" of little Bobby Frank in 1924; the murder of Verna Klink was Harrisburg's sensational crime of 1927. New Yorkers and Harrisburghers were now thumbing through the same magazines (*Time, Readers Digest, *and the* New Yorker *itself), listening to the same music (George Gershwin's "Rhapsody in Blue," Hoagy Carmichael's "Star Dust," and Eddie Cantor's "Makin' Whoopee"), and reading the same books (F. Scott Fitzgerald's* The Great Gatsby, *Ernest Hemingway's* A Farewell to Arms, *and Sinclair Lewis'* Babbitt*).*

It was a good time to take an accounting of city life, because as President Coolidge had said, the business of America was business. How else would we know, but for the Greater Harrisburg Chamber of Commerce's Industrial Survey of 1928, that 146,657 dozen shirts and 46,044,675 "cigar units" were manufactured locally in 1925 (26 stogies per pocket), or that Dauphin County produced 936,702 gallons of ice cream the same year, but that York County made all the cones.

March 31, 1928:

The Chamber's mimeographed report, compiled during February and March 1928, estimated that Harrisburg's population in July would be 86,900, up 1,200 since January. The suburban population was 52,000.

Eighty-eight percent of the city people were native-born whites, seven percent were black, and five percent were foreign-born whites (most of those were from Russia, Italy, Germany, Hungary, England, and Ireland, in that order).

Close to two-thirds of all adults were married. Each family averaged 4.0 members, but each dwelling 4.5 residents.

Beth-El Temple has served the Jewish community since the late 1920s. (HSDC)

There were 43,936 members of 81 churches, or about half of all men, women, and children, led by 13,500 Lutherans, 6,259 Methodists, 5,552 Presbyterians, and 5,465 Roman Catholics.

There were 2,040 mules in the county.

There were 33 elementary schools, parochial and public, for 8,800 pupils. Within the city limits there were 13 theaters showing films and vaudeville, 22 hotels, 12 service clubs, and three major newspapers. Four thousand people played in the 1,100 acres of parks each day.

Every 24 hours 142 passenger trains and 126 freight trains passed

FINK'S PRIZE BEERS

ONLY AMERICAN BEER AWARDED
GRAND PRIZE FOR QUALITY AT
BRUSSELS EXPOSITION 1910.

A Beer Brewed to Ship Around the World.

FINK BREWING COMPANY
HARRISBURG, U. S. A.

through the city, or about one train every five minutes. During peak hours 87 streetcars ran in the metropolitan area.

Rent for a six-room house started at about $20 a month. A new brick rowhouse could be bought for about $4,000, or $300 down and $50 a month. Sixty percent of all homes were owned in 1927, up from 36 percent in 1920 and almost half of Harrisburg's families had their own telephones.

The city's 16,000 employed men and women made an average wage of $1,300 per year with about 80 percent of all men employed and about 25 percent of all women.

Among the over 2,000 retail establishments in the city were 30 places to buy firewood, coal, and ice, 114 shops selling candy and ice cream, and 250 cigar and tobacco counters. There were 410 corner grocery stores, 51 pool halls, and 56 junk dealers. Harrisburghers spent more money annually on musical instruments than they did on either funerals or gasoline, and they bought more hats than sporting goods. Indeed, they spent more per capita on goods and services than residents of any other county.

The survey pronounced "optimism." Energy from gas and electricity was "unlimited." The city had an "unusually satisfactory labor market." Employers had "no difficulty whatever in securing more labor, both male and female, than they can use." Harrisburg was an "open shop town" and "American-born labor predominated." There was "no serious labor trouble at any time" and "no interference from organizers." Coincidentally, "The church attendance in Harrisburg is high," they said, "which indicates a good class of labor." There was "general order" throughout the city.

Greater Harrisburg's industrial outlook in 1928 was "encouraging," they concluded.

And the Depression came.

In 1919 the Harrisburg Tech football team (right) trounced the Portland, Maine, football team (left) to become national high school champions. A close inspection of the players on both teams, especially Harrisburg's, suggests that either some of the players spent quite some time in high school or else got there late. (HSDC)

Left: *Local breweries once added to a town's sense of community and civic pride. Harrisburg's Fink Brewing Company, like today's beer industry, tried to use the image of an attractive woman to sell their product. This postcard dates to pre-World War I. (PHMC)*

The staff of the Hill Post Office poses with visiting
dignitaries in this late 1930s photo. (HSDC)

XIII
TWO TALES OF A CITY

In Greater Harrisburg and elsewhere, the Thirties were as rough as the Twenties were roaring. The stock market crash of 1929 and the Depression that followed were largely democratic in their effects. In 1930, 1,300 banks closed in the United States; by 1932, 5,000 had closed. Industrial production was at half-volume and so was the total of wages paid. About 12 million Americans, or 25 percent of the workforce, were unemployed. Charles Lindbergh's son was kidnapped, the "Hindenburg" dirigible exploded, and Amelia Earhart's plane disappeared. More than 32,000 Americans were killed in auto accidents in 1938. The 1936 flood in Harrisburg was the worst to date.

But there were silver linings. The New Deal heartened most of the people, even if it didn't stop the Depression. Boulder Dam was completed, the Queen Mary was launched, and the Golden Gate Bridge was opened. The movies were better than ever, maybe the best ever: "It Happened One Night," "Mutiny on the Bounty," "Gone With the Wind" (all Clark Gable triumphs), "Captains Courageous," "Boys Town" (Spencer Tracy's Academy Awards), and "Stagecoach" (John Wayne's opening night). The Forties would start off with "The Grapes of Wrath" and "The Philadelphia Story."

In 1939 the World's Fair opened in New York, showing how the future might be planned. Its theme was the "World of Tomorrow." They planned for the future in Harrisburg that year too, and suffered in the present.

July 14, 1939:

The Municipal League's Report of 1939-1940, "Planning for the Future of Harrisburg," proclaimed the second phase of Greater Harrisburg's improvements. In the main, the area was probably well-served by this report. Malcolm Dill, Resident Regional Planner, and E.S. Draper Associates, Consultants, both employed by President Vance McCormick and Secretary J. Horace McFarland of the Municipal League, had done a professional job. They offered 129 recommendations to modernize the larger metropolitan area, the inner city, and the suburban fringe. Having designed the "City Beautiful" successfully, now the planners and the League would build the "City Practical"—a progressive, well-coordinated, rational place to live that would accommodate Harrisburg's new "automobility."

It seems the planners were "doc-

toring" a city: in their report's words, they "diagnosed ailments" and wrote "prescriptions." Perhaps it was such hubris that led the planners to say that there was never any "valid reason" for the city's narrow house lots, which led to "endless rows of monotonous houses predominately without architectural merit." Perhaps that judgment bespoke the planners' tastes more than the residents'. The planners stated that these rowhouses would be unattractive "in the eyes of the coming generation, which is witnessing construction of an increasing number of attractive single-family dwellings, set on adequate-sized lots"—not foreseeing the monotony and troublesome ecology of Levittown.

The planners said Harrisburg's housing pattern led to "crowded conditions for automobile parking," especially downtown, where there was "indiscriminate parking" and

A rifle team, in Civil War uniforms, fires a salute for Memorial Day in a Harrisburg cemetery in 1938. (HSDC)

"inexcusable double parking" that would "destroy the value of a lane of moving traffic." But they did not realize that cities made easy for drivers would become cities driven by cars.

The planners insisted that Harrisburg needed "zoning," their "form of publicly-applied insurance against cupidity and selfishness." The planners said the city needed to build new neighborhoods, such as the "Harrisburg Housing Authority's plan for a development for white people between Sycamore and Hanover Streets on 13th Street," not realizing that all "white"

neighborhoods were the problem, not the solution.

The planners said the city should manage its pedestrians better, and recommended "admonition by amplifiers," such as a "not-too-loud-speaker" telling "the young woman in the red hat to wait for the green light." This order "would receive embarrassed compliance." "Technique is important," they said.

They planned, and Greater Harrisburg progressed, but did the consultants ever consult ordinary residents? Dorothy Day, visiting social worker, was not concerned about making the city safe for a Chevy.

The Pennsylvania Railroad introduced the famous GG-1 electric locomotive in 1934. Designed by the great industrial designer Raymond Loewy and engineered by John V.B. Duer, they were so reliable and durable that many are still in service. In Harrisburg during World War II, they were the principal means of intercity travel. (HSDC)

The square in Hummelstown was the scene of the Homecoming Parade in the late 1930s. Hummelstown is typical of the east shore small towns that ring Harrisburg. "Homecoming" was held to welcome natives of the town who had moved away— including those who succumbed to the lure of the big city in Harrisburg. (HSDC)

Here in Harrisburg there just isn't any toilet. You go next door to the neighbors. And there was no running water until a week ago. Most of the houses on the block have no running water. The neighbors pay one man down the street for the privilege of getting pails of water from his house. Our place, the Blessed Martin Home, is two rooms, now scrubbed clean . . . There is paint and linoleum on the floor, the linoleum donated out of her salary by a colored cook who works all day and comes over to help us in the evening. There is a faucet in the kitchen now, but no sink. We are begging for that.

Toilets bothered her. Reporting to the Catholic magazine *Commonweal* on poverty in Harrisburg, she wrote on July 14, 1939:

Her Catholic Workers had given some families the Blessed Martin as a temporary lodging. They put up

Harrisburg's elite has traditionally belonged to either Pine Street or Market Square Presbyterian churches. The Pastor's Aid Society of the Pine Street Church posed at this meeting on May 18, 1934. Mrs. Vance McCormick (second from left) and Mrs. James Cameron (fourth from left) were probably the richest Harrisburg socialites. (HSDC)

"two white families with thirteen and seven children respectively and one colored family with seven children," she wrote.

How they got along in two rooms with no water and no toilet is hard to understand. . . . In one case the children were rolled out of bed and left in their night things as the clothes and bedding were loaded on the van.

Dorothy Day had other saint-simple stories to tell about her Catholic Workers and the poor of Harrisburg, some just too sad in their details, such as the story of "Lucille," whom they found Job-like and dying in an empty house. "Lucille grew up on the streets," Day said. "She and her brothers and sisters just prowled around, living

as best they could." Father Kirchner of St. Patrick's baptized and anointed her before she died.

Day observed,

The greatest difficulty in Harrisburg is to find a home to live in, even when a family is on relief and has money to pay rent. Housing seems to be the greatest immediate problem of the city.

The Municipal League planners knew that too, in a way. They began compiling their report that same July. Their recommendation in favor of slum clearance and "eventual Neighborhood Units" said that the "present dwelling shortage, from a social and economic standpoint, has reached a rather serious stage." But there was no room or reason for intimate evidence in their report.

Activities on the "Home Front" give some idea of the enormous national commitment to World War II. In Harrisburg, the local USO (United Service Organization, which was created to boost the morale of service personnel) maintained a Floating Club, moored in the river at Locust Street, where there was dancing to live music every night. (HSDC)

*Maris Harve Taylor lived to be over 100 years old, and by the
1960s he was a Harrisburg institution. He is pictured here
receiving honors from Governor Scranton for his long service
to the public. (PHMC)*

XIV
HARVE TAYLOR'S
SECRET DIARY

The post-war history of Greater Harrisburg deserves its own book, for what happened to this area in the last 40 years is what happened to America at large since 1945. Harrisburg's city population climbed to more than 89,000 by 1950, then declined to around 53,000 by 1980. This was also true of other northeastern cities. Greater Harrisburg's suburbs and neighboring towns grew like toadstools on spring bluegrass. This was also true of other cities across the country. Harrisburg struggled to renew itself, and so did Baltimore. Steel and railroads became less prosperous here, and likewise so in Pittsburgh. The place of state government expanded in Harrisburg, as it also did in Albany. The interstate highway system (the largest construction project in the world's history) tied all the major cities together even tighter, and proved again that you have to put your finger on Harrisburg to make the knot. And when the nation or the state were prosperous, Greater Harrisburg was too, usually with one of the lowest unemployment rates in the states.

But as we point out the parallel paths that America and Greater Harrisburg have followed in their recent history, we must be careful not to miss a deeper truth: this area is more notable for its stability than any dynamism up or down. South central Pennsylvania has one of the lowest rates of emigration—people leaving—of any state in the nation. These people don't have their heads in the clouds or in the sand. They are the most middle western of Easterners.

Perhaps the quickest and most penetrating way to cover modern change, and the lack of change, is to try to see it through some observer's eyes. So I have taken the liberty to imagine what Harve Taylor, the quintessential Harrisburgher, might have written in a diary during these years. Who can better represent us—not at our best or at our worst—but at the good balance we would be?

May 3, 1946 – June 4, 1981:

May 3, 1946. Stopped by Shipoke on a good Spring day. Joe and Dom Caldarelli are home from the war now, along with about 7,000 other boys from the area. They moved back in with their folks on Pancake Row. There used to be renters moving in'n'out all the time on the block, but since the war nobody's budged an inch. Roy and Mary Houser are on the corner at 100 Conoy, the nine Snavelys at 102, Ralph and Elsie Schlitzer and their daughter at 104, Henrietta Carroll and her child at 106, the six Shearers at 108, the nine O'Keefes at 110, Ross and Mary Hart at 112, and Vince and Carrie Caldarelli and their two heroes at 114, across the street from where I was born. That's about 4 baseball teams squeezed in between home plate and second base. When I grew up here you never had the privacy to be lonely. And when your neighbor had bread, everybody had bread.

December 25, 1949. Merry Christmas, and John O'Hara's novel present to us this year was *A Rage to Live.* Everybody's been tryin' to figure

out who's who and what's what in it. I'm not sure how many local friends he'll have left when this is over, but I'd bet he'll know more lawyers.

January 25, 1952. Well, they dedicated "me" today. What does it mean when they name a bridge after you while you're still alive? If it's the thought that counts, that's what worries me! Ha! I told them I would do my very best to keep living up to this honor.

March 3, 1957. Today they announced they'll tear down the old County Prison at Walnut and Court. I remember back in the Gay Nighties when they locked you up in there if you even looked at loitering. More than a thousand guys arrested one year. I'm surprised the joint didn't fall down back then from the sheer weight of all that civic concern.

January 19, 1958. They opened up the new Jewish Community Center up on Front Street today. They opened up their own country club, the Blue Ridge, about 20 years ago after they found out every other place was restricted. There's a real story there—what the Jews have done for this town, even though they didn't owe us many favors.

June 18, 1958. Get packed! They're going to clear the slums! About 200 houses and stores are going to be bulldozed in Shipoke to make way for the South Bridge and the ramps—80 on Race Street and everything south of Tuscarora. And they're taking down about 180 houses up at 6th and Boas. You can't say they aren't trying to do their leveling best.

July 21, 1958. There were 89,554 people in Harrisburg in 1950, about 93,000 in 1957, and today the *Evening News* predicted there'll be

Harve Taylor was at the height of his influence in the 1950s when he posed for this and innumerable other pictures with Dauphin County worthies. (PHMC)

The State Theatre was Harrisburg's last movie palace. In the 1970s the theater was torn down and Locust Court replaced it. (PHMC)

At the turn of the century, Shipoke was decidedly a working-class neighborhood. The eight-to-ten-room houses were too small to accommodate a middle-class family and its necessary corps of servants. Conoy Street at the corner of Front (south of the section where Front Street is a busy thoroughfare) was dusty and quiet. Courtesy, Michael Barton

In recent years, the eastern side of Shipoke has been obliterated by Interstate 83 and its ramps, but the western part has become an enclave for people united by a common fondness for living in houses in an urban area. The houses along Conoy Street remain attractive, some because of continuous maintenance, others because of restoration. New sidewalks and paving make the place less dusty than in earlier times. Courtesy, Michael Barton

97,000 in 1965 and 100,000 in 1975. I won't bet you can expect Republicans to be that prolific. Now Democrats, that's another thing.

July 28, 1961. Paul Beers wrote in the paper about Front Street today. The street went one-way in 1956, the Wallower Mansion (once Harrisburg Academy) started to come down in 1959, the old Governor's Mansion in 1960, and now on Front from Division to Market it's about half commercial where all the big homes used to be. Maybe Second Streeters are behind this. Better view of the river over the parking lots.

November 7, 1964. What can I say? We got beat, that's what. At least I did it in the primary and missed the rush. But Nibs Franklin brought his ward in for the Grand Old Party. The Goldwater Blacks, they are, the only Negro ward in the country to go Republican this year. That's the party of Lincoln for you.

June 23, 1969. Trouble up on Allison Hill today, big trouble. Race trouble. There are two main problems in Harrisburg—white people and black people.

January 24, 1972. The boys will say Pop-Pop's got it made now, because today I'm in the *New York Times.* Their reporter Homer Bigart came in to report on our "Hairy Seven" trial. You know, there's more radicals in this town than you'd think, and they run their own newspaper. Not bad. Anyway, they naturally sent Homer to see me to find out what makes the place tick. I said to him, "You say your name's Homer Big-City?" He

asked me what Harrisburg thought about Vietnam, and I said Front Street supports Nixon but Shipoke is against it because they "don't want their sons drafted and because they want to live on relief." That's the way he quoted me. Hope nobody in Shipoke reads the *Times.* Mainly because he spelled it "Shypoke." I bet somebody told Homer that waterbird story. You don't see "Shite-poke" in the paper anymore.

May 7, 1972. They opened up the new Hersheypark today. What a park! What a town. Everybody's so sweet in Chocolate Town they've forgotten about the strikes in '37 and '53. If you were going to let somebody set up his own country in America, it might as well have been

The worst part of any flood is its aftermath. Any flooding river carries with it ton upon ton of soil—slimy mud when it is wet and microscopic dust when it is dry. The flood that followed Tropical Storm Agnes in 1972 carried devastation from New York to Maryland, but just as bad was the ubiquitous mud it left behind as it receded. (HSDC)

In 1973, the Penn Harris Hotel, once the pride of Harrisburg, yielded to urban renewal soon after its neighbors. (HSDC)

Milton Hershey. The place almost makes you wish your pop had run away with the circus so you could be an orphan. Or it almost makes you look forward to gettin' sick—brand new gorgeous hospital and medical school have been there about six years now. Sort of shaped like a horseshoe. As if this place needed the luck.

June 24, 1972. My third big flood. The mess is horrible, and I'll tell them the smell afterwards is going to be even worse. Somebody said the water will drown 5,000 rats. Baloney. There were never more than 2,000 lobbyists in town at one time.

August 13, 1973. They blew up the Penn Harris Hotel today. There'd have been more fun if they'd have let it burn down the way the old Grand Opera House did on just about the same spot in '09. I'll never forget how excited people used to get about fires, like the Capitol in '97, and the Packing House in '07. Or accidents too, like the Lochiel Train Wreck in '05. Great town for insurance. But where is a fellow going to make a deal now around the Capitol? You can't make a deal in a "motel," even if the place is brand-new and high-priced. If they're to believe what you're promising, you've got to be standing under a high ceiling.

April 15, 1979. At least there's something to smile about in this TMI mess. The kids are wearing some pretty good one-liners on their tee-shirts.

I have that radiant look—I live near TMI.
I survived Three Mile Island—I think.
Gone fission.
Hell no, we won't glow.
I survived the Sooper Dooper Leaker.
We are a nuclear family—we live near TMI.

The Metropolitan Edison people threw one back at them, a tee-shirt that says "Three Mile Island Staff—we stayed behind to save yours." You know what worries me—their insurance isn't that good. That should tell you something. All things considered, you knew what to be afraid of with candles and coal.

June 4, 1981. Well, I'm 105 parties old today. The only one I can't remember is the first one. Probably wasn't much fun for me anyway. Just about everything's changed around here since then. I've seen

The towers of Three Mile Island loom up behind an explanatory panel at the plant's visitor observation tower, located across Route 441 from the facility. The panel gives no explanation for the 1979 accident, however. Courtesy, Mark H. Dorfman

much go down and even more go up—Strawberry Square, all the office buildings and the state buildings, the bridges, all the suburbs and the shopping malls. A boy's not likely anymore to jump school and work in iron and steel the way I did. What would a kid do nowadays at AMP or Berg? Stoke up the computers? And today if your neighborhood's old, you're in luck. Used to mean you were just poor. But the bricks aren't the main thing—a town is people. And I wonder if all the newcomers will be givers or takers. At least two things will stay the same, for sure—straight Harve and that crooked river.

The Harrisburg area suffered financially when Olmsted Air Force Base closed in the 1960s. Governmental agencies helped find other uses for parts of the former base: the base headquarters, shown here, became the Capitol Campus of the Pennsylvania State University. This campus now has 2,500 students. Courtesy, Capitol Campus, Pennsylvania State University

Harristown has been reshaping the face of downtown Harrisburg since the 1970s. Strawberry Square, the shopping mall, has become the town center of the development. It was designed to attract suburbanites downtown for business again. Courtesy, Harristown Development Corporation

XV
EPILOGUE
THE MOVING ROAD
THAT MIGHT BE

Those are all the "written snapshots," far too few but perhaps enough to understand the past of Greater Harrisburg a little better, how it started as a ferry crossing, developed to a proper town, succeeded as a capital, matured as a workman's center, turned itself into a modern city, then became an old city growing suburbs, now begun renewing.

The physical frame, the natural border—the whole story has been the Susquehanna River, the same as Chicago's has been Lake Michigan, Lincoln's the plains, Denver's the Rockies, and San Francisco's the Bay. Greater Harrisburg, however, has not been determined by its environment so much as presented with possibilities. People built this metropolis once, and they will build it more.

The next history will start with the two dozen shopping malls, a tri-county area which is the fastest growing market in the Northeastern United States, the 12th leading market in the nation in per household income ($26,617), and by all measures the 24th most attractive medium-sized metropolitan area in the country in which to live (rated higher than either Lancaster or York counties). It will be the history of Conrail, Hershey Foods, Harsco, Berg, Rite-Aid, Bethlehem Steel, AMP, TRW, HERCO, and PPG. It will be about Harristown and the Redevelopment Authority. It will see if Paul Beers' Eight Commandments are still true: that we have an "obsession with eating, prudent conservatism, congenital obliviousness, small-talk enterprise, clear gender distinctions, contented prosperity, hatred of the cold, and a dark underside." And the next history will still be about the river.

But if the Susquehanna has tenure here, no city is guaranteed endurance, which is earned. And years and years from now, when Phoenix and San Diego are scouting historic districts, applying for redevelopment grants, and coordinating urban sprawl, one can hope that Greater Harrisburg will have grown older youthfully, and usefully, so that they might come to ask us for advice, and we will know that we are practiced to reply.

*The Old State Capitol in
Harrisburg, circa 1890, is
depicted here in a rare and
unique reverse painting on
glass. Thin sheets of mother-
of-pearl are used for the
windows to give a glowing
effect. The Capitol, designed
by architect Stephen Hills and
constructed between 1818 and
1822, was remodeled many
times by the time this painting
was completed. Courtesy,
Private Collection,
Woodbourne, New York*

The first depiction of the attempted burning of John Harris was painted by William S. Reeder in about 1839. Reeder reputedly consulted with Robert Harris about the event, but his stylistic inspiration comes from Benjamin West's famous painting of William Penn's treaty with the Indians. Reeder's oil painting currently hangs in the governor's mansion. (PHMC)

That Harrisburg was for most of its history a small town set in rich farmland is emphasized in this painting of "Whitehall Farm," done about 1880 by amateur artist Ellen Winebrenner. Note the old capitol at the far right; built to the designs of Stephen Hills between 1818 and 1822, the building burned in 1897. The present Capitol covers its foundations. (HSDC)

In the mid-19th century Charles Magnus depicted this view of Harrisburg from Bridgeport (now Lemoyne). At the center is the Camelback Bridge and to the left is the Cumberland Valley Railroad Bridge. (HSDC)

Fleming Residence and Bird's-eye View of Susquehanna River, Harrisburg, Pa.

The Fleming Mansion, now the home of the Harrisburg Civic Club, was the only residence left standing when the River Front Park was created. Behind it stands the old city waterworks. (HSDC)

This novelty postcard provides a conjectural view of mid-19th-century travel in Harrisburg. (PHMC)

At the turn of the century Market Street was filled with pedestrians, horse-drawn vehicles, and trolley cars. (PHMC)

Residence, Reservoir Park, Harrisburg, P

Reservoir Park blooms with children and flowers in this World War I era postcard. (PHMC)

Sadie Hepford and Leonard Sparver married in 1888. The kewpie dolls and the napkin date from their 50th wedding anniversary in 1938. (HSDC) Photo, Mark Dorfman

October 4, 1906, was the date of the dedication for the new capitol. Legislators wore these splendid badges to the ceremonies where the guest of honor was President Theodore Roosevelt. (HSDC)

Harrisburg was an important manufacturer of blue-decorated, saltglazed stoneware. The most famous potters were Cowden and Wilcox, makers of the jug on the right. The water cooler on the left was made by the less well known John Young and Company. It probably belonged to the Cameron family. (HSDC)

This early 20th century postcard shows St. Patrick's Cathedral on the mall that was once State Street. (HSDC)

This couple finds spooning in Paxton Park in 1913 more attractive than playing tennis. (PHMC)

The oldest portion of the Harrisburg City Hospital is presented in the moonlight in this early 20th century postcard. (PHMC)

The Harrisburg Public Library maintains an extensive collection for the use of area residents.

This scenic building houses the Harrisburg Area Chamber of Commerce.

The present state capitol, completed in 1906, stands on the site of the old one, overlooking the Susquehanna.

The Rockville Bridge, a National Historical Landmark, is the longest stone arch bridge in the world with a length of 3,810 feet.

The Trinity Evangelical Lutheran Church is a long-standing house of worship in Lemoyne.

John Harris built the Harris Mansion in 1796. Later it would be remodeled by Simon Cameron. It now houses the Historical Society of Dauphin County.

Visitors enter the William Penn Museum through the Grand Hall. Inside are the many artifacts and exhibits preserving Pennsylvania history.

Along with new buildings, Harrisburg's downtown revitalization includes many restored townhouses.

The city of Harrisburg is still impressive today in this view from a West Shore vantage point that inspired 19th century graphic artists. Photo, Mark Dorfman

The revival of downtown Harrisburg includes these new multi-story office buildings.

Medical facilities in the Harrisburg area include the Milton S. Hershey Medical Center in Hershey.

The Pennsylvania National Horse Show at the Farm Show Arena was graced with this performance by the Royal Canadian Mounted Police Musical Drill Team.

Along with sustenance and economic vitality, the Susquehanna River has long provided Harrisburghers with recreational possibilities.

*The Federal Building in Harrisburg is a classic example of
Bauhaus-influenced design.*

XVI
GREATER HARRISBURG NEIGHBORS

By Mark H. Dorfman

Commerce and industry unite the communities that constitute greater Harrisburg, Pennsylvania's capital area. Geography and history have split it into two distinct regions. Ethnicity and other social forces have fragmented greater Harrisburg into a collection of individual jurisdictions and prevented it from developing into a large, cohesive, powerful urban center.

To the north and east are Derry, Lower Paxton, Susquehanna, and Swatara townships. This sector includes Hershey, Hummelstown, Paxtang, Pennbrook, and other communities. To the southeast are Londonderry and Lower Swatara townships, Middletown, Royalton, Highspire, and Steelton—each with its own identity and heritage. Across the river is the West Shore, itself a complex collection of municipalities and neighborhoods.

These are not just bedroom suburbs of Harrisburg. Thousands of state workers do commute daily to the city from the surrounding areas, yet these are distinct communities—each with its own histories and social institutions. Many have their own industries and commercial identities as well. They are part of greater Harrisburg because bridges and highways make travel convenient and because state government is so pervasive an influence. They, like the business and professional firms, industries, associations, and institutions of central Pennsylvania, are Harrisburg's Partners in Progress.

LOWER PAXTON TOWNSHIP

Paxton Township was the American frontier. Settled primarily by Scotch-Irish immigrants in the early 18th century, it was the setting for countless tales of heroism and adventure. When first surveyed in 1729, the township included all of the contemporary Upper Paxton, Middle Paxton, Swatara, and Susquehanna townships as well as the city of Harrisburg.

Paxton Church was founded in 1722. Its services were one of the few touches of civilization in the wilderness. The Scotch-Irish settlers always referred to themselves as God-fearing, peace-loving people. But they were no strangers to fighting. In Scotland, they had rebelled against Britain. In Philadelphia, they feuded with the Quaker government. On the frontier, they warred with the Indians.

The Indian Wars produced a source of continuing controversy in Paxton Township. Elsewhere in the country, historians refer to the Paxton Boys with loathing and to their 1763 massacre of the Conestoga Indians as a low point in American history. Nobody questions details about the raid or the follow-up attack at the Lancaster workhouse where surviving Indians had been offered protection by Lancaster County authorities.

But in Paxton Township, the Paxton Boys will always have their defenders. As one local historian wrote in a bicentennial work, "We find our Paxton Rangers much maligned in history books where they are too often depicted as a villainous bunch of cutthroats, rather than the brave, God-fearing, hard-working men they actually were," Lower Paxton is loyal to its own.

MIDDLETOWN

Middletown is the oldest established community in Dauphin County. Named for its location mid-way from Lancaster to Carlisle, the town was an important stopping-off point on the way west. Through the American Revolution, the town remained the most populous and most important commercial center in the county.

It is a patriotic community. Records of a July 4th celebration held on July 5, 1798, record 15 toasts drunk to various aspects of American life. The celebrants started by drinking "to the anniversary!" and "to the President!"; they ended by drinking "to the arts and sciences!" and "to the fair daughters of America!"

Penn State University architectural historian Irwin Richman likes to point out that Middletown has several restaurants and taverns that have been in continuous use as public houses since the town's days as a stop on the road west and as a terminus of the Union Canal. St. Peters Kirk (church) has been in continuous use as a house of worship since 1767.

On March 28, 1979, Middletown was shaken from its 19th-century complacency by a 20th-century accident. Three Mile Island Nuclear Plant is located just to the south. Early reports of trouble at the plant stunned the community. School closings, rumors, and conflicting reports rapidly added to the confusion. As reporters descended on the community, many residents packed a few precious belongings and evacuated, believing that they might never be able to return. Middletown residents still live with memories of their anger, shock, and fears, as well as uncertainties about long-term effects from the radiation.

STEELTON

Steelton was incorporated in January 1880. But a far more important date in local history is September 22, 1865, the day that the Pennsylvania Steel Company was formed. For Steelton, like Hershey, was a company town.

Two other towns, Baldwin and Ewington, sprung up nearby, but without the support of the company these speculative real estate ventures were short-lived. The company housing was in Steelton, along a stretch of North Front from Locust Alley to Mulberry Street. So too was the company store, located on the river side of the Pennsylvania Canal, facing Locust Street.

The people of Steelton are sturdy and well-tempered. Their bakeries, sausage makers, and other ethnic shops are reminders that Steelton was populated by Eastern European immigrants who came in the closing years of the 19th century. A special census of 1898 listed 33 nationalities in the community.

Like miners, steelworkers learn to live with impending tragedy. Accidents in the plant were common, their cost always high. Local residents learned to live with other forms of disaster as well.

Steelton lies low and close to the river. In 1889, 1902, 1904, 1936, and 1972 destructive floods swept the town. But the most vivid local disaster memory is the Lochiel Train Wreck. On May 11, 1905, the Pennsy's Cleveland Express collided with a freight train carrying dynamite. The toll—22 dead, 130 injured. But Steelton's people always endure—always carry on.

HERSHEY

Derry Township was among the first parts of Dauphin County to attract white settlers. Derry Church was founded in 1729. Its land patent was signed by sons of William Penn in 1741. But when millions of visitors descend on Derry Township each summer, they do not come to study the distant past but to tour and play in Chocolatetown.

Hershey, Pennsylvania, is not a city, a town, or a village. Only its post office carries the official designation, "Hershey," but the "town square" of this community in Derry Township is formed by the intersection of Chocolate and Cocoa avenues. The street lights are shaped like chocolate kisses. On many days, the sweet aroma of cocoa fills the air. Official or not, this is Hershey.

The history of Hershey, Pennsylvania, is the history of Hershey Chocolate. Like Steelton, Hershey was a company town—built along with the factory to house and support the workers. And while the firm provided a street railroad from Hummelstown to Campbelltown, Hershey has remained the center of the world for generations of central Pennsylvania workers.

Milton S. Hershey, founder of the chocolate company, was born in 1857 near Hockersville in Derry Township. In 1900 he sold his Lancaster Caramel Company, manufacturer of "Crystal A" caramels and other popular sweets, for one million dollars. But he reserved the right to keep making chocolate candy.

On January 28, 1903, a corps of surveyors arrived in Derry Township to begin surveying for a factory, streets, houses, water mains, sewage system, trolley lines, and a park. Hershey had decided to build not only a new chocolate factory, but a town to go with it.

The impressive public buildings of Hershey, its community center (now executive offices for Hershey Foods), Hotel Hershey, the high school, and the sports arena were all built by the company during the Great Depression—in part to keep local construction workers employed, in part because the cost of building materials was very low. For the rest of his life Milton Hershey remained proud that "no man... was dropped by reason of the Depression. And no salaries were cut."

All has not always been idyllic in Chocolatetown. There have been strikes and ethnic conflict, even during the lifetime of the founder. In recent years, the transformation of the chocolate company to a complex modern corporation has altered the relationship between the town and the firm—residents have taken more responsibility for their own political and economic affairs.

HUMMELSTOWN

Founded around 1740, Hummelstown is one of the older communities in Derry Township. A small, quiet, primarily agricultural community between Harrisburg and Hershey, Hummelstown became the focus of national attention late in 1955 when one of its residents defied the right of the United States government to tell her how to run her farm.

Elsie Mumma was charged in September 1955 with overplanting her wheat acreage quota by 18 acres. The government assessed $403.20 in fines and penalties; she decided to fight. The image of this lone farmer standing her ground against the government will always be remembered as former *Patriot* writer Bern Sharfman told it.

The Mumma family came to the United States in 1624. Elsie Mumma was graduated in 1922 with the first coeducational class at Gettysburg College. She later learned to fly airplanes, danced with Bill (Bojangles) Robinson, and performed at Madison Square Garden with Barbara Hutton. Pictures of her appeared in *Vogue* and *New Yorker* magazines. She became the first woman to join the National Association of Life Underwriters' Million Dollar Round Table.

When her father died in 1948, Elsie Mumma promised him that she would maintain the farm. She came home to keep the promise. And when the government tried to enforce crop controls, she rebelled. "As long as I own the land, pay my taxes, pay my debts, and ask for no aid, the land is mine ... to protect, to plant, to harvest." Hummelstown agreed.

THE WEST SHORE

West Shore real estate is among the most valuable in central Pennsylvania. From a historian's viewpoint that is surprising, because for many years almost nobody wanted it.

Today the West Shore consists of a large and diverse group of municipalities: Camp Hill, Lemoyne, New Cumberland, Mechanicsburg, Shiremanstown, Wormleysburg, West Fairview, Enola, Marysville, Hampden Township, East Pennsboro Township, Lower Allen Township, Fairview Township, and other communities. Yet under early plans for the region, much of this land—the core area between the Yellow Breeches and the Conodoguinet creeks, from St. Johns Road to the River—was a single unit known to the Penn family as Louther Manor.

Archaeological evidence and historic records suggest that local Native American tribes were only passively interested in West Shore lands. The Susquehannock (Conestoga) Indians set up a few camps in the area as early as 1616. The Iroquois Nation conquered the area around 1675. And the Lenape (Delawares) were resettled there by the Iroquois toward the end of the century.

The Penn family offered to sell the lands from Silver Spring to the river to John Harris, Sr. But Harris was pleased with his more valuable East Shore location, and found the price of 5,000 pounds (about 50 cents an acre) excessive. The Penns then offered it to the Shawnee in an attempt to get them out of Paxton Township. But, perhaps because they had already been granted privileges in the area by the Iroquois, the Shawnee rejected the Penns' offer.

Despite the refusal of the Shawnee to accept their offer, the Penns tried to prevent white settlement in the area. This may have been a prudent attempt to use the West Shore as a buffer zone between the German settlers of York County to the south and the Ulstermen to the north (Perry County) and east (Paxton Township).

Louther Manor had been explored and surveyed for the Penn family by Peter Chartier, a son of French pioneer Martin Chartier and his Indian wife. Peter Chartier was an exception to the Penns' "no white settlement" policy; he was granted title to lands in Louther Manor between the Yellow Breeches and what is now 16th Street, New Cumberland.

The second exception (and first permanent structure) was William Kelso's Tavern, opened in 1734. The tavern became a West Shore terminal for the ferry John Harris had begun operating one year earlier.

But the land remained largely unoccupied, what West Shore historian Robert Crist has described as "an island in a sea of settlement." It was not until 1770 that the Penns started granting patents from Louther Manor. Only in 1771 did Robert Whitehill construct the area's first stone building, his house at what is now 19th and Market streets in Camp Hill.

Shortly thereafter, some settlement formed along the roads through the region, especially along the road from the "lower crossing" (used by westbound traffic), Simpson's Ferry. Eastbound traffic used the "upper crossing" at Harris' Ferry. Later, those who could afford the toll used the Camelback Bridge from Harrisburg to Bridgeport (now Lemoyne). The area near Trundle Springs along the Simpson Ferry Road became known as Mechanicsburg in recognition of its wagon builders, wheelwrights, and repair shops.

The Civil War's Gettysburg campaign produced some anxious moments for Harrisburg, and some actual confrontations around the West Shore's Bridgeport and Oyster Point. Mechanicsburg was actually occupied by the Confederacy for four days. It was not the town's finest hour. As local historian Norman Keefer describes events, local leaders took down the town flag and surrendered it to the rebels when threatened with a destructive search.

And "farmers' wives baked themselves into a state of exhaustion to supply bread and cake for the invaders."

The war was just one in a long series of reverses for West Shore inventor Daniel Drawbaugh, whose Eberly Mills birthplace is identified by a state historic marker. According to biographer Warren Harder, Drawbaugh was born poor and died poor, but his life was a remarkable series of "almosts" and "potential." He came within a controversial 4-3 vote of the U.S. Supreme Court of being recognized as the inventor of the telephone. He was a major stockholder in the company that "almost" replaced American Bell. Drawbaugh later invented a wireless voice transmitter (it sent signals through ground and water) that "almost" replaced Marconi's radio.

Historic markers also denote the location of Fort Couch at Eighth and Ohio streets in Lemoyne. The breastworks there were thrown up to resist the expected Confederate advance during the Gettysburg campaign. According to the marker, "a few Confederate scouts neared here but withdrew." A marker on State Highway 641 just west of Camp Hill identifies Peace Church. The 1798 stone church, one of the oldest in Cumberland County, is near the site of an old Indian graveyard.

A lasting tribute to those who passed through the Harrisburg area on their way to build new lives is the brief, understated historic marker on Simpson Street near Walnut Street in Mechanicsburg. It marks the Simpson Ferry Road, "Built about 1792. It extended from Michael Simpson's Ferry on the Susquehanna to Carlisle.... Used by many persons traveling to western part of State." And to a new world.

The smartly dressed staff of a tailor shop pose in front of their store at S. Third Street and Blackberry Alley in this 1900 photo. Small-scale entrepreneurs have always contributed a great deal to Harrisburg, including a strong foundation for the area's commercial community. (HSDC)

XVII
PARTNERS IN PROGRESS

Harrisburg was destined by geography to be a distribution center, and the highway network that so efficiently ties these diverse communities together is itself part of the regional heritage. Natural roads travel north-south, skirting the eastern edge of the Appalachian mountain range. And the best east-west route through the mountains also crosses Harrisburg.

During the great canal era of American commerce, greater Harrisburg was a hub and trans-shipment center. The Pennsylvania Canal crossed the Susquehanna at Clarks Ferry; the Penn Lock was located near Walnut Street in the capitol complex. And the Union Canal joined the Susquehanna at Middletown, connecting to the Schuylkill River at Reading.

Harrisburg's highway network now includes the Pennsylvania Turnpike and several other major interstate highways. They continued the tradition (and usually follow the same routes) of the Indian paths, pioneer roads, and canals that preceded them. Amtrak and Conrail transport passengers and freight along rights-of-way once followed by trains of Conestoga wagons.

German immigrants pushing west from the crowded lands of the Atlantic Coast area knew that by following the black walnut trees, they would find the richest, most fertile soils. That custom led them to Lancaster County, then up the Susquehanna Valley to Harrisburg and into the West. That rich soil and agricultural heritage have made central Pennsylvania a leading food producer. Agriculture, food processing, and food distribution are still the way many area residents earn their daily bread.

Greater Harrisburg is a complex society. State government dominates the region, but private industry remains powerful and active. The people of central Pennsylvania are proud and hard working. There is a tradition of self-reliance, productivity, and craftsmanship that goes back 150 years or more.

Change comes slowly in central Pennsylvania, for there is respect for the old—the known, tried, and proven. Only when newcomers—new people, new industries, new ideas—prove themselves are they accepted fully as community partners. Yet there is also a real belief in progress and a desire to be up to date and in tune with the times.

Local social customs require gracious understatement and modesty. Harrisburg's business and professional leaders are reluctant to parade their achievements. But there is also respect for family and associates, and a deep appreciation of history.

The pages that follow are a tribute to past generations of vision, work, and dedication. They are offered so that future generations may understand and share greater Harrisburg's traditions, heritage, and community pride.

CHAMBER OF COMMERCE OF THE GREATER HARRISBURG AREA

Since the 19th century when its predecessor was known as the Board of Trade (incorporated in 1886 under president W.W. Jennings), the Chamber of Commerce of the Greater Harrisburg Area has worked to advance commerce and industry in cooperation with the public sector.

As the Chamber's first president, George B. Tripp, wrote to the city council on January 26, 1914, "The policy of the new organization will not be one of criticism or complaint. . . . There are many ways, we believe, in which the Chamber of Commerce and the City Council can work together."

Incorporation proceedings were concluded on March 9, 1914. Commercial realities, especially prices, were a little different in those days. Among expenses incurred in the process were $10 for eight days of typewriting (Miss Shumaker), 10 cents for paper clips, $79.50 for food, and $19.60 for cigars. The new association leased offices in the Kunkle Building for $64 per month, including light, heat, and elevator service.

The Chamber's headquarters was totally destroyed by fire in 1923 and almost all files and records were lost. Only the minutes of board of directors' meetings, membership lists, and dues invoices were saved. The Chamber purchased and occupied its current headquarters building at 114 Walnut Street in 1940.

In 1972 flood waters spawned by Hurricane Agnes again destroyed Chamber files and records. After the waters receded staff members were faced with their own personal problems but dedicated themselves to coordinating the regional clean-up and revival effort.

To Matt Douglas, current president of the Chamber, none of that was as trying as the U.S. Defense Department's decision to phase out Olmsted Air Force Base in the early 1960s. Many in the greater Harrisburg area thought that the community was

The Old Home Week Industrial Day Parade of 1905 was sponsored by the Board of Trade, predecessor to the Chamber of Commerce of the Greater Harrisburg Area. Thousands of former Harrisburg residents returned for the week's festivities, enjoying parades and celebrations in the decorated city.

facing economic disaster. Douglas recalls the efforts to convince Pentagon officials to change their minds—efforts that continued even as a second committee started work attracting new industries to replace jobs lost with the Middletown military installation.

From that effort emerged Penn State Capitol Campus, the Fruehauf plant, and the new airport in Middletown; the Book-of-the-Month distribution center in Camp Hill; and other newcomers to the vicinity. Working through the specially created Harrisburg Area Industrial Development Corporation, the Chamber, in cooperation with municipal authorities and other groups, turned near economic catastrophe into community revitalization. Douglas recalls it as one of the Chamber's great triumphs.

Douglas sees the local economy expanding. "This area will continue to

be economically viable," he says. "We have more going for us than any other community in the state, or most other parts of the Northeast." Such economic vitality in the future will result from continuing the Chamber's tradition of a progressive alliance of civic and commercial leadership.

The Walnut Street headquarters of the Chamber of Commerce has changed little since this 1948 photograph. Built in 1842, the building was the Fager School and the Harrisburg City Hall before the Chamber of Commerce purchased it in 1940.

EARL LATSHA LUMBER COMPANY

Give most men a chain saw and they'll cut a little firewood. When Earl Latsha took hold of some chain saws shortly after World War II, he used them to clear a tract and build a great lumber business.

Latsha was a farm boy, a native of Dauphin County's Lykens Valley. He came to Harrisburg "because it was the only place where anything was happening." He had an old farm truck that he used to trade first in produce, and then cattle.

When an associate defaulted on a loan, Latsha claimed the chain saws. He began his venture aided by Johnny Demarco, who still works for Latsha as one of 60 employees at the Latsha lumberyard. At first the two used the old cattle truck to haul wood; by 1948

Earl Latsha, owner and president of the lumber company that bears his name.

they had a new International; today they have a fleet of vehicles.

Latsha Lumber produces the kind of custom-milled fine hardwood specified by exclusive interior designers. Latsha's millwork has gone into many corporate boardrooms but his own office still has a more rough-hewn and rugged appearance.

The lumberyard is located on Linglestown Road, north of the city. Its 45-acre site was a farm before Latsha bought it in 1951. The office and planer used to share the barn. Where the main mill shed now stands, there was an apple orchard. "We just took a bulldozer and pushed back the trees," remembers Latsha.

The plant features an automated sawmill that trims giant logs down to rough-cut boards. The bark is ground for mulch; chips are sold to paper mills; the sawdust is sold as bedding material.

A Christmas Eve fire destroyed the main shed in 1968. More than 125 firemen from 10 companies fought that blaze, one of the biggest in Harrisburg history. Memories of that fire still show in redesigned buildings and in Latsha's stories.

The sawmill sits on the northern edge of the lumberyard, surrounded by logs waiting their turn. From there, it is just a short walk to the planing mill. The dry kiln is housed in the same building as the maintenance operation.

Latsha hurries past the Sheetrock and commercial plywoods, explaining that the yard has to stock all contemporary building supplies needed by area contractors and do-it-yourselfers. But he stops to admire and show off the stocks of fine timbers, moldings, hardwoods, and other prized products of the lumberman's craft. He runs his hands fondly over a beautiful sheet of walnut plywood. "Look at this," he says. "There's not a flaw on it." This is a man who understands both the costs and benefits of progress. That understanding has helped make his contribution to greater Harrisburg unique and valuable.

Earl Latsha Lumber Company, Linglestown Road, Harrisburg.

MERCHANTS AND BUSINESS MEN'S MUTUAL INSURANCE COMPANY

The President of the United States is provided with a fully insured home. But even the President must provide his own coverage on personal properties. Dwight D. Eisenhower chose Harrisburg's Merchants and Business Men's Mutual Insurance Company to provide the fire and extended benefits coverage on his Gettysburg farm while he was away living and working in the White House.

The company was created January 3, 1895, in Wyalusing, Pennsylvania. Its founders were E.A. Strong, president; R.J. Fuller, vice-president; George T. Ingham, secretary; and E.D. Lewis, treasurer. These officers joined with friends and neighbors to form Merchants Mutual Insurance Company.

Twelve years later, a similar group

The 1967 board of directors of Merchants and Business Men's Mutual Insurance Company was comprised of many of Harrisburg's leading citizens. Standing, left to right, are William S. Miller, Jr., John A. Blessing, Chester M. Sheffer, William D.P. Holcomb, L.B. Smith, Robert L. Bennett, and Dr. J.B. Bittenbender. Seated, left to right, are J. Robert Elser, W.W. Dodson, Sr., and J. Axe Miller.

founded Business Men's Mutual Fire Insurance Company in Towanda, Pennsylvania. In 1920 the firms merged, forming Merchants and Business Men's Mutual Insurance. Soon the Towanda company was offering insurance protection throughout Pennsylvania, Maryland, and West Virginia.

Today Merchants and Business Men's Mutual Insurance Company and its allied firms—Penn Allen Mutual Insurance Company (founded in 1843 and acquired by Merchants and Business Men's in 1965) and the M & B Agency—conduct business in 17 states and the District of Columbia. The organization covers the Eastern Seaboard from Florida to Massachusetts, as well as much of the adjacent area. It employs 150 people, most of whom work in the Harrisburg corporate headquarters.

President W.W. Dodson, Sr., brought his entire staff of eight people to Harrisburg in 1929. His small group leased office space in half of the first floor at 321 North Second Street, a building then owned by a local welfare association. He soon became deeply

The floods that followed Hurricane Agnes in 1972 caused devastation throughout central Pennsylvania. Merchants and Business Men's Mutual Insurance experienced the problems firsthand in its Front Street, Harrisburg, headquarters. At its highest, the flood rose almost to the top of the first-floor windows.

involved in his new community, working with such area leaders as Vance McCormick, Milton Hershey, and Harvey Taylor. One of the organizers of Capital Blue Cross, Dodson served as president of the Harrisburg School Board and on the council of St. Mathew's Lutheran Church. He also was a director of the Central YMCA, and a member of the boards of United Way, Children's Home, and Polyclinic Hospital.

W.W. Dodson, Sr., was president of the company from 1926 to 1958 and was succeeded by W.W. Keay (1958-1963), J. Axe Miller (1963-1970), J. Robert Elser (1970-1977), and W.W. Dodson, Jr., the current president.

The company's headquarters building at 2201 North Front Street was built by Harrisburg lawyer Horace King in the mid-1920s. Once boasting a swimming pool and bowling alley in its lower level, this lavish Greek revival mansion has become a Harrisburg landmark. King died shortly after completing the facility. It had several other tenants before Merchants and Business Men's Insurance purchased and occupied it in 1947. The south wing was added in 1952.

All insurance companies know and understand catastrophe and disaster. Merchants and Business Men's is no exception; the firm protects clients against losses from fire and countless other risks. It worries about hurricanes and sinkholes in Florida and mine subsidence in West Virginia. Through participation in reinsurance pools the company has been involved in such diverse tragedies and events as the Las Vegas fire in the MGM Grand Hotel, and the destruction by terrorists of three jet airliners in the Libyan desert.

But the staff of Merchants and Business Men's is most familiar with the damage caused by Hurricane Agnes in 1972. The rampaging Susquehanna River rushed past, and then through, the company offices,

W.W. Dodson, Sr., was president of Merchants and Business Men's Mutual Insurance Company from 1926 to 1958.

threatening staff and records vital not only to the firm but to all its clients.

Sweeping flood waters into the onetime King family swimming pool helped gain a vital few minutes' delay. Massive cooperation by the entire staff carried the rest of the day, as records were moved first to higher shelves, and then to a higher floor. The Coast Guard later evacuated president (now board chairman) J. Robert Elser and

W.W. Dodson, Jr., is the current president of Merchants and Business Men's Insurance Company.

three other employees who helped complete the protection work.

All needed current records were saved from the river. A file system of cartons, boards, and cinder blocks sheltered IBM cards and other records, replacing submerged file cabinets. Just three days after the flood crested, Merchants and Business Men's was back in business. The company was fortunate to have experienced so little damage; it had no flood insurance at the time.

The tradition of community service established by W.W. Dodson, Sr., is still closely observed by officers of Merchants and Business Men's Mutual Insurance Company. Board chairman Elser has been president of the Mechanicsburg Area Library and of the board of managers of the West Shore YMCA, and a member of the board of the area YMCA. He is an elder of the Mechanicsburg Presbyterian Church.

President W.W. Dodson, Jr., joined the firm as general counsel in 1952, following service as a pilot in World War II and the Korean War. He has been a vice-president of the Harrisburg Symphony, board member of the Harrisburg Area YMCA, president of the council of Trinity Lutheran Church, and currently is a member of the board of directors of Polyclinic Hospital and a trustee of the Harrisburg Academy.

Merchants and Business Men's Insurance remains a true mutual insurance company. The corporate owners are the policyholders, all of whom receive dividends.

"Harrisburg has been a good home for us," says president Dodson. "We hope to stay here and to continue to support the community." Certainly the company has prospered since president W.W. Dodson, Sr., first brought it to Harrisburg, and the community has benefited from the company's contributions. This has been a fine partnership.

GANNETT FLEMING, INC.

It is impossible to spend time in Harrisburg and not feel the impact of Gannett Fleming, Inc. Have you crossed the Susquehanna on the South Bridge, or driven Interstate Highway 83 south of York? Gannett Fleming engineers worked with both, along with other area highways. Have you had a drink of water? Gannett Fleming designed much of Harrisburg's water system. And when all else is said and done, Gannett Fleming also designed the Harrisburg incinerator and the wastewater treatment plant.

Or you may be familiar with several other Gannett Fleming projects such as the Lindenwold High Speed Line in the Philadelphia area, the Southeast Freeway and Metro in Washington, D.C., and dams throughout Pennsylvania, Ohio, and West Virginia.

But few area residents know about such other Gannett Fleming productions as its environmental impact study of development on the Senegal River Basin in West Africa, the water supply system developed for Quito, Ecuador, or the Tel Aviv to Ashdod Highway in Israel.

Gannett Fleming , Inc., headquarters its worldwide operations in Camp Hill. It has more than 20 regional offices throughout the United States, 17 affiliated companies, and a total of more than 1,000 employees.

The firm's work includes virtually all consulting engineering services. The Gannett Fleming logo includes ancient symbols for ether, air, earth, fire, and water. The company works in concert with all of these elements, expanding man's domain but with a profound respect for the laws of nature and the environment.

Founder Farley Gannett was born in Washington, D.C., the son of Henry Gannett, chief geographer of the U.S. Geological Survey and a founder of the National Geographic Society. Farley Gannett was chief engineer of Pennsylvania's Water Supply

Commission when he backed Bull Moose presidential candidate Theodore Roosevelt in 1912; the state Republicans backed W.H. Taft. Gannett resigned shortly after Taft's victory, starting his own firm in 1915.

Gannett's principal assistant, Ted

The Farley Gannett Engineering Center in Camp Hill, Pennsylvania, is the headquarters complex of Gannett Fleming, Inc.

Seelye, left the water commission to become Gannett's partner. Samuel W. Fleming, Jr., joined the partnership in 1916. The other senior members of the firm, William Howard Corddry, James Donald Carpenter (the only Harrisburg native), and Frank H. Eastman, assumed executive positions with Gannett Fleming following World War I.

The company's first office was in Harrisburg's Telegraph Building. Its

first jobs included the design of a multipurpose dam for Gifford Pinchot on his Pike County estate (Pinchot later became twice-governor of Pennsylvania), a flood-control job at Erie, and a public utility rate study for the towns supplied by the Ohio Valley Water Company, near Pittsburgh.

Today Gannett Fleming is ranked among the top 10 consulting engineering organizations in the United States. Harrisburg can take great pride in the work of this partner—not only in the region's progress, but in progress throughout the world.

PATRIOT-NEWS PUBLISHING COMPANY

Harrisburg has always been a newsy town. Its first newspaper, *The Harrisburg Advertiser,* was started in 1791 when the population was only 500. By 1830 the city had 4,000 people and 11 newspapers.

Columnist and historian Paul Beers finds it impossible to date the birth of *The Harrisburg Patriot.* Its oldest ancestor was *The Dauphin Guardian* of 1805. Another choice would be the 1843 merger of three papers into *The Democratic Union.* The name "Patriot" first appeared in Harrisburg with *The Pennsylania Patriot* in March 1854.

Harrisburg journalism entered its modern era shortly after the turn of the century. Edward J. Stackpole bought *The Telegraph* in 1901. Vance McCormick bought *The Patriot* a year later. A classic American newspaper war was on. McCormick started *The Evening News* in 1917 as direct competition for *The Telegraph.*

The Stackpoles and Vance McCormick not only reported the news—they made and controlled it. They were actively involved in politics, business activities, and civic affairs. From one perspective they were active local owners; by another standard, they were "walking conflicts of interest."

When McCormick purchased *The Patriot,* it was housed on Market Street, just west of where Pomeroy's Department Store now stands. The newspaper was moved to Market Square in 1906.

Construction of the present building in 1953 came under the ownership of the late S.I. Newhouse, who had acquired *The Patriot, The Evening News,* and *The Telegraph,* and subsequently merged the newspapers by closing *The Telegraph* on March 27, 1948. Edwin F. Russell has been president of the Patriot-News Publishing Company since 1946. In 1949, under his direction, the Sunday *Patriot-News* was introduced to central Pennsylvania.

John H. Baum became publisher

In 1902 Vance McCormick, who was active in Harrisburg politics, business, and civic affairs, purchased *The Patriot.*

Publisher John H. Baum watched closely as in-plant production resumed on July 12, 1972. Because of Hurricane Agnes and the resulting flood, production was shut down for the first time in the history of *The Patriot-News.*

and vice-president of the newspapers in 1968. A native of Lemoyne, Baum was an outstanding, almost legendary leader of Harrisburg civic affairs. He died in 1981 and was succeeded by Raymond L. Gover.

Hurricane Agnes caused a major crisis for the newspapers in 1972. With the presses submerged under 28 feet of water, the papers missed publication from June 22 to June 28. Publication was resumed with the help of newspapers in the neighboring communities of Allentown, Chambersburg, and Lancaster.

On July 12, after removing 1,200 tons of soggy newsprint from the building, local production was resumed. Never before had *The Patriot-News* failed to publish.

The progress of greater Harrisburg has been reported in the pages of its newspapers for almost 200 years. Over the past 30 years *The Patriot-News* has expanded and modernized as it met the challenges of contemporary Harrisburg life and its responsibilities as the home paper for the seat of Pennsylvania government.

PENNSYLVANIA NATIONAL MUTUAL CASUALTY INSURANCE COMPANY

Many Pennsylvania threshermen and farmers were angry in 1914. The state had just passed a law that could have prevented traction engines and threshing machines from using state highways. In response, a group of 35 men, including farm implement businessmen, led by J.A. Rose, W.F. Hovetter, and Frank Moyer met in Harrisburg to form the Pennsylvania Threshermen and Farmers' Protective Association.

One month later, over 400 threshermen and farmers from throughout the state attended the new association's first general meeting. They organized quickly and effectively. The offending automobile law was repealed in 1915, replaced by a new version passed with the blessing of the PT&F Protective Association.

The association organized its Pennsylvania Threshermen and Farmers' Mutual Casualty Insurance Company in 1919. This was the beginning of today's Pennsylvania National Mutual Casualty Insurance Company and its affiliated companies of the Pennsylvania National Insurance Group. The first board of directors included Harrisburgers Rose and Hovetter, Spencer Barber of Paxtang, and Ira M. Hart and Charles Wilson of Mechanicsburg. The first policies were issued April 1, 1920, offering Pennsylvania business firms "Owners' Coverage" and workmen's compensation coverage for employees.

The protective association had been a part-time activity for its organizers; the insurance company became a full-time occupation for Rose, its first secretary/treasurer and general manager. One of his first actions was moving the insurance company to its own quarters—an office in the Kunkle Building (now the Feller Building) at Third and Market streets.

The first convention of the protective association and its insurance company was held in 1921. Because of the group's political importance, its

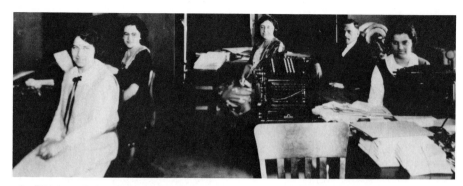

By 1923 the staff of Pennsylvania Threshermen and Farmers' Mutual Casualty Insurance Company had expanded to include Jacob Rose and five clerical assistants. The company was still in its Market Street quarters.

annual meetings became major Harrisburg events until they were discontinued during World War II. The conventions often featured speeches by Pennsylvania's governors and United States senators, as well as presentations by leaders in agriculture and insurance.

In 1929 the company branched out, offering a new policy protecting automobile owners. Automobile underwriting would quickly become an important activity for PTF Insurance, and the firm eventually became a major insurer of automotive businesses as well as individual owners and drivers. When the 1972 flood struck the Commonwealth, Pennsylvania National policies protected many of the Harrisburg

area's automobile dealers. As a present company officer remembers, "We had to buy a lot of new—but totally ruined—cars."

The company reached beyond Pennsylvania in 1932, expanding first to Maryland, then to the District of Columbia, where the first branch office was opened. Today the Pennsylvania National Insurance Group conducts business in 18 states with regional offices in Harrisburg; Pittsburgh; Kansas City, Kansas; and Greensboro, North Carolina.

In 1933 PTF Insurance moved its corporate headquarters to a newly

The first board of directors of Pennsylvania Threshermen and Farmers' Mutual Casualty Insurance Company met in Harrisburg. They are (left to right, seated) A.H. Brubaker, H.S. Lee, W.F. Hovetter, J.A. Rose, Ira M. Hart, W.B. Crawford, S.U. Kepple, F.R. Moyer, J.E. Irwin; (left to right, standing) Kinney Stephens, E.S. Strasbaugh, Spencer Barber, H.L.R. Anderson, J.W. Bagshaw, Charles Wilson, W.S. Weaver, and E.S. George.

purchased facility on 18th Street, Harrisburg. The same year, the firm once again expanded its coverage by offering insurance to anthracite and bituminous coal mine operators. A general line of public liability policies soon followed—as did the need to expand the headquarters building.

In 1944, through the purchase of Blair County Fire Insurance Company and a modification to its charter, PTF added general fire coverage to its other casualty lines. Once again the organization was faced with the realization that expanding business required additional office space. PTF moved to its current headquarters at 19th and Derry streets in 1949. Speakers at the dedication included Pennsylvania Governor James Duff, Harrisburg Mayor Claude Robins, and Daniel Casey, secretary of the Chamber of Commerce of the Greater Harrisburg Area. Today three buildings at that location contain the home offices of Pennsylvania National Insurance Group.

The Pennsylvania National Life Insurance Company was incorporated in 1962, further expanding the line of policies offered by PTF Companies. In

1963 the Pennsylvania National name replaced PTF, ending the public tie to the old Pennsylvania Threshermen and Farmers' Protective Association. In 1967 the transformation was completed, as a series of mergers begun in 1963 with the acquisition of the Mutual Insurance Company of Pennsylvania, Collegeville, Pennsylvania, concluded with consolidation into the Pennsylvania National Mutual Casualty Insurance Company.

Founder Jacob Rose died in 1941, and his duties were split among three men—W.F. Hovetter and Frank Moyer, cofounders, and J.G. Feinour. In 1954 Rose's daughter Marjorie Rose Thomas, manager of the workmen's compensation department, wrote a history of her father's company. Thus it was she who recognized that steady growth and expansion had resulted from one crucial and consistent management policy. "Many times," she wrote, "it had to be decided whether to stand still, retrench, or go forward into new fields. Each time . . . new lines of coverage were added, new territories were entered."

PTF was founded in 1920 with $54,000 in cash ($19,000 borrowed), and two part-time employees. In 1982 Pennsylvania National Insurance Group companies had nearly 1,100

employees and assets of over $400 million.

Those companies now include Pennsylvania National Mutual Casualty Insurance Company; Pennsylvania National Life Insurance Company; PENCO Consumer Discount Company (founded 1973); ESL, Inc. (founded 1980); and Inservco Insurance Services, Inc. (founded 1980).

Never underestimate the power of a group of angry farmers!

J.A. Rose, founder of PTF Mutual Casualty Insurance Company.

An artist's rendition of the national headquarters complex of Pennsylvania National Insurance Group on Derry Street in Harrisburg.

RITE AID CORPORATION

The headquarters building of Rite Aid Corporation, greater Harrisburg's newest billion-dollar-plus company, is a stylish, streamlined, contemporary structure. There is a smooth and energetic sense of corporate efficiency that pervades the nerve center of a marketing empire.

Rite Aid, the third-largest drugstore chain in the country, employs more than 15,000 people in operations extending across much of the United States. The organization employs about 1,200 in the Harrisburg area at its headquarters and distribution centers. The company operates more than 1,000 drugstores in 18 states (more than 200 in Pennsylvania alone).

The company has also become involved in specialty retailing with the addition of Circus World Toy Stores, the fifth-largest toy store chain in the country, and Heaven, a small group of contemporary variety stores. Other corporate divisions include Super Rite Foods, Inc., a wholesale grocery business which today accounts for about five percent of profits, and Sera-Tec Biologicals, a chain of nine plasmapheresis centers in the eastern United States. Rite Aid also owns 28.2 percent of Superdrug Stores P.L.C., a 143-store chain based in Great Britain.

Rite Aid had its roots in a small Harrisburg grocery business started in 1927. But the company didn't really begin to expand to its present size until the firm moved outside its traditional boundaries.

Alex Grass, chairman of the board and president of Rite Aid, joined the firm in 1953. Under his leadership, the company expanded rapidly in a series of new directions. For the first time, additional product lines including dairy, candy, and cigarettes were added to the firm's offerings. Along with the new merchandise came aggressive marketing.

The health and beauty aids business had its beginning in 1958, when Grass

first took the company beyond grocery sales. Ironically, he found golden opportunity in the same supermarket chains that were becoming competitors to the wholesale grocery business. The supermarkets had begun offering shoppers nonfood merchandise and Grass realized that health and beauty aids would be commanding growing consumer attention. He decided to begin Rack Rite Distributors, Inc., a rack jobbing service that would add a new and larger dimension to the wholesale grocery business. Dave Sommer was hired to help manage this new venture.

The rack jobbing concept involved providing grocery retailers with pre-priced merchandise on specially designed racks. To the store owner, it means that little time, effort, space, or investment is needed to increase sales. For the company in 1958, it created outlets for their lines of health and beauty aids, stationery, housewares, and toys wherever they could place, supply, and service their racks.

The division grew so rapidly during its first four years of operations that it was forced to move to expanded quarters four times. By 1962 it was apparent to Grass that another shift in direction was required to take full advantage of the division's potential.

The "fair-trade" concept (under which it was illegal to sell many kinds of merchandise below "list" prices) was under attack by consumer interests in the early 1960s. The age of price controls was rapidly giving way to the discount era in 1962, when Rack Rite Distributors opened its first discount health and beauty aids store. Named Thrif-D Discount Center, the Scranton outlet was an immediate success. Two years later the chain boasted 12 stores with total corporate sales of approximately $20 million and net income of over $400,000.

The rapidly expanding company changed its name to Rite Aid and made its first public stock offering in

Top:
The "Thrif-D" stores marked the beginning of Rite Aid's discount health and beauty aids stores. One of the first was located in Allentown, Pennsylvania.

Bottom:
When Rack Rite became Rite Aid, the stores adopted the company name and many added prescription services.

June 1968. Sales had almost doubled in the previous four years. The chain had 60 stores, and the public (including many Harrisburg-area investors) were impressed by the accomplishments of Rite Aid management. The initial offering of 350,000 shares sold briskly at $25 per share. Less than a year later there were more than 100 stores in the chain and the stock split two-for-one. In 1970 the stock began trading on the New York Stock Exchange. Since then, there have been three more stock splits and today there are 12 shares for each originally issued share of stock.

Rite Aid has grown through acquisitions as well as internally generated expansion. In 1968 the corporation purchased the 10-store Martin's chain in Philadelphia. In 1969 it acquired Daw Drug, a 47-store chain based in Rochester, New York, and its largest acquisition came in 1977 with the addition of the 99-store Reed Drug chain in Baltimore. Rite Aid also added new distribution centers in Rome, New York, and Nitro, West Virginia, to handle the increasing volume. There have been many others and the future should continue to see new ones.

One of Rite Aid's newest stores in downtown Harrisburg.

Alex Grass, president and chairman of the board, Rite Aid Corporation.

COMMONWEALTH NATIONAL BANK

Commonwealth National Bank has witnessed a great deal of Harrisburg history from its Market Square vantage point at the center of the city. When the bank first opened, the borough had a population of 2,500, the state capitol had not yet been built, and transportation was by horse, canal, or stagecoach.

The Harrisburg Bank (as it was first known) was organized on June 13, 1814, at the "Wheat Sheaf" tavern at Front and Market streets. Tavern owner John Schoch became one of the bank's first directors. Also among the founders was Robert Harris, son of Harrisburg pioneer John Harris.

Other early directors of the bank were Thomas Elder, president of the Harrisburg Bridge Company and, later, attorney general of the state; iron manufacturer and land developer Jacob Haldeman; and Theodore Burr, designer of the famous "Camelback" bridge. General John Forster, second cashier of the Harrisburg Bank, was a state senator. Stockholder Francis R. Shunk was governor from 1844 to 1848; stockholder Alexander Ramsey was later governor and United States senator from Minnesota. James Buchanan became a stockholder in 1822 and a director in 1831, but resigned before his election as President of the United States.

Technological progress was actively pursued by early directors. The bank helped finance the Harrisburg Canal Company, the Union Canal, and the Pennsylvania Canal. Later, it provided funds for The Harrisburg, Portsmouth & Mount Joy Railroad; the Cumberland Valley Railroad; and the Lebanon Valley Railroad. The bank was an early supporter of and major investor in the Pennsylvania Railroad.

The Harrisburg Bank has actively supported local educational and civic institutions. It provided financial support and leadership to the Harrisburg Academy, the Harrisburg Female Seminary, and the Harrisburg

This old print is of the Harrisburg National Bank, which was built in 1854 on the site of the property purchased in 1817 from the Philadelphia Bank.

School Board. Other institutions that originated with bank assistance include the local YMCA (1854) and the Harrisburg Benevolent Society (1835), predecessor to the United Way. The Harrisburg Hospital was organized at a meeting held in the bank (1873) and Dorothea Dix had her headquarters in the bank as she worked to establish the State Hospital for the Insane.

The Harrisburg Bank received a national charter in 1864, shortly after passage of the National Banking Act. The Civil War was raging, and it was a frightening time in Harrisburg. During the Gettysburg campaign, gold bullion held as reserves by the bank was removed to New York. Bank records were taken to Philadelphia as Confederate troops advanced toward the city.

Jacob S. Haldeman, son of New Cumberland pioneer and bank founder Jacob M. Haldeman, was president of the bank during those critical years of war and reorganization. He was succeeded by Judge Valentine Hummel (1868-1870) and Dr. George W. Reily (1870-1892), whose families would establish a long and continuing tradition of leadership of the bank.

The bank—with the city—has weathered numerous major crises since the Confederate Army threatened. In 1933, during the Bank Holiday, the Harrisburg Bank shipped gold to the Federal Reserve to help stabilize national currency. After normal banking activities resumed, deposits jumped sharply in a remarkable show of confidence by customers.

During Hurricane Agnes in 1972, the Uptown Office was the hardest hit among flooded branches. Soaked currency and records as well as safe-deposit boxes were removed to the main office for cleaning, drying, and for the opening of the boxes by customers.

In 1979, as area residents fleeing possible disaster at Three Mile Island nuclear plant strained regional resources to the limits, Commonwealth anchored central Pennsylvania's banking system. Massive amounts of currency were demanded as residents closed accounts and sought travel funds. Commonwealth served as a conduit for currency to banks throughout the area. Largely as a result of Commonwealth's efforts and the cooperation of many other banks, none were forced to disappoint customers.

The evolution of the Harrisburg Bank to Commonwealth National Bank occurred through gradual and carefully controlled growth. In 1893 directors of the Harrisburg National Bank founded the Harrisburg Trust Company with a state charter. The two banks remained closely associated, sharing many facilities. They thus offered area financial interests the benefits of both state and federal banking systems.

Throughout the late '50s and early '60s a series of mergers and acquisitions expanded the holdings and facilities of the bank and the trust company. Banks in Penbrook, Highspire, Mechanicsburg, Steelton,

Shiremanstown, and Middletown had become part of the Harrisburg Bank by 1961, when the bank and the trust company merged to form Harrisburg National Bank and Trust Company.

The "Commonwealth" name was adopted after the 1969 merger of Harrisburg National, Conestoga National Bank (Lancaster), and The First National Bank of York. The tricornered logo of Commonwealth National symbolizes the three regions involved in that merger. Cumberland Valley is now also served by a division of the bank.

The holding company, Commonwealth National Financial Corporation, was formed in 1982.

John R. Biechler is currently chairman of the board and chief executive officer of the holding company and the bank. He succeeded Spencer G. Hall, a director of the bank since 1949 and chairman of the board of directors of the corporation since its formation. Hall died on April 16, 1983. Charles F. Merrill is president and chief operating officer of the holding company and the bank.

The founding directors of the Harrisburg Bank recognized back in 1814 that their own fortunes were tied to those of their community. They knew that the selection of Harrisburg as the state capital offered them an outstanding opportunity, and worked with imagination, courage, and dedication to take the bank through difficult and complex times. Their success can be measured by the progress of their community. The vitality of the greater Harrisburg area today is the result of this 170-year partnership.

General John Forster was cashier of the Harrisburg Bank from 1815 to 1833.

Judge Valentine Hummel, who was president of the bank from 1868 to 1870 and director from 1843 to 1870, was related to many succeeding officers of the bank.

ICELAND SEAFOOD CORPORATION

The fish are caught in frigid North Atlantic waters off Iceland and served on tables throughout the world. But before reaching millions of consumers, a big portion of the catch is processed at Iceland Seafood Corporation in Camp Hill. More than 45 million pounds of fish—12 percent of the total United States market for processed seafood—passed through the Camp Hill plant in 1982.

Yet the Iceland Seafood name (or its "Samband" brand) is known to few consumers. For the company does little retail business. Its product is sold to schools, industrial plant kitchens, restaurant chains, and health care institutions. And while the test kitchens of Iceland Seafood have produced an excellent, imaginative cookbook to help chefs prepare their product, it too is not for the private home; most of its recipes result in 100 or more servings.

Iceland Seafood's first office opened in 1951 in New York City. It had three employees, including Gudjon B. Olafsson who is now president. One client was a processing plant located in an old Steelton, Pennsylvania, brewery. The plant also processed small quantities of fish for distribution under the Samband label.

In 1959 Iceland Seafood purchased the plant and moved its headquarters from New York to Steelton. Rapid expansion quickly outdated the inefficient facility. Working with the regional industrial development corporation, the firm opened a new plant in 1966. Iceland Seafood moved its 50 employees to the newly constructed plant in Camp Hill. The latest addition to the plant was completed in 1981, doubling processing and storage space to over 200,000 square feet.

The expanded, energy-efficient plant provides work space for the company's 400 employees and subzero frozen storage space for over 10 million pounds of fish. Its loading dock can handle up to 10 semitrailers at a time.

Iceland Seafood is jointly owned by the Federation of Iceland Cooperative Societies (Samband) and by the 35 fish-processing plants that are members of Samband's Fish Products Division. Member plants sell all of their products to Iceland Seafood. It is an unusual corporate setup, reflecting Iceland's blend of economic systems. But as a result of this cooperative effort, about 20 percent of the haddock, lobster, cod, pollock, turbot, flounder, and other fish from Iceland's 850-vessel fishing fleet is processed and distributed through the Camp Hill plant. Over 1,500 fishermen and 2,000 shore-based workers in Iceland have become partners with workers in Camp Hill.

Central Pennsylvania is known throughout the world for its agricultural production and food processing. Iceland Seafood is one of the greater Harrisburg area's most important ingredients in this tasty and nutritious tradition.

The Iceland Seafood Corporation plant in Camp Hill, Pennsylvania, houses processing, storage, and shipping facilities serving customers throughout the United States.

Gudjon B. Olafsson—president of the Iceland Seafood Corporation.

KESSLER'S, INC.

Pass through the plant doors at Kessler's, Inc., of Lemoyne and you are greeted with the pungent, spicy aromas of smoked hams, hot dogs, and sausages. The machines and techniques here are modern, yet there is a relaxed, bustling camaraderie. It reminds you that Kessler's may be a major meat packer, but it is still very much a local, family-owned business.

Back in 1916, a young lady named Guenther gave her family's recipe for Easton-style bologna to George A. Kessler, Sr. Kessler was an ambitious merchant with a coffee, butter, and egg route that he serviced by horse and buggy. With his new recipe in hand, he started the Guenther Bologna Company.

Kessler's, Inc., has now become an important central Pennsylvania meat processor. The firm's "Nittany Lion franks" and other meats are popular throughout central Pennsylvania and northern Maryland. And while Kessler's no longer makes Easton bologna, it once again is supplying customers with a wide line of other food products, just as George Kessler did in the early days.

George and Emma Kessler brought their meat-packing business from Easton to Lebanon, Pennsylvania, in the early '20s, and to Lemoyne in 1928. They also first opened their stands at Harrisburg's Broad Street Market and at the Carlisle Farmers' Market that year.

The plant moved to its present site at 1201 Hummel Avenue in 1940, when the firm added a slaughterhouse. That part of the business was later phased out and Kessler's now buys all of its meats from other suppliers.

During the early years, the entire family was involved in the business. While caring for their eight children, Emma Kessler baked beans and made the potato salad that the company sold at market. When the stands were closed, she drove Kessler's products around the area, selling out of the

In 1939 the Lemoyne homestead of the Kessler family included a retail store and was located next door to the plant. The retail store was closed in 1940.

trunk of her car. Robert Kessler, the firm's current president, remembers hand-stuffing sausages and peeling casings off skinless franks after school as well as helping out at market.

Today Kessler's, Inc., offers its products exclusively on a wholesale basis. The Kesslers' stands in Carlisle, Lemoyne, and Harrisburg are now a separate operation run independently by other members of the family.

Kessler's has always been a family business. After George Kessler, Sr., retired in 1945, son John P. Kessler became president. After his death in 1961, son-in-law Charles L. Zoll took

over. Robert Kessler, another son of the founder, has been president since Zoll's death in 1967. The other owners of the corporation are Dale Zoll, Fred Kessler, and Charles Zoll, Jr.

The makers of Nittany Lion franks, incidentally, are not graduates of Penn State. But they do support the university generously and enthusiastically. Robert Kessler is especially pleased with the Penn State Nittany Lion football team's 1982 national championship. "Our franks have always been number one," he says. "It's nice that the football team is, too."

In 1916 George A. Kessler, Sr., had a coffee, butter, and egg route in Easton, Pennsylvania, that he serviced by horse and buggy.

HOOD, LIGHT AND GEISE, INC.

John Hood had been a press aid for Pennsylvania Governor Gifford Pinchot, state manager for the Associated Press, and general manager of *The Harrisburg Telegraph* when he decided to start his own advertising and public relations agency. He created Associated Advertisers in 1935.

Ben Light had been a sportswriter and columnist in his native Lebanon, Pennsylvania, and in Harrisburg. Shortly before *The Telegraph* ceased publication in 1948, Light agreed to work for Hood. But he insisted that he would only handle press relations assignments, claiming no interest or skills in advertising. That distinction quickly blurred and Light became one of Harrisburg's finest craftsmen of the sponsored word.

George Geise is a graduate of Harrisburg's John Harris High School, a local boy who studied commercial art at New York City's Pratt Institute. When he joined the firm in 1955, Associated Advertisers took the name Hood, Light and Geise. He is now president and one of the firm's two principals.

George Geise, shortly after joining Hood, Light and Geise in the 1950s.

Terry Bush, the other principal, joined the agency in 1963. A graduate of Elizabethtown College, Bush served a hitch with Army Intelligence, worked with the advertising departments of several area newspapers, and was on the staff of the Pennsylvania Farm Bureau before joining the firm.

Hood, Light and Geise has worked with many business firms and trade associations in Harrisburg. In a way, the city itself has been a client of the agency. For such actual clients as the Chamber of Commerce of the Greater Harrisburg Area, Strawberry Square, and the Downtown Shoppers' Garage all have benefited from agency programs.

Agency chronicles include numerous other success stories. The Eastern Sports and Outdoor Show has become the biggest event at the Farm Show complex, with help from Hood, Light and Geise. Two other clients have won national awards from the Freedom Foundation and the American Advertising Federation in recognition of promotional campaigns.

The agency has moved around a great deal during its half-century of operation. It first opened for business with a suite in the Kline Building, moving to the Telegraph Building in 1940. Subsequent moves took it to 315 North Second Street (1946), 329 North Second Street (1951), 101 Locust Street (1963), 111 North Front Street (1967), and 129 State Street (1974). The office is now at 509 North Second Street.

In all, the agency has had eight offices over its 48 years. But then there's nothing like a housewarming party for good public relations.

Friends and associates of John Hood (seated, center) gather for this rare photo. Rita Hood, with the family cat, stands behind her husband. Ben Light stands between the Hoods.

George Geise puts the finishing touches on this 1967 message. Ben Light (left) and Terry Bush (right) complete the promotional picture.

McNEES, WALLACE AND NURICK

Shortly before his death in 1959, Sterling G. McNees wrote of his law firm, "We have never erased from our shield the words Integrity, Industry, and Intelligence. Our present practice is built on them and in that order." The law firm McNees built on that credo, McNees, Wallace and Nurick, is the largest in the state based outside of Philadelphia and Pittsburgh.

McNees was born in 1887 in Armstrong County. A graduate of the University of Pittsburgh Law School, he became a circuit-riding lawyer in his home region. McNees came to Harrisburg in 1920 "on a temporary basis" as an assistant to the superintendent of public instruction. The following year he was appointed a deputy attorney general of Pennsylvania, and three years later moved to Harrisburg permanently and entered private law practice.

The practice was very successful and in 1931 McNees employed Gilbert

Nurick, a recent graduate of Dickinson School of Law, as an associate. An early advocate of strengthening bar disciplinary procedures, Nurick is respected throughout the country for his work in this field.

Charles H. Hollinger, the longtime chief of the Bureau of Corporations of Pennsylvania, joined McNees and Nurick in 1935 and the partnership of McNees, Hollinger and Nurick was formed. Hollinger died in 1937.

David M. Wallace, a native of Middletown, a 1917 graduate of Dickinson School of Law, and a veteran of the American Expeditionary Force in France during World War I, joined the firm in 1942. Its name was changed to McNees, Wallace and Nurick at that time. McNees died in 1959 and Wallace in 1967, but the firm continues to carry their names.

To provide individual and corporate clients with a full range of legal services, the firm has added lawyers with expertise and experience in an increasing range of specialized fields. Several attorneys with the firm have

served such government agencies as the Securities and Exchange Commission, Interstate Commerce Commission, and National Labor Relations Board. McNees, Wallace and Nurick attorneys also have been drawn from the staffs of the Pennsylvania Public Utility Commission, the Board of Finance and Revenue, and the Department of Environmental Resources.

The firm has 50 lawyers, 8 paraprofessionals, and an administrative and secretarial staff of 50. The areas of practice cover nearly the entire spectrum of legal services except for a few narrow specialties.

The practice of law has long been an important business activity in Harrisburg, the county seat and state capital. For more than a half-century McNees, Wallace and Nurick has played a major role in the legal and community life of Harrisburg and central Pennsylvania.

Sterling G. McNees

Gilbert Nurick

UNITED REPUBLIC LIFE INSURANCE COMPANY

The headquarters complex of United Republic Life Insurance Company dominates a hilltop overlooking the Eisenhower Interchange southeast of Harrisburg. Its large, brightly lighted sign has become an area landmark.

The corporation behind the sign is one of the youngest of the Harrisburg-based life insurance companies. Yet United Republic Life already is licensed to conduct business in 38 states and the District of Columbia; its more than 1,500 agents sell their leading-edge "Universal Life" policies throughout an area ranging from Pennsylvania and Delaware south along the Eastern Seaboard to Florida and west to Indiana.

United Republic first was licensed by the Pennsylvania Insurance Department in 1966, and began selling its policies in January 1968. Its corporate headquarters was the first floor of a Front Street, Harrisburg, house. The executive offices were the front porch. The internal communications system was a hand bell. But by 1982 United Republic had more than $100 million in assets, and by 1983 more than one billion dollars of insurance in force.

Throughout its history, the company has employed agents on a "flex-time" basis. More than 80 percent of its sales staff are teachers or coaches. Former professional baseball player Gary Clemens was a physical education teacher when he joined the firm as an agent. He became president of United Republic Life in 1981.

United Republic Life moved from Front Street to the former Seybolds Hotel Bar and Restaurant (across Maclay Street from the Farm Show complex) in January 1973. The staff of 15 braved weather and traffic to move into their new offices during Farm Show week. Marlan Molinelli, chairman of the board and one of the original founders of the company, remembers that sometimes discouraging early period. "Files and supplies were located in the old kitchen. The barroom was occupied by the underwriting and accounting departments. One of the first jobs was to fumigate the place."

Molinelli also remembers the flood of 1972. "Thirty thousand policy files were under water for five days and swollen papers jammed the cabinets shut." The firm already owned the land it now occupies; that hilltop became the site of salvage activities. As Molinelli recalls, "We got into the files with can openers, and used clothes-lines and microwave ovens to dry the papers." The new headquarters opened the following year.

Monumental Corporation of Baltimore, Maryland, acquired United Republic in July 1981. Americana Life was merged into United Republic in 1983. Subsidiary companies include United Data Co. and United Sun Life. This corporate restructuring concluded the first chapter of United Republic's history. It also promises a dynamic and exciting future.

This Front Street, Harrisburg, house was the corporate headquarters of United Republic Life until 1973.

The present home office of United Republic Life, completed in 1973, is located on a hill overlooking the Eisenhower Interchange.

STEPHENSON'S FLOWER SHOPS

Harry L. Stephenson, Sr., president of Stephenson's Flower Shops, smiles with a deeply felt warmth as he recalls his early memories of the flower business. "I was always fascinated with the miracle of growth," he says. "I guess I was six or seven when I started hanging around Granddad and watching plants take root and grow.

"Granddad gave me a corner of a bench. He called it 'Harry's corner,' and no one else was allowed to touch anything in that space. I'd grow little plants. Then I'd pot them, and Granddad would put them in a box and take them to market. When Granddad came home, I'd look in the box to see how many plants were gone, and he'd give me a nickel for

each one. I guess he taught me that if I worked, and took care of the plants, the plants would take care of me."

J.W. Miller, Harry Sr.'s great-grandfather, started the family business around 1890 in the Cumberland County village of Keeneytown. Around the turn of the century Miller moved his growing enterprise to Shiremanstown, where he had access to the railroad and a larger population.

J.W.'s son, L.F. Miller, took over the business when his father died in 1932. It was L.F. Miller who started retail selling at farmers' markets. His daughter Marie and her husband Frank Stephenson took over around 1942, running the company until Harry Sr. was able to take over in 1948. Marie still manages the retail store at the West Shore Farmers' Market.

Harry Sr. was only 23 years old when he took control and began

Three generations of the family still actively involved in the business pose in one of their greenhouses. They are (left to right) Marie Stephenson, Harry Stephenson, Jr., and Harry Stephenson, Sr.

modernizing the business. His wife Betty took over the books; she now is treasurer of the corporation.

Between 1950 and 1960 Stephenson's moved heavily into retail. Today the firm relies on computers to keep track of activities at its eight locations, including its headquarters and full-service wholesale/retail operation at Shiremanstown, its newest retail store in Hershey, and its new greenhouse complex near Franklintown.

Harry Stephenson, Jr., is the fifth generation of his family to be a florist. Like his great-great-grandfather, he is primarily a grower. A company vice-president, Harry Jr. heads the greenhouse and growing operations and the garden shop. His wife Janet is assistant bookkeeper and computer supervisor. Connie Stephenson Grainger handles personnel. The company employs from 160 to 200 people, depending on the season.

Family patriarch J.W. Miller once was known as "King of the Primroses." Five generations later Stephenson's no longer grows or sells this once most-popular of all American house plants. But it still is greater Harrisburg's first family of florists.

Mr. and Mrs. J.W. Miller founded the business that is now Stephenson's Flower Shops. Around the turn of the century, Miller was known as the "King of the Primroses."

PENNSYLVANIA CREDIT UNION LEAGUE

The Pennsylvania Credit Union League represents the more than 1,500 state and federally chartered credit unions throughout the state. Nearly two million Pennsylvanians are members of credit unions with assets of more than $2.5 billion. In the greater Harrisburg area alone, some 150,000 residents belong to more than 50 credit unions.

Credit unions are nonprofit associations of individuals who pool their savings to provide each other with a source of financial assistance. The members are tied together by a "common bond," typically a shared profession, employer, residential community, or other affiliation.

The League is owned and directed by member credit unions, just as credit unions themselves are owned and democratically controlled by their

Joseph Moore, pioneer credit union volunteer and leader of the Pennsylvania movement, speaking before the 1954 annual meeting.

members. Founded in 1934, the Pennsylvania League has helped make this state an important part of the national credit union movement.

The credit union movement grew out of the age-old struggle between those with excess capital and those in need. It became popular in its native Germany where urban-based banks were unwilling to help farmers or small businesspeople. It gained support in the United States primarily as an antidote to loan sharks and other usurious lenders who often charged extraordinarily excessive interest rates.

The original idea was simple. Groups of people sharing common experience and ideals could pool their savings—a little at a time—and make funds available to any of their number who needed financial assistance. Loans would be made without collateral; credit union members would pledge only their good names and reputations. There was no intention to make a profit through credit unions. Earnings, if any, would be shared by members as dividends. Credit union officers and directors would serve without pay.

The modern credit union came to the United States in 1909. The drive to organize American credit unions was financed by Boston merchant/philanthropist Edward Filene and led by credit union evangelist Roy Bergengren. Like many reform movements, it was staffed primarily by volunteers.

Before credit unions could become part of the Pennsylvania banking structure, legal authority to charter this new form of financial institution was needed. The drive to pass such a state law was led by Harrisburg resident Andrew Hanemann; it lasted 10 years. Governor Gifford Pinchot signed the Pennsylvania Credit Union Act in 1933. Less than a year later the federal government also passed a credit union law.

National credit union pioneer Roy

Bergengren helped form the state League in Harrisburg in December 1934. Unfortunately, the depths of the Great Depression proved to be a poor time to form a new financial association. There was little money available to the League; member credit unions found it difficult to pay League membership fees and the League fell behind in its dues payments to the Credit Union National Association. Survival of the young League seemed doubtful.

In July 1936 Bergengren's assistant, Tom Doig, returned to Harrisburg to reorganize the state League. With the help of Harrisburg resident Mattis Pottiger (who became acting managing director) and several other forceful and imaginative leaders from throughout the state, the League was reborn. Its new leaders would include Pottiger, Joseph Moore, William W. Pratt, and Frank Tokay, among others.

Progress proved rapid, both for the League and for the Pennsylvania credit union movement. In 1934 there were 17 credit unions in the state; by 1940 there were 546, and the League had its first full-time managing director, Julia

Michael J. Judge, president of the Pennsylvania Credit Union League.

Connor. It also had a new office, having left its rented room in Harrisburg's Kline Building and moved to larger quarters in Philadelphia.

Bill Pratt, an active credit union volunteer from the Philadelphia area, became executive director in 1942. Under Pratt's leadership, the League moved its headquarters back to the capital city, purchased the building at 4309 North Front Street in 1951, and has made its home there ever since. The rear extensions were added in 1961 and 1974.

The professional staff of the League is headed by president Michael Judge, who succeeded Pratt in 1965. Under Judge's direction, the League works to organize new credit unions, assists existing groups in solving operational problems, maintains public relations and advertising programs, provides educational and training activities,

prepares a wide range of publications, and works with the state legislature.

The credit union movement is voluntarism in action. Leadership in the movement is motivated by a desire to serve people. No director, committee member, or other credit union officer (except the treasurer) is paid. "Not for profit, not for charity, but for service," has long been the motto of the movement.

The League provides the professional support needed to supplement volunteer activism. But League directors, like credit union directors, serve without compensation. This unique combination of volunteers and professionals is a source of great strength to the movement.

The Pennsylvania Credit Union League operates in conjunction with its subsidiary service corporation, Pacul Services, Inc. Pacul Services fulfills supply needs, provides

electronic data processing, and offers specialized financial services to the Commonwealth's credit unions. It was created in 1965 as a supply affiliate, and reorganized in 1973 to offer a full range of support services.

The organized credit union movement is a partnership of volunteers and professionals, of borrowers and lenders, of urban and rural communities. "The primary purpose of the credit union," said its pioneering American leader Roy Bergengren, "is to prove the practicality of the brotherhood of man." It is the commitment to such a philosophy that has made the Pennsylvania Credit Union League so special a partner in the progress of the greater Harrisburg community.

The headquarters building of the Pennsylvania Credit Union League—4309 North Front Street— as it appeared in 1952.

William W. Pratt, standing, executive director of the Pennsylvania Credit Union League (1942-1965), with Roy Bergengren, seated, leader of the national credit union movement.

PENNSYLVANIA BLUE SHIELD

The ravages of the Great Depression cut deeply during the 1930s—many victims of unemployment and depleted savings were forced to deny themselves medical care, and many doctors' bills went unpaid. To the general public, medical practitioners, and social reformers alike, the situation was unacceptable.

The organization that eventually became Pennsylvania Blue Shield was born in those difficult years just prior to World War II. The high cost of medical care was a subject that generated bitter controversy. Some leaders resisted all change. Others proposed plans ranging from prepaid group practice to socialized medicine.

Dr. Lewis T. Buckman, an eye, ear, nose, and throat specialist from Wilkes-Barre who was chairman of the Pennsylvania Medical Society's Medical Economics Committee, heard about hospital bill prepayment plans being tested in New Jersey. Investigating further, he learned that the idea (Blue Cross) had spread to parts of

Pennsylvania as well. He began seeking ways to extend the concept to doctors' bills.

In 1938 Dr. Chauncey L. Palmer proposed the idea of prepaid doctor care to the Pennsylvania Medical Society House of Delegates. He quickly won support from Dr. Buckman and other influential leaders of the medical community. Dr. Palmer became the first president of Pennsylvania Blue Shield on April 3, 1940.

Not everyone favored the creation of Medical Service Association of Pennsylvania (now Pennsylvania Blue Shield). One irate physician responded to a circulated draft of the plan (and its standardized fee schedule): "The medical profession is entirely too holy to have placed upon it the foul, unscrupulous, politically warped hands of many members of the New Deal." The Dauphin County Medical Society rejected the proposed plan without comment. But most of the state's doctors were impressed by the plan and willing to launch it on an experimental basis.

With the active support of the state medical society, the legislature passed a law enabling incorporation of the

Medical Service Association of Pennsylvania on September 5, 1939. Lester H. Perry, an executive with the Pennsylvania Medical Society, became executive director and secretary of Medical Service Association of Pennsylvania on April 3, 1940, in addition to his other duties.

The Association began enrolling members in 1940, and immediately began assisting people of limited income who needed medical care. Participating doctors contracted to accept payment from the Association as payment in full for services performed in hospitals for member patients. Because of the experimental nature of its programs, the Association limited activities to the western part of the state.

Then known as Medical Service Association of Pennsylvania, Pennsylvania Blue Shield had its first offices on the second floor of this building at 222 Locust Street, Harrisburg.

Public response was enthusiastic when Blue Shield began active promotion of its services after World War II.

Completed in 1983, the newest headquarters complex for Pennsylvania Blue Shield is on Center Street, Camp Hill.

Response to the new company was disappointing to its supporters. At the end of its first year, the Association had only 967 members and 122 participating doctors. Growth continued to be slow during World War II.

In 1944, with fewer than 14,000 subscribers, the Association decided to extend the program statewide and to undertake a more aggressive sales campaign. Agreements in 1947 with several Blue Cross Plans in various areas of the state (which offered coverage for hospital bills, but not doctors' fees) provided an instant network of enrollment, advertising, billing, and collection agents. This arrangement soon proved extremely successful; enrollment in Pennsylvania Blue Shield soared.

In its initial years, the Medical Service Association of Pennsylvania borrowed $33,000 from the Pennsylvania Medical Society to help finance its operations. So successful was Pennsylvania Blue Shield that the money was repaid by 1948.

The enrollment explosion continued. Blue Shield moved from a rented second-floor office on Locust Street in downtown Harrisburg to its own building on Front and Radnor streets in 1949. It had one million members in 1959 and two million in 1962, when the continued enrollment expansion forced the addition of a new wing.

Continuing rapid growth soon mandated another move. In selecting its next location, Pennsylvania Blue Shield made a decision that opened a new chapter of Harrisburg history. The Association decided to cross the Susquehanna River and relocate in East Pennsboro Township. Construction started in 1957, and in 1959 Blue Shield became the first major organization to move to the West Shore.

The 1960s witnessed many changes for Blue Shield. Under Medicare and Medicaid, Blue Shield saw its early mission of prepaid doctors' care for low-income families taken over in part by government but it contracted with federal and state agencies to process claims. In 1966 Blue Shield signed an agency agreement under which Capital Blue Cross assumed enrollment, billing, collection, advertising, and record-keeping tasks in the 19-county central Pennsylvania region. This completed the statewide system of agreements with Blue Cross Plans begun in 1947.

Pennsylvania Blue Shield expanded to include its white building off Erford Road in East Pennsboro Township in 1974, and opened its new headquarters complex on Center Street in 1981. All Blue Shield operations were relocated to the Center Street complex when it was completed in 1983.

Pennsylvania Blue Shield is a not-for-profit corporation. The president is Leroy K. Mann; the chairman of the board is Harry V. Armitage, M.D. As provided by its enabling legislation, the board of directors consists of both doctors and subscribers in equal proportions.

With more than six million subscribers in the Commonwealth, the Pennsylvania company is the largest Blue Shield Plan in the world. Its 2,200 employees make it one of the largest private employers of Harrisburg area residents. And, with more than $1.8 billion in annual revenue, it is one of the region's biggest businesses. This experimental plan for paying doctors' fees approved by the legislature in 1939 has produced an extraordinary history of accomplishment.

CAPITAL BLUE CROSS

When William Edwards needed an appendectomy in 1938, he faced one less worry than any Harrisburg area hospital patient before him. He knew that his policy with Capital Hospital Service would pay his bill. He was the first patient to receive benefits from the new Plan and his $95 bill for a 15-day stay at Harrisburg Polyclinic Hospital was paid in full. He did have to pay his 50-cent phone bill himself.

Justin Ford Kimball, vice-president of Baylor University in Dallas, Texas, devised a hospital care prepayment system in 1929 that eventually became the model for Blue Cross Plans. His idea was imitated, expanded, and modified by Plans in Sacramento, California; Essex County, New Jersey; and then throughout the country.

In 1937, at the urging of the hospital association and of the medical profession, the Pennsylvania Legislature passed the Non-Profit Hospital Plan Act enabling the creation of similar plans in the state. Capital Blue Cross, then called Capital Hospital Service, was organized in February 1938 by representatives of Harrisburg Hospital, Harrisburg Polyclinic Hospital, Carlisle Hospital, and the Dauphin County Medical Society.

When it first opened for business,

the Plan had four employees and leased two rooms of Harrisburg's Ebner Building at Second and Locust streets. The Plan proved popular from its inception, and by 1943 it had more than 100,000 members. By 1946 the Plan was paying almost $1.5 million in annual benefits.

Capital Hospital Service moved to 116 Pine Street in 1949. It moved to its current headquarters at 100 Pine Street in 1967. Capital Blue Cross shares that building with the law firm founded by Sterling G. McNees. That is most appropriate; McNees and insurance executive W.W. Dodson were among the community leaders who helped create the Plan in 1938.

Today, under the leadership of chairman of the board Franklin W. Ruth, Jr., and president Richard D Rife, Capital Blue Cross has over 525 employees and serves 19 counties in south central Pennsylvania. The Plan has offices in York, Lancaster, Reading, Pottsville, and Sunbury, in addition to its Harrisburg headquarters. From 7,500 subscribers and $6,200 of claims (including the $95 for William Edwards) paid in 1938, Capital Blue Cross has expanded to over 1.2 million

subscribers and well over $290 million in claims paid during 1982.

The distinctive blue cross symbol and Plan name have a unique history of their own. E.A. van Steenwyk, chief executive of Minnesota's Hospital Service Association, created a visual symbol for his organization which included the blue cross, an adaptation of the international symbol for help for the sick and injured. The symbol captured the popular imagination; people began calling van Steenwyk's group the "blue cross plan." Other regional associations quickly adopted the symbol.

From 1939 to 1972 the American Hospital Association (AHA) set and administered standards for use of the blue cross name and mark. AHA superimposed its own ornate seal— including a variety of medical symbols and the phrase "nisi dominus frustra," Latin for "without God, all is lost"—in the center of the cross.

In 1972 the Blue Cross Association, the coordinating organization for Blue

The Ebner Building at Second and Locust streets was the home of Capital Hospital Service from 1938 to 1949.

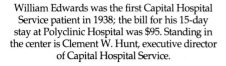

William Edwards was the first Capital Hospital Service patient in 1938; the bill for his 15-day stay at Polyclinic Hospital was $95. Standing in the center is Clement W. Hunt, executive director of Capital Hospital Service.

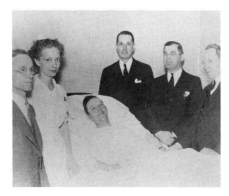

Cross Plans, assumed the AHA role and modified the symbol once again, replacing the AHA seal with the stylized human figure that is now superimposed on the center of the cross.

While Capital Hospital Service began using the blue cross symbol early in its history, it officially changed its name to Capital Blue Cross only in 1965.

The Harrisburg area's Capital Blue Cross is widely respected as one of the most innovative Plans in the nation. In 1945 Capital Hospital Service became one of the first two Blue Cross Plans in the country to offer a comprehensive contract without a dollar limit. In 1974 the Plan became the first to provide alcoholism rehabilitation as a standard benefit. In 1981 Capital Blue Cross joined with Blue Cross of Northeastern Pennsylvania and Pennsylvania Blue Cross to use computerized processing for major medical claims.

Over the years Capital Blue Cross has expanded to provide a wide range of supporting services. Now, not just room charges but almost all additional services received from the hospital—either on an inpatient or outpatient basis—are covered in full, regardless of cost.

In recent years much of Capital Blue Cross' effort has been dedicated to containing hospital costs. With inflation of health care costs accelerating, many of the Plan's efforts have been directed to encouraging subscribers to receive necessary care in the lowest possible cost setting. Thus the Plan has been promoting preadmission testing, same-day surgery, home care, and the use of outpatient services. In 1938 William Edwards' appendectomy required a 15-day hospital stay. Today a four-day stay is typically sufficient.

As another part of its concern for constraining costs, Capital Blue Cross has traditionally engaged in extensive health education efforts. The Plan distributes free literature and films on a wide range of health education subjects. Tel-Med, a telephone service providing free, taped health information, is sponsored by Capital Blue Cross in 13 of the 19 counties served by the Plan. Thus the Plan continues to fulfill its historical mission of serving the community both by encouraging people to take better care of themselves and financing hospital care whenever needed.

The present Capital Blue Cross headquarters is at 100 Pine Street, Harrisburg.

The Benmar Building at 116 Pine Street was the home of Capital Hospital Service from 1949 to 1967.

NATIONWIDE INSURANCE COMPANY

Nationwide Insurance is one of the largest insurers of automobiles in the United States; it is one of the two most active in Pennsylvania. From its headquarters complex near Interstate Highway 81 just north of Harrisburg, one of 12 regional centers throughout the United States, 850 Nationwide employees service the firm's Eastern Pennsylvania Region.

The company was started in Ohio back in the 1920s. As farmers joined the switch from horses and buggies to automobiles, they discovered the need for insurance. It's not that buggies never had accidents, but they had been less expensive to repair. They also discovered that existing city-based insurance companies charged farmers the same premiums as urban drivers—even though rural driving posed significantly fewer hazards. In response to the farmers' needs, the Ohio Farm Bureau Federation created Farm Bureau Insurance (renamed "Nationwide" in 1955) in 1926. Its

national headquarters still is in Columbus, Ohio.

The Pennsylvania Farm Bureau Federation invited the Ohio company to Harrisburg in 1929. Its first Pennsylvania office opened in the State Chamber of Commerce building early in 1930. It was staffed by just four people: one claims adjuster, an agent, and two secretaries.

Interest in Farm Bureau Insurance was light until a 1934 advertisement in *The Pennsylvania Farmer* brought an unexpected, massive response. The resulting sales push made Farm Bureau Insurance a going concern in Pennsylvania, and established a major place in the company's structure for its

Harrisburg office. By the end of 1935 the Pennsylvania office had 35 employees, 400 agents, and 45,000

Douglas Arthur, manager of the Eastern Pennsylvania Region, Nationwide Insurance.

Present at the 1952 ribbon-cutting ceremony for the expanded headquarters at the onetime Derry Street shoe factory were (left to right) Mrs. R.N. Benjamin, wife of the executive secretary of the Pennsylvania Farm Bureau Co-op Association; Artemas C. Leslie, Insurance Commissioner of Pennsylvania; Harrison Nolt, director of Farm Bureau Insurance Companies; and Mrs. Nolt.

policies in force.

Such growth demanded expanded office facilities, and in 1935 Farm Bureau Insurance opened a new Pennsylvania regional office at 3607 Derry Street in suburban Paxtang. It was the middle of the Great Depression. Prosperity still was just around the corner. For its new offices, Farm Bureau Insurance made do with an old shoe factory. Only slightly remodeled to meet the firm's needs, the shoe factory won a lasting place for itself in Farm Bureau Insurance history.

By 1950 Farm Bureau Insurance had grown to more than 600 employees based in the Harrisburg office and 700 agents throughout the state. It already had outgrown the shoe factory. Several departments were housed in offices at other locations, most notably at Court and Cameron streets.

But there was an acute shortage of

office space in Harrisburg, and the company liked its Derry Street location. Farm Bureau Insurance decided to build new offices at the Derry Street site. To avoid temporary dislocation, the new building was designed and engineered in order to allow business to continue in the old factory even during construction of its replacement.

The result was an L-shaped, four-story office complex built in and around its predecessor. The September 18-19, 1952, dedication of the completed Farm Bureau Insurance building was a Harrisburg gala featuring presentations by many national, state, and local leaders. For the firm's employees it was business not quite as usual. Farm Bureau Insurance moved to a "late-shift" operation for the two days so the staff could attend morning ceremonies and still work a full day.

In 1935 the entire Harrisburg staff of Farm Bureau Insurance stands in front of the former shoe factory that became the headquarters for the Eastern Pennsylvania Region.

Even as the new building was dedicated, the national headquarters team was planning a major change for its Pennsylvania office. As part of a corporate reorganization plan the Pennsylvania region was split, and the Harrisburg office became the headquarters unit for the Eastern Pennsylvania Region.

This reorganization was the beginning of a process that had major impact for the Harrisburg group. First the auto insurance business was decentralized; then the same procedure was followed for the Farm Bureau Mutual Fire Insurance Company and carriers of other lines of Farm Bureau insurance. As a result, the Eastern Pennsylvania Region acquired substantial new responsibilities for the additional lines of Farm Bureau Insurance.

Since that reorganization the Eastern Pennsylvania regional office in Harrisburg has handled auto insurance, fire and casualty, health, and life insurance on behalf of the Nationwide group of companies including Nationwide Mutual Insurance, Nationwide Mutual Fire, Nationwide Life, and Nationwide General.

Since 1970 Nationwide's Eastern Pennsylvania Region has been under the management of Douglas Arthur, a vice-president of the corporation. Arthur is a graduate of Millersburg High School and Susquehanna University. He joined Nationwide in 1949 as a claims adjuster in the Philadelphia area. Arthur is a member of the board and the executive committee of the Insurance Federation of Pennsylvania. He has been chairman of the insurance committee of the Pennsylvania State Chamber of Commerce. He is a director of the Chamber of Commerce of the Greater Harrisburg Area and a trustee for Susquehanna University.

One of Arthur's earliest responsibilities was leading the company through the intense claims activity that followed the flooding from Hurricane Agnes in 1972. Nationwide catastrophe teams moved into the flood zone to help speed benefits to policyholders. Special claims adjusters were empowered to write checks on the spot, providing immediate assistance to flood victims. In all, more than 2,300 claims were paid by the company in Eastern Pennsylvania, for a benefit total of $8 million for storm and flood damage.

The Harrisburg center has expanded rapidly in recent years—both in activity and in physical requirements. The main office complex at 1000 Nationwide Drive, Harrisburg, was completed in 1976. The extensive addition was opened in the fall of 1981.

In addition to the regional headquarters building itself, the Eastern Pennsylvania Region maintains 35 satellite offices, including the Harrisburg district sales and claims offices (located in the headquarters center) and an office in Mechanicsburg.

The Eastern Pennsylvania regional office also administers Nationwide's assigned-risk policies from a 20-state district. The assignment-risk program provides a pool of insurers who share responsibility for underwriting policies for individuals who otherwise would be unable to obtain suitable coverage.

By January 1983 Nationwide had more than 900,000 policies in force in the Eastern Pennsylvania Region, including policies on 512,000 automobiles and 174,000 homes. The 110,000 life insurance policies represent $1.37 billion of coverage and $15.8 million in premium income.

This volume of business has a major impact on the Harrisburg area and Eastern Pennsylvania economy. Nationwide's Harrisburg payroll totals over $14 million, and commissions paid to agents throughout the region totaled $17 million in 1982.

Other Nationwide activities are less visible, but also important. Through the Insurance Federation, Nationwide continues to work with the state legislature to provide needed reform of insurance laws as well as other, related areas. Nationwide was active in its support of strong anti-drunk driver legislation, and continues to support strengthened no-fault auto insurance.

Nationwide's Eastern Pennsylvania regional office has made itself a vital element of the community. Following a long-established tradition, more than 60 Nationwide people volunteer each year to work with the United Way. Clearly they, like those members of the Pennsylvania Farm Bureau in the 1930s, see themselves not just as local employees of a national organization, but as a central part of greater Harrisburg.

The present Eastern Pennsylvania regional headquarters of Nationwide Insurance at 1000 Nationwide Drive, Harrisburg.

HARRISBURG AREA COMMUNITY COLLEGE

"I believe that the community college in the Harrisburg region can stimulate a resurgence of education and cultural activity which will touch upon the lives of all citizens in the area," said Clyde E. Blocker in May 1964 when he accepted the presidency of Harrisburg Area Community College (HACC).

Blocker was a nationally respected leader of the community college movement. Under his leadership, HACC became the flagship of the Commonwealth's community colleges. He retired in 1975 and was succeeded by S. James Manilla, who served until 1977.

HACC was the first public community college in Pennsylvania, chartered in 1963 to serve residents of Cumberland, Dauphin, and Perry counties. Under the leadership of chairman Bruce E. Cooper and vice-chairman James W. Evans, the trustees selected administrative officers; in September 1964 the college enrolled 433 students as its first class. A year later Hershey Junior College closed and most of its faculty—along with their students—transferred to the new community college.

The first HACC campus was on North Second Street at the site now used by the University Center at Harrisburg. The first buildings at the current 157-acre campus opened in 1967.

The HACC campus was created on land that once was part of Wildwood Park. Before World War II the Wildwood gardens and zoo were a favored place for family outings. But the zoo closed during the war, and the park was largely abandoned. When the site was given to the college by the City of Harrisburg, part of it had become a trash dump.

More than $2.5 million in gifts, low-interest loans by a consortium of area banks, and the concerted efforts of many community leaders have transformed the abandoned park and onetime ash heap into a gracious college campus. Approximately 6,000 students now study there each year.

During the presidency of James Odom (1978-1983), the college extended its efforts to serve the area, reaching out and making its facilities available to individuals and groups throughout greater Harrisburg. More than 60,000 people each year now attend seminars, debates, films, theatrical performances, continuing education classes, conventions, or other public events on campus.

Community support for the college has been continuous and extensive. The Hall Foundation, Trustees of the Mary Sachs Estate, Ray Shoemaker Scholarships, Leon Lowengard Scholarships, and other similar funds assist students directly. Two buildings, the McCormick Library and Rose Herman Lehrman Arts Center, were financed primarily by individual and foundation gifts to the college.

This close relationship of community and college is the result of 20 years of dedicated effort based on mutual respect. In 1983 HACC ended an era with the resignations of Cooper and Odom. Its new chairman of the trustees and president inherit a college that in its brief history has already built solid foundations and a tradition of progressive community leadership.

Attending the laying of the cornerstone for the Harrisburg Area Community College in 1966 were (left to right) John F. Matsko, Helen Swope, Raiford E. Spencer, James H. Rowland, Sr., Bruce E. Cooper, Jacob L. Snyder, Clyde E. Blocker, James W. Evans, and Robert L. Rubendall.

BENATEC ASSOCIATES, INC.

Ralph Peters, president and chairman of the board of Benatec Associates, Inc. (Photo by The Camera Box.)

The name Benatec Associates (from "Best ENgineering, Architecture, and TEChnology") is new, adopted in July 1982. Many clients and local residents still call the Camp Hill company Berger Associates, the name it had carried since it was started in 1952 by Dr. Louis Berger.

One of the most energetic community leaders in central Pennsylvania is Ralph Peters, president and chairman of the board, who has worked for almost three decades with more than 25 different civic, educational, charitable, and professional associations.

Benatec is a leading full-service architectural/engineering/planning firm. Clients include major international corporations like IBM, Bell Telephone, AMP, and HERCO; federal agencies such as the U.S. Army Corps of Engineers and the Department of Energy; and numerous state and local governments.

Benatec projects are as varied as the restoration of General Knox' Headquarters at Valley Forge, the design of Penn State University's liberal arts building, and the aerial mapping of the flood plain for the Three Mile Island nuclear plant.

The company was incorporated in 1953 as Berger Associates. Its first major contract was designing a section of the northeast extension of the Pennsylvania Turnpike. That road led the way to the establishment of the Berger companies. In 1954 Dr. Berger created a New Jersey corporation, Louis Berger & Associates, as the basis for national expansion; in 1958 the group launched its international operations from the Harrisburg base.

At the end of 1969 Dr. Berger sold all of his companies to Leasco Data Processing Equipment Corporation of New York. The following year he repurchased the overseas division of Louis Berger, Inc., but Leasco temporarily retained ownership of the two domestic companies—Berger Associates in Pennsylvania and Louis

Berger & Associates in New Jersey.

A group of vice-presidents headed by Peters purchased the domestic groups late in 1971. While they soon resold the New Jersey company to Dr. Berger, Peters and his associates retained ownership of the Pennsylvania corporation, including its branches in other states. Benatec currently maintains offices in Columbus, Ohio, and Charleston, West Virginia, in addition to its Harrisburg headquarters.

The other principal executives of Benatec include architect and restoration specialist Tomas Spiers, senior vice-president, Professional Services; Wesley Norris, senior vice-president, Technical Services; A.D. Santeusanio, senior vice-president, Administration and Finance; Hendrik Jongsma, vice-president, Engineering/ Harrisburg; and William Wallace, vice-president, Engineering/ Columbus.

The Benatec name may be new, but the progress of greater Harrisburg—in its civic, educational, and social affairs as well as its roads, buildings, and physical environment—has long involved the planning of Ralph Peters and his company.

The corporate headquarters of Benatec Associates, Inc., is located at 101 Erford Road, Camp Hill.

ALBERT L. ALLEN COMPANY, INC.

The Albert L. Allen Company, Inc., has its roots deep in the heart of Pennsylvania, down in the shafts of the anthracite and bituminous coal mines of the Commonwealth. When Albert L. Allen founded the company in 1919, he offered self-insurance contracting and guidance to mine owners and operators.

Allen had directed the Workmen's Compensation Bureau in Massachusetts when that state started requiring the insurance, and later initiated the program for New York. When Pennsylvania decided to start a similar program, Allen was brought to Harrisburg. Tiring of the political arena after experience in three states, he soon decided to offer his expert knowledge to the private sector as a consultant.

In November 1919 ads in *The Patriot* and *The Evening News* announced the opening of his agency and its allied coal mine self-insurance service with offices in the Telegraph Building. Success and expansion came quickly. In 1923 the agency started its companion corporation, Allen Registry Bureau, Inc., an insurance agency specializing in travel insurance for groups.

The Registry Bureau also was responsible for the unusual but popular "Sportsman's Policy," an accident insurance policy that cost one dollar per year and paid up to a $1,000 benefit if the holder was injured while on a hunting or fishing trip. But most of the firm's activities were along more traditional insurance lines. Albert L. Allen, Jr., son of the founder and current president of the company, still remembers hearing his father talk about the Cambria County coal mine explosion at Sonman Shaft. Forty miners died in that accident. Albert Sr. traveled to the site, where he worked with the injured survivors and families of the dead miners to settle claims.

In 1930 the firm took a suite in the Kline Building, where it was located

Albert L. Allen, Sr., founder of the Albert L. Allen Company, Inc., at the firm's Second Street office.

until 1944 when it moved to 319 North Second Street. Albert L. Allen, Jr., joined his father in the Second Street offices in 1946, following service during World War II. He has been with the company ever since, becoming president in 1952 when his father died. In 1958 the firm moved to its current offices at 121 State Street.

Other key executives of the organization include vice-president William S. Hench, Jr., vice-president Robert J. Hall, and secretary/treasurer Wilbur B. Lupton.

In 1956 Albert L. Allen, Jr., began the American Sentinel Insurance Company, a firm that now has more than 500 agents in Pennsylvania. American Sentinel writes "special risk" health insurance, specializing in

such unusual groups as summer camps, athletic teams, and volunteer firemen.

Even though the agency stopped providing workers' compensation service for self-insured employers in 1972, the Allen family has two major reminders of its history. The first is that several of the firm's original clients are still with the Allen Company. And second, Harrisburg attorney Heath L. Allen, a brother of Albert, now practices law in the same Kline Building suite once occupied by the Albert L. Allen Company.

THE QUAKER OATS COMPANY

The Quaker Oats Company makes some of the most widely distributed products in the world. Its "Quaker Man" trademark is a familar figure in the market. Yet the extent of activity at Quaker Oats' Shiremanstown plant is realized by few Harrisburg area residents.

The Shiremanstown plant is the third-largest manufacturing facility in the Foods Division of Quaker Oats, and the corporation's largest distribution center for foods and pet foods in all of its worldwide operations.

Quaker Oats/Shiremanstown manufactures Cap'n Crunch, Life and Cinnamon Life, Corn Bran, and Halfsies cereals. In one section of the plant, Puffed Wheat and Puffed Rice are explosively treated with steam—a process that gave life to the famed advertising slogan, "The cereals that are shot from guns!" Other food products manufactured at Quaker Oats/Shiremanstown include Aunt Jemima Regular and Lite syrups and Flako baking mixes.

The Quaker Oats Company was founded in 1901. Among the founders was Robert Stuart, grandfather of Robert D. Stuart, Jr., current chairman of the board. The president and chief executive officer of Quaker Oats is William D. Smithburg; president of the Foods Division is Hedrick E. (Pete) Rhodes.

The giant international corporation is best known for its food products, but it also manufactures pet foods and Fisher-Price Toys, and operates a "Direct-to-Consumer" Division with retail and catalog sales including Brookstone Hard-to-Find Tools, Herrschner's crafts products, and Jos. A. Bank Clothiers. In all, Quaker Oats operates 65 manufacturing plants in 15 states and 14 foreign countries. The corporation is headquartered in Chicago.

Quaker stockholders first learned of corporate activities in Shiremanstown

from the 1954 annual report, which said that the company was "operating a large distributing warehouse at Shiremanstown, Pennsylvania. . . . It is a very modern installation and will provide greatly improved service to our customers in the East."

The Shiremanstown plant began operations in May 1954. It was expanded in 1957 to produce animal feeds (including Ken-L-Ration dog foods and Ful-O-Pep farm animal feeds), and again in 1959 to produce Puffed Cereals, Pancake Mix, Round

A familiar array of Quaker Oats products, some of which are produced at the firm's Shiremanstown facility.

Oats, and Corn Goods. Animal food production was later dropped so that the plant could be used exclusively for the production of food for humans.

Quaker added new facilities quickly as the Shiremanstown facility established a reputation as an efficient and reliable plant. In 1965 Cap'n Crunch came to town. Subsequent arrivals included Aunt Jemima Syrup and Life Cereal (1966), Flako (1973), Corn Bran (1978), Lite Syrup (1980), and Halfsies (1982). In 1977 the

warehouse was expanded and distribution activities increased sharply. New production facilities are planned for 1983 or 1984.

Taking full advantage of the outstanding combination of rail and highway facilities that have attracted many industries to Harrisburg, the local Quaker Oats center distributes hundreds of products to markets in much of the Northeast. Military commissaries throughout the United States and Europe are served from this center, as are all commercial grocery

stores in a region bound on the west by Harrisburg and blanketing the Eastern Seaboard from New York City south to Norfolk and Richmond, Virginia. The plant ships 16 million cases of foods (including pet foods) each year. As many as 150 semitrailers and up to 30 rail cars each day bring raw materials (and finished products from other plants) to Shiremanstown, and carry them off for redistribution.

Warehouses in Bethel, Connecticut, and Huntington, West Virginia, are administered from Shiremanstown. The group is responsible for shipping 16 percent of the $1.2 billion in food

Vast quantities of Quaker products move through the distribution center at their Shiremanstown plant.

Aunt Jemima syrup is among the products manufactured at Quaker Oats' Shiremanstown plant.

produced by Quaker Oats' Foods Division.

Quaker Oats/Shiremanstown employs 450 local residents. Its work force has an unusual record of reliability and loyalty; the average hourly employee has 16 years of service. Of the 40 people hired when Quaker Oats first moved to the area, nine still work at the plant.

Plant manager of Quaker Oats/ Shiremanstown is Ken Dykes, a youthful and dynamic executive who has been with Quaker Oats since 1974. A native of Missouri, Dykes assumed the top position at the Shiremanstown

facility in 1983, having worked previously at the St. Joseph, Missouri, foods plant, as well as the Danville, Illinois, and Shiremanstown plant. Dykes enjoys youth programs with his family, including basketball and soccer, and is also a member of the Masonic Lodge.

Quaker Oats/Shiremanstown is a massive facility: Railroad boxcars line

After repeated expansions, the Quaker Oats/ Shiremanstown plant has become a massive complex. It takes full advantage of the excellent railroad and highway systems that serve the Harrisburg area.

one section; tank cars full of raw materials for syrup production wait along another wall; a 15-bay loading dock dominates a third section of the distribution center. The complex includes 384,000 square feet of warehouse and 184,000 square feet of manufacturing space, much of it occupied by stacks of pallets loaded with Quaker products. And it's there just so we can all enjoy a little breakfast and an occasional snack.

AMP INCORPORATED

You may not know it, but AMP Incorporated is part of your daily life. If you ride in a car, boat, train, or plane, watch television, or make a phone call you are probably using AMP products. And if you play a video game or use a computer, connectors manufactured by AMP, an international corporation based in Harrisburg, tie it all together.

AMP (pronounce it as one word, "amp," not as three initials) is the world's leading producer of electrical/ electronic connection devices. Whenever electrical wires, cables, printed circuit boards, or components must be connected, AMP makes a device and related production or installation tools and machines that will handle the job with sophisticated engineering.

AMP Incorporated has a Puerto Rican manufacturing affiliate, Pamcor Inc. (identical shareholder ownership), and 25 wholly owned subsidiaries in the United States, Canada, Latin America, Europe, and the Far East. It has more than 20,000 employees

worldwide including more than 8,000 at its over 60 plant and office facilities in central Pennsylvania. The company holds more than 2,000 patents. AMP's 1982 sales totaled nearly $1.25 billion.

It all started with uninsulated electrical terminals intended for use by aircraft and marine manufacturers. The terminals and their hand-operated application tool were designed to replace expensive and slow hand soldering. It was a simple system but proved to be a major contribution to production processes. In 1966, its 25th anniversary year, the company that produced that system joined the *Fortune Magazine* list of America's 500 largest corporations. (AMP ranked 256th on the 1983 list.)

The founder of AMP was U.A. Whitaker, son of a Missouri educator, legislator, and minister. Whitaker was born in Kansas in 1900. He received degrees in mechanical engineering from MIT, electrical engineering from Carnegie Tech (now Carnegie-Mellon University), and law from Cleveland Law School. He attended Carnegie while employed at Westinghouse in Pittsburgh, and law school while an engineer and administrator with the Hoover Company in Cleveland.

Lessons learned at those institutions and industries were later applied at

AMP. At Westinghouse, patent-producing engineers were allowed great creative freedom. Finding talented people and giving them room to work later became a guiding principle at AMP. Hoover made only one product, vacuum cleaners, but employed 130 people in its engineering department. Whitaker learned the lesson well. To maintain leadership in an industry, take one product and engineer it to perfection. That is a key philosophy at AMP.

In January 1939 Whitaker moved to New York City to assume a senior engineering position with American Machine & Foundry. Later, with the financial backing of Midland Investment Company (a family investment company established by financier Joseph M. Hixon), Whitaker founded Aircraft-Marine Products on September 15, 1941.

Legends about the first offices and plant of AMP abound. Actually, the company's office was in a small building AMP shared with a Greek restaurant, and its first plant was across the street from the giant Elizabeth, New Jersey, Phelps-Dodge plant.

On December 7, 1941, the Japanese attacked Pearl Harbor and AMP moved to a war footing. As the

Opened in mid-1983, this newest headquarters complex for AMP Incorporated is located near the Eisenhower Interchange, overlooking the Harrisburg East Mall.

manufacture of aircraft, ships, and radio products accelerated, so did the AMP production lines.

In 1942 the rapidly expanding AMP production facilities moved from New Jersey to an abandoned shoe factory in Glen Rock, a small town in York County, Pennsylvania, and Whitaker began looking for a new corporate home.

The search for a new plant and headquarters facility first focused on York, but suitable buildings were not available. Harrisburg looked attractive; many skilled tool and die workers lived in the area, and several possible plant sites were available. But early approaches to the Chamber of Commerce produced a reply that "The town had no housing available and would not desire any new enterprise in the community."

R.J. Szukala, AMP's plant site investigator, persisted. He saw Harrisburg as a transportation hub and liked its hotels, shops, modern office buildings, and state government complex. The streets were well-paved and clean. He thought it a pleasant

community in which to relocate.

Finally, the Chamber changed its tune. Szukala was shown several locations including an old automobile agency building at 1521-31 North Fourth Street. He was concerned because "Harrisburg suffers extraordinary floods every 50 years, which do a great amount of damage," but was convinced that the Fourth Street site was on safe ground. (The 1972 flood later proved both the accuracy of Szukala's concern and the prudence of his selection. The Fourth Street plant was undamaged.)

The move to Harrisburg was completed by the end of 1943. The future looked great. AMP sales were accelerating rapidly; the 1943 gross of $2.2 million doubled the 1942 volume. But the costs of a fire at the Glen Rock plant and the expense of moving to Harrisburg held profits below one percent.

Almost hidden by the year's activity was the invention of AMP's preinsulated terminal. This device and the special crimping tool that facilitated its installation became one of AMP's most important products. The system's widespread popularity helped assure the company of long-term leadership of the solderless terminal market.

Transition to a postwar economy proved stressful for the young company. Profits and production dropped sharply. In 1946 only massive cutbacks and economy measures prevented drastic losses. Continued operation was possible only with additional capital investment from Midland. AMP experienced other difficult periods but never again would things look so dark. From this point, the only way was up, as the company changed its emphasis from military to commercial markets. The way was led by a new AMP product system—strip-formed terminals complete with semi-automatic application machines.

The 1950s produced rapid and enthusiastic expansion. In 1952 AMP created subsidiaries in Puerto Rico (Pamcor Inc.), France, and Canada as well as the marketing subsidiary now known as AMP Special Industries. During the decade, product lines expanded to include pin and socket connectors, coaxial cable connectors, printed circuit board connectors, and other new systems. New facilities were built throughout central Pennsylvania and foreign subsidiaries were opened

U.A. Whitaker, founder of AMP Incorporated.

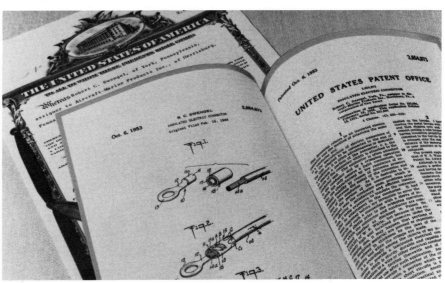

This insulated terminal was a major breakthrough in connector technology and helped make AMP the industry leader.

George A. Ingalls, a long-term close friend and key adviser to Whitaker who joined AMP as controller in 1957, took over as president in 1961. (Whitaker continued to serve as chairman of the board.) S.S. Auchincloss, who became a director and consultant in 1962, became president in 1965 and Ingalls was elected vice-chairman of the board. Brenner was elected president in 1971 and chief executive officer in 1972.

Whitaker died in 1975. Fredricksen was elected chairman and Brenner continued as president and chief executive officer. That same year

This Fourth Street building was the first Harrisburg home of AMP Incorporated. Now a plant, it is still in active use. Photo circa 1955.

Two former chairmen of the AMP board of directors are Cleve J. Fredricksen (left), and Joseph D. Brenner.

in Australia, England, Holland, Italy, Japan, Mexico, and West Germany.

Growth was guided by a series of policies that are still followed. The company grew by expansion—not acquisition. Because of Whitaker's desire to minimize AMP's visibility and impact on its hometown, plants were kept moderately sized and located throughout the region.

Through the 1950s, AMP was guided by a group of executives who had been with the company since its early days. Whitaker headed the executive team, which included S. Wilson Pollock (operations), G. Earle Walker (sales), and Cleve J. Fredricksen (finance). In 1956 Aircraft-Marine Products became a publicly held corporation and changed its name to AMP Incorporated. Late in October 1959, AMP stock was approved for listing on the "big board," the New York Stock Exchange.

New faces started appearing in the executive suite during the early 1960s. Joseph D. Brenner, who had joined the company in 1947, was elected vice-president/manufacturing in 1960.

Auchincloss retired from the board and two of a new generation of leaders were elected to the board: W. Smith and W.F. Raab. Willard Smith, an engineer who joined AMP in 1951, became vice-president/operations in 1970 and was elected a director in 1975. He died in April 1979. Walter F. Raab, a graduate of Wharton School and a certified public accountant who joined AMP in 1953, was elected treasurer of the corporation in 1969, vice-president in 1971, and a director in 1975.

In early 1981 Fredricksen retired and Brenner was elected chairman. Raab was elected vice-chairman and Harold A. McInnes, who joined the company as an engineer in 1965, was elected president and a director. Raab became chairman of the board and chief executive officer when Brenner retired in 1982.

Most of the systems that lead the market for AMP products today were not even conceived when the company was created. The insulated connector and crimping tool that helped make AMP's reputation are still manufactured. But today's products include complex advanced connectors for coaxial cables, ribbon cables, fiber-optic cables, printed circuit boards, and flexible circuitry; cable assemblies;

The current leaders of AMP Incorporated are Walter F. Raab, chairman and chief executive officer (left), and Harold A. McInnes, president.

miniature electronic switches; and membrane switches and keyboards.

Aircraft manufacturers and other industries that were the company's earliest clients are still valued customers. But AMP now also supplies manufacturers of computers, telecommunications devices, home entertainment systems, and such high-technology mass-transportation concepts as the 200-m.p.h. French TGV railroad and the Washington Metro. Today more than 25,000 manufacturers use AMP's 100 product lines including over 200,000 part numbers.

The firm has consistently maintained a 15-percent average annual growth rate since the 1950s. It has outgrown its corporate offices several times. Its first Harrisburg home was at the Fourth Street location. Later locations include 2100 Paxton Street (1951-1956) and Eisenhower Boulevard (1956-1983). The current corporate headquarters center opened at 470 Friendship Road in 1983.

AMP is an unusual new-era corporation—an engineering-oriented company whose business is not labor, materials, or capital intensive. It is geographically diverse with domestic plants clustered around hubs in central Pennsylvania, North and South Carolina, New England, the Shenandoah Valley area of Virginia, and two facilities in Florida. Its international activities, initiated in the 1950s under Whitaker's leadership, have been expanding rapidly and now include facilities in 25 countries.

AMP's future will be intimately connected with the next phase of technological revolution—micro-miniaturization of electronics, laser devices, and fiber optics all hold new challenges and opportunities. Indeed, 21st-century central Pennsylvania residents will still be grateful that the Chamber of Commerce changed its mind and decided to welcome this new corporate citizen back in 1943.

TRW, INC.

"A company called TRW" is a 20th-century industrial giant, a leading supplier to the automotive, aviation, and aerospace industries. Its Cameron Street, Harrisburg, plant—home of the Turbine Airfoils Division—is a key corporate component. With over 1,200 employees, it is a vital part of the local economy.

TRW was founded in 1901 in Cleveland, Ohio; its headquarters is now in a nearby suburb. Originally called Cleveland Cap Screw Company, its main products were nuts and bolts. But at the beginning of the automobile age, the firm created valves that smoothed the operation of the internal combustion engine. Soon its valves were part of every automobile engine.

When the internal combustion engine was adapted for aircraft, sales took off. The company's valves were in the engines that powered the French Spad fighters during World War I, and a specially redesigned valve helped power the *Spirit of St. Louis* on Lindbergh's historic solo Atlantic crossing.

It was the jet age that propelled

The Hurricane Agnes flood of 1972 caused major problems for TRW. While the main plant escaped serious damage, the computer center in the administration building was destroyed.

TRW (then known as Thompson Products) into national industrial leadership. Just as its valves had become part of every automobile engine, Thompson Products gas turbine components became standard in jet engines.

The Cameron Street plant was at the center of this development, and TRW Harrisburg played a vital role in the growth of its parent corporation. None of that was foreseen when the plant opened in August 1951.

Needing expanded production capability to meet Korean War needs, the company was lured to Harrisburg by the state's offer of a suitable plant complex and the availability of skilled, reliable labor. Under general manager Stan Johnston, 38 employees came to Harrisburg from Cleveland to transform an obsolete state automobile maintenance garage (other buildings included liquor control board offices and William Penn Memorial Museum storage) into a high-technology plant.

After the war TRW Harrisburg shifted quickly to civilian aviation. As commercial jet transport came of age in the late 1950s, TRW Harrisburg led the support industry with advanced engineering and technology. First the plant made casings for jet engines. Then it shifted to the vanes and blades

Dr. John Gadd, vice-president and general manager of the TRW, Inc., Harrisburg facility.

---

that still are its most important products.

TRW Harrisburg was a leading profit center for its parent corporation, generating capital to support investment activities. One corporate venture was the 1953 purchase of a half interest in an exciting and promising aerospace firm, Ramo-

The General Electric CF6-50 engine, with its many locally manufactured parts, was on display at the TRW Harrisburg's 30th anniversary open house in July 1981. Seen with it are (left to right) Terry Lyden of TRW; Jill Ann Shaffer, Miss Pennsylvania; and Bob Allen, General Electric's manager of Airfoils Contract Administration.

Wooldridge Corporation. That acquisition led directly to the 1958 merger of Thompson Products with Ramo-Wooldridge, the foundation of TRW in its modern form.

Now operating as the Turbine Airfoils Division, TRW Harrisburg continues to be a valued component of TRW. The plant is one of the world's largest manufacturers of jet turbine components and the second-largest vendor repairing turbine components. Widebody jet aircraft—McDonnell Douglas DC-10s, Boeing 747s, and Lockheed L-1011s—all have TRW Harrisburg parts in their engines, as do the smaller DC-9s and B-727s serving Harrisburg International Airport.

Two divisional "strategic business units" comprise the Turbine Airfoils Division: Airfoil Finishing (original equipment manufacture) and Airfoil Overhaul/Coatings. The latter unit refurbishes used engine parts and

handles TRW Harrisburg's prized airfoil-coating operations. The low-pressure plasma spray-coating system used by TRW Harrisburg is a state-of-the-art, high-technology process involving an artificial atmosphere of inert gas. Through its application the useful life of metal components is dramatically extended.

The Airfoil Finishing unit sells to a select group of corporate clients. Companies like Rolls Royce, General Electric, Pratt & Whitney, and SNECMA (France) use engine turbine airfoils made in Harrisburg. Airfoil Overhaul customers include all of the world's major airlines.

TRW Harrisburg covers 24 acres, including 8.5 acres of enclosed manufacturing and office space. Its facilities include more than 2,000 machines, some worth more than one million dollars apiece. Turbine Airfoils also has a plant in Singapore performing airfoil overhaul work for clients in the Middle East, Asia, and the Far East.

Stan Johnston served as general manager of TRW Harrisburg until 1961. He was followed by Ray Whitmore (1961-1965), Paul Hazen

(1965-1975), and Steve Dardick (1975-1980). Metallurgist Dr. John Gadd, a scientist turned businessman, has headed the plant since 1980.

Dr. Gadd, vice-president and general manager, is interested in his division's past, but fascinated by its future. "The air transport industry is going to grow and TRW intends to grow with it," he says. Acknowledging the difficulties that have plagued commercial aviation in recent years, Dr. Gadd looks to new aircraft, engines, and technologies that are now emerging.

"TRW Harrisburg grew up with jet aviation," he says, "and we will continue to develop together. As jet engine technology has skyrocketed, TRW has always supplied the industry and met its needs. We were here in the past when they needed us. They are going to need us, and we will be here in the future."

TRW Harrisburg's newest machine is this low-pressure plasma spray device used to apply special coatings to blade and rotor airfoils.

NOVINGER'S, INC.

There is no American equivalent to the British boast, "by appointment to Her Majesty, the Queen." If there were, Novinger's, Inc., the Harrisburg-based interior/exterior systems contractor, would be entitled to use it. Novinger's has done lath and plaster work for the White House (during the Truman Administration) and interior walls for the Gettysburg farmhouse of President Eisenhower. Other Novinger jobs include the State Department Building in Washington, the new Governor's Mansion, the Labor and Industry Building, the William Penn Memorial Museum, and the Dauphin County Courthouse and Founders' Hall in Hershey.

James Dewalt Novinger, founder of the company, began his lathing and plastering career when he was 14 years old. Born in a log cabin near Fisherville, Pennsylvania, the elder Novinger started a lathing-contracting business in 1924 (in partnership with Herman Wagner), added plastering in 1933, and formed the venture that is now Novinger's, Inc., in 1947. The White House contract was an early break, the result of a bid submitted by Novinger in partnership with Washington contractor James Kane. Success and rapid expansion soon followed. After Novinger's retirement, the firm was headed by son-in-law Bob Gulden. Grandson James David Novinger assumed control of the company in 1980.

For many years Novinger worked out of a basement workshop and living room office in his Shell Street, Harrisburg, home. In the 1950s Novinger's built its first major facility at 6 North Progress Avenue on land received from a bankrupt client. In 1970 the firm moved to Linglestown Road, 10 miles east of Harrisburg. Novinger's has well over 100 employees.

The current main warehouse and corporate headquarters, a 20,000-square-foot facility located at 1213 Paxton Church Road, was completed in 1980. The 60,000-square-foot plant where Novinger's manufactures its own exterior panel system is located on Miller Lane in Harrisburg.

Novinger's works exclusively with commercial construction and while the company is no longer active in Washington, a list of current contracts is still impressive. Current projects include work on Caesar's Palace in Atlantic City and a housing project in Huntington, West Virginia. Locally, the firm just completed work on the massive new Pennsylvania Blue Shield complex in Camp Hill.

The construction business has changed radically since the elder James Novinger first lathed out a wall. There is not much plastering done now.

Instead, suspended ceiling systems, steel stud, and drywall, and a wide range of other, new materials have replaced wooden lath and plaster. Novinger's interiors now even include access floors and coordinated furniture systems, specially designed and installed to complete the new office environment. And for exteriors, Novinger's works with its own prefabricated wall panel in a wide range of insulated exterior finishes.

But some things don't change, especially the tradition of quality materials and skilled workmanship at this proud Harrisburg business.

James Dewalt Novinger, founder of Novinger's, Inc.

INCLINATOR COMPANY OF AMERICA

We all know that life is full of ups and downs. But some take that concept more seriously than others. In 1923 C.C. Crispen, owner of Harrisburg's Cadillac dealership (Crispen Motor Car Company), decided that the automobile market was saturated and that it was time to go into some other business. For some people a decision like that might be a real downer. For Crispen it turned out to be a highlight.

Crispen loved telling the story, for from then on instead of selling automobiles, he invented, manufactured, and sold a movable seat that traveled up and down stairs on a rail, powered by regular household current.

In the great American tradition, Crispen built his first prototype in his basement. The folding footrest and seat, designed to save space on his narrow stairway, have remained distinctive features of the INCLIN-ATOR® and Inclinette® ever since.

Crispen incorporated the firm in 1924 and sold his first production model to a handicapped friend. The friend's doctor was fascinated and had one installed in his own home. Like the INCLIN-ATOR® itself, sales rose smoothly. When Westinghouse had an INCLIN-ATOR® installed in its "Electric Home" on Atlantic City's Boardwalk, the company's future was assured.

In 1928 Crispen added the "Elevette"®, a private residential elevator for homes with winding staircases, to the firm's product line. As the Inclinator Company of America celebrated its 60th anniversary in 1983, INCLIN-ATOR® and "Elevette"® remain the major products manufactured and sold by the company.

Crispen remained with the firm until his death in 1979 at the age of 103. Inclinator Company of America is owned jointly by Hibberd R. Crispen (now retired), the son of the founder, and Paul R. Krum, the current president.

Krum joined the venture in 1929 as a part-time worker while attending

business college. Crispen offered him a permanent job with Inclinator in 1930. Krum accepted the offer and he has been with the company ever since.

Over the years, INCLIN-ATORs® have risen to many special occasions. Director Billy Wilder made a star of the INCLIN-ATOR® in *Witness for the Prosecution.* The "Elevette"® also appeared in *Ruby* and *Ladies' Man,* starring Jerry Lewis. Groucho Marx used to joke about his home elevator, an "Elevette"®, on *You Bet Your Life.*

Company products continue to sell primarily for in-home use, though recent efforts to help handicapped people overcome architectural barriers have led to Inclinator Company products being used in churches, schools, and other public places under new "authorized use" regulations.

We all know that life has its ups and downs. But it took C.C. Crispen and Inclinator Company of America to create a useful product and successful business based on that simple idea.

C.C. Crispen, inventor of the INCLIN-ATOR® (a movable seat that traveled up and down stairs on a rail), and founder of the Inclinator Company of America.

The INCLIN-ATOR® had a starring role in *Witness for the Prosecution,* along with actor Charles Laughton.

WERT BOOKBINDING, INC.

At Wert Bookbinding, Inc., available technology includes futuristic computerized typesetting, sophisticated paper deacidification processing, and ultrasonic welding for paper encapsulation—but these advanced processes are all dedicated to preserving the past. And although the firm works on more than 300,000 volumes yearly, each is custom crafted, some completely by hand.

John Wert was working in the bindery division of the McFarland Company, a Harrisburg printer, back in 1960 when his employer decided to phase out the bookbinding division. Wert bought the equipment, paying for it with weekly paycheck deductions while operating the bindery on a part-time basis in a garage behind the old Linglestown Post Office.

By 1963 the equipment was fully paid for. With a staff consisting of his wife, Kathryn, and one of his sons, Wert went into bookbinding full time. His first major contract was the 1963 John Harris High yearbook. That was only 20 years ago, but the company now typically employs about 80 people, has contracts with more than 100 libraries, and is ranked among the nation's top 10 custom library binderies.

Wert really tied it all together when he won a contract to bind all state-owned books. At the time he had neither the facilities nor the staff nor the financial backing to handle that volume of business. He quickly acquired a new location (behind a food market on Jonestown Road), some new equipment, a group of new employees—and a new bank loan.

Wert Bookbinding's accounts today include the state contracts for New Jersey and New York as well as Pennsylvania. The firm also does all work for the libraries of Penn State, Princeton, Temple, the University of Pennsylvania, and other major colleges and universities, and has

handled special contracts with the Library of Congress and the National Library of Medicine. But just as when Wert first started, the company still rebinds single books for private collectors and often works on family bibles or other heirlooms.

township on U.S. Highway 22 near Grantville. From 1968 to 1983 the firm was in the industrial park at Harrisburg International Airport. But wherever it is located, this company will help keep greater Harrisburg a tightly bound community.

John Wert died in 1971. The organization is now headed by his two sons, Gary L. Wert (president) and Rodney D. Wert (vice-president), and his brother, Paul B. Wert (treasurer). Kathryn Wert is now secretary of the corporation and its principal stockholder.

Gary Wert sees Wert Bookbinding's main task as "paper conservation," protecting and preserving books, documents, letters, maps, and other paper artifacts. Some books are taken apart and treated one page at a time. The process may cost several hundred dollars, but adds centuries to the book's endangered life.

In 1984 Wert Bookbinding will move to new quarters in East Hanover

The owners and corporate officers of Wert Bookbinding are (left to right) Kathryn Wert, secretary; Rodney Wert, vice-president; Gary Wert, president; and Paul Wert, treasurer.

THE FARMERS BANK AND TRUST COMPANY OF HUMMELSTOWN

Hummelstown, Pennsylvania, is a peaceful, quiet small town—the kind of community people remember and romanticize. Step inside Farmers Bank and Trust Company offices on the north side of the town square. You'll find yourself in the kind of bank that you may have thought had gone the way of the corner drugstore, the nickelodeon, and the ice cream parlor.

Farmers calls itself "The Community Bank." It is proud of its heritage as a "locally owned, independent bank that is not affiliated with any other institution." Tradition continues to guide policy. As the 1983 annual report says, "Deposits have been and will continue to be used prudently for granting loans in our communities. There will be no change in this philosophy."

The bank occupies land that once was owned by Colonel George T. Hummel. Hummel built his mansion in 1873; it was sold by his estate in 1877 and purchased by the Farmers Bank of Hummelstown when it was organized early in 1885. The bank at first occupied only one first-floor room of the mansion.

The Sun, Hummelstown's weekly newspaper, reported bank affairs regularly. April 3, 1885: "The new and beautiful carpet on the floor—was made and lain by our townsman, C.P. Haehnlen, who is known as a fine weaver." May 8, 1885: "A handsome safe weighing nearly five thousand pounds was this week received by the Farmers Bank. It is one of the most secure and best safes now manufactured and nothing can be more secure than that deposited within its irresistible sides."

Jack Straub's jewelry store occupied part of the first floor in 1891. Straub shared facilities until 1894 with Snyder's Barber Shop. When Snyder left, the bank expanded with help, as *The Sun* reported, "from the paintbrush artistically wielded by Joseph Dasher." The second story

In 1916 Farmers Bank of Hummelstown remodeled its headquarters in the Hummel Mansion on the Center Square.

became "an inviting and nicely furnished room and is fitted up for the Republican Club where the members meet to discuss subjects most important for the day." In 1910 the third floor of the building became the Masonic Lodge. The building was remodeled in 1916.

Christian Hoffer was the first president of Farmers Bank. Drs. W.C. Baker and Thomas G. Fox were vice-president and cashier, respectively. Dr. William H. Lodge is the current chairman; State Representative Rudolph Dininni is president; William L. Shoap is executive vice-president and chief executive officer. Shoap joined the bank in 1947 as a teller, one of four bank employees at the time

(there are 80 now). He was promoted to cashier in 1957 and has held his present post since 1969.

Farmers Bank was granted trust powers in 1959 and changed its name at that time to The Farmers Bank and Trust Company of Hummelstown. It since has added branch offices at Rutherford (1963), Linglestown (1967), and East Park Center (1974). Bank assets now exceed $80 million. The bank has come a long way since it opened in the former parlor of the Hummel Mansion. But it is still an independent hometown bank, devoted to serving its community.

R.J. ROMBERGER & SONS

"People's lives mean something. They should have a marker so that others remember that they lived," asserts Larry Romberger. Larry and his older brother, Robert L. Romberger, are stonecutters. They own and operate the Penbrook monument company established by their father, Russell Joseph Romberger, in 1929.

R.J. Romberger came to Harrisburg in the early '20s to work in the Enola railroad yards. He had been employed by his father in a monument business in Berrysburg on the northern edge of Dauphin County, and soon started a part-time monument business in the garage of his 24th Street home. In 1929 he quit working on the railroad and made the monument company his full-time occupation.

R.J. Romberger was a master stonecutter and engraver. But his sons were raised in the trade and both brothers can still hand cut a monument when needed. Today the only calls for handwork are occasional requests to match or repair old stones. Otherwise the granite slabs are engraved by sandblasting. "Hand-chiseled letters are not as deep," says Robert. "Even though they're wider, they're not as visible. You can do more with the new technique."

"Dad used to pay me 10 cents each to cut the letters out of the tape before we sandblasted. That's how I got interested in the business," recalls Larry. Today it's Bob who does most of the shop work. Larry usually handles sales and office duties, but the brothers can switch if necessary.

Bob was in the army, and materials were hard to obtain when R.J. built the Romberger plant in 1942. He designed most of the equipment himself. His special top-opening sandblast room has been imitated by many other stonecutters.

Russell Joseph Romberger (1898-1975), founder of R.J. Romberger & Sons.

R.J. Romberger & Sons is one of the top 25 dealers in the nation for Rock of Ages, a popular Barre, Vermont, quarry and monument manufacturer. But it will use any of a wide variety of granites. One favorite is a dark, almost black rock quarried in Pennsylvania, between Reading and Philadelphia.

Stonecutting is still a fine art—even with the semiautomated technology available today. To watch Bob in his plant is to see a skilled craftsman at work. The skills required to cut the patterns and control the cutting process are complex and precise.

The Romberger brothers specialize in personalized monuments and have fulfilled many unusual requests. One truck driver has a picture of his rig engraved on his stone. A coach and referee has a football on his; an FBI agent killed during the Shade Gap kidnaping has the Bureau seal. One couple has a picture of the farm they worked together engraved on their shared gravestone.

This 1933 photo shows the Romberger delivery truck decorated for a Harrisburg parade.

BERMAN, BOSWELL & TINTNER

A small, but extremely versatile, law firm has for more than 40 years been a leader in the Bar of the central Pennsylvania area. Berman, Boswell & Tintner, which has actively participated in both the longest civil (antitrust) and criminal (turnpike contract fraud) cases in the central Pennsylvania area, can truly state its mark in litigation. Variety in its interests and endeavors plus expertise, is the mark of this law firm.

Berman, Boswell & Tintner is a general practice firm. The member lawyers devote personal and individual attention to the full range of their clients' legal problems. No sign, not even a discreet professional shingle, identifies their Front Street Office. However, their clients—including local major foundations, multinational and international corporations, many family-owned businesses, and persons involved in those businesses—know exactly where to find them whenever they need legal help. The representation involves matters of local, national, and international scope.

The venture was started in the early 1940s by Earl V. Compton and Samuel Handler, both experienced lawyers with distinguished private practices. World War II intervened in the formative years and interfered with their plans, but Samuel Handler, with the able assistance of his cousin, Earl Handler, maintained the fledgling practice until Colonel Compton returned and reactivated the original firm of Compton & Handler.

Arthur Berman and William D. Boswell joined the concern in 1945 and early 1946, respectively, and Leonard Tintner in 1959. When the Handlers left to form their own enterprise in 1966, Arthur Berman, William D. Boswell, and Leonard Tintner reorganized the firm. Other attorneys who have subsequently associated with the firm include Pennsylvania State Representative

This 1976 watercolor by Henry Koerner shows the law offices of Berman, Boswell & Tintner at 315 North Front Street, Harrisburg.

Jeffrey E. Piccola, Jeffrey R. Boswell, and Sondra T. Berman.

The mansion at 315 North Front Street occupied by Berman, Boswell & Tintner since 1976 has a fascinating history of its own. The land upon which the mansion now stands was sold by the son of the founder of Harrisburg, John Harris, to American Revolution hero General ''Mad'' Anthony Wayne who, according to local legend, had a hunting and fishing cabin there and used it in the summers from the late 1780s into the 1790s. The main brick structure was erected in approximately 1840, with additions built in 1870 and 1900. During the early 1900s, the mansion was the manse for the Pine Street Presbyterian Church. The firm has taken great care to restore and preserve much of the interior detailing and character of the original mansion, in Early American style.

The partners are deeply committed to the Harrisburg community. Six of the seven attorneys are Dickinson School of Law graduates. Members of the firm are active with the Children's Home of Harrisburg, the Tri-County United Way, the Tri-County Welfare Council, the Dauphin County Unit of the American Cancer Society, and the Chamber of Commerce of the Greater Harrisburg Area, with members serving in executive capacities during their tenure.

They are also very active within their profession. Leonard Tintner was elected secretary to the Pennsylvania Bar Association in 1982. Both William D. Boswell and Leonard Tintner have served as presidents of the Dauphin County Bar Association. And in 1981 Jeffrey R. Boswell became the third member of the firm (and second generation of his family) to serve as president of the Dauphin County Young Lawyers' Association.

Their clients, however, are the first interest of the members of this small, but effective, law firm.

PENNSYLVANIA MEDICAL SOCIETY

We Americans take comfort in the assumption that our doctors are well-trained, highly skilled professionals. We know that our laws regulating medical education and professional licensure are rigorous and demanding.

Such has not always been true. One 17th-century autopsy proved conclusively that the patient had died from witchcraft. Bloodletting with cups or leeches was a popular 18th-century cure that doubtless killed more patients than it saved. Even through much of the 19th century, quackery and unprincipled behavior were common. Virtually anyone could hang a sign and claim to be a medical doctor. Patent remedies were sold by traveling hucksters working from medicine shows.

The American Medical Association, formed on May 7, 1847, in Philadelphia, was part of a nationwide effort to heal the ills of professional medicine. Pennsylvania's physicians soon followed the AMA lead. Their objectives, identified during early proceedings, were to advance medical knowledge, elevate professional character, protect the interests of physicians, extend the bounds of medical science, promote all measures adapted to the relief of suffering, and improve the health and protect the lives of the community.

The initiative to form a statewide medical society was first offered by Wilmer Worthington, M.D., at the December 1847 meeting of the Chester County Medical Society. Members of the Lancaster County Medical Society greeted the idea with enthusiasm and proposed holding a convention in Lancaster.

The convention met in April 1848 at the Methodist Episcopal Church. Under the leadership of Samuel Humes, M.D., of Lancaster, its first president, the association adopted purposeful membership rules that set high standards of medical education, practice, and ethics.

The new society was opposed by some doctors who feared its powers or disliked it on philosophical or political grounds. Its early progress was careful and slow. Seeking meaningful vital statistics, the society won state legislative approval for an 1851 law requiring physicians to register the births and deaths they witnessed.

Thirty years later the society won legislation requiring the registration of physicians. In 1885 the state created its first Board of Health and Vital Statistics, empowered to investigate

The society's first permanent headquarters building was at 230 State Street.

epidemics (including those of domestic animals) and "the effects of localities, employments, conditions, habits, food, beverages, and medicines on the health of the people . . ."

The crowning legislative

The headquarters of the Pennsylvania Medical Society is at 20 Erford Road, Lemoyne.

Samuel Humes, M.D., was the first president of the Pennsylvania Medical Society.

instituted a continuing medical education requirement for membership.

In 1977 the society founded its own medical liability insurance company. The Pennsylvania Medical Society Liability Insurance Company (PMSLIC) was started when most commercial carriers refused to write medical liability coverage for Pennsylvania physicians. Through its physician-oriented philosophy and initiatives, PMSLIC is continuing the society's mission. David S. Masland, M.D., is chairman of the PMSLIC board and its president is A. John Smither.

Lester Perry, executive director of the society for many years before his retirement in 1969, describes the early work of the Pennsylvania Medical Society as a dedicated effort to improve health care delivery. In the '40s and '50s, he says, the society became concerned with improving the business aspects of medicine. More recently, the work of the society has been dedicated to improving public understanding of the medical profession and its work.

Until 1922 the Pennsylvania Medical Society traveled. It was headquartered wherever its executive secretary lived. The first permanent home of the society was at 230 State Street, Harrisburg. In 1934 the society remodeled the building, taking over the entire structure for its own use. In 1953 the offices were expanded to include 226 State Street. The society started construction of its current headquarters complex on Erford Road, Lemoyne, in 1965. An addition was completed in 1982.

The Pennsylvania Medical Society is a nonprofit corporation representing 15,000 physicians throughout the state. Executive vice-president of the Pennsylvania Medical Society is John F. Rineman. The president of the society (1983-1984) is John Y. Templeton III, M.D.

achievement in the early history of the medical society was the Medical Practice Act, passed in June 1911. This comprehensive law gave legal definition to medical practice, created a State Board of Medical Education and Licensure, and prescribed the educational requirements for licensure in Pennsylvania as a physician.

During the 1930s the society turned its attention to medical economics, an effort that resulted in the Medical Services Act. That law made possible

Pennsylvania Medical Society creation of the company that eventually became Pennsylvania Blue Shield.

In the postwar 1940s and throughout the 1950s, the society conducted extensive scientific sessions and programs. At first these sessions functioned to bring physicians returning from World War II up to date on advances in clinical medicine. Subsequently, they served a continuing medical education function, to keep doctors informed of the latest research and procedures. In the 1960s state and national specialty societies to a large extent assumed this role, although the society in the 1970s

SHAMMO'S QUALITY FOODS

Truffles, wild rice, and escargot. For more than 80 years, Shammo's has been giving life in Harrisburg special flavor all its own.

Imported preserves, white asparagus, and sweet chestnuts. When it comes to specialty food items, local gourmet cooks claim, "If you can't find it at Shammo's, you can't get it in Harrisburg." Calder R. Shammo, Jr., the current owner and third generation of his family to operate Shammo's Quality Foods, says that his customers may exaggerate a bit. But he's proud of the reputation his family store has earned during its long history.

Turtle soup, smoked oysters, and caviar. The store was started by Luther C. Shammo back in 1900. It was located at 609 East State Street, on the current site of the Forum. Luther's son Calder joined the business after a few years. As L.C. Shammo & Son, the two sold groceries and produce to customers throughout Harrisburg.

The firm was known as Shammo Brothers' Grocery from 1910 to 1923. Henry L., Charles A., and William J. Shammo joined the business, which

---

Luther C. Shammo founded the family business in 1900. He ran it with his son Calder at the State Street location until 1920.

became a major retailer and wholesaler with five wagons on the road, supplying stores and markets throughout the area.

Exotic teas, coffee, fine chocolates, glazed fruit, nuts, and fancy cookies. The firm shifted to become a leading purveyor of specialty foods around 1920. Calder Shammo, Sr., and his brother Charles were the active partners at the time, and the store had moved to 17th Street at Walnut in East Harrisburg. Shammo's Quality Foods stayed at that Walnut Street location in a store built by Luther and Calder Sr. until 1970.

In 1971 Shammo's moved to its West Shore location on Trindle Road. The oldest specialty grocer in the region, Shammo's is the sole survivor of an era that featured fancy food stores like S.S. Pomeroy, Koon's Grocery, J.W. Wilson, and Gilbert Sourbeer.

Today Shammo's is perhaps best known for its premium quality fancy fruit and produce—especially its fruit baskets. At holiday times, the store prepares thousands of them—many for local consumption and others for delivery throughout the country. Visiting celebrities often find Shammo's fruit baskets in their rooms, provided by gracious and thoughtful

Calder R. Shammo, Jr., current owner and operator of Shammo's Quality Foods on Trindle Road in Camp Hill.

---

hosts or hotel managers.

Shammo's does not carry sugar, flour, or other staple groceries. "People used to want top-quality beans, grains, corn—the basics," says Calder Shammo. "Now they are using a lot of unusual or imported gourmet foods." But no matter how you slice it (or dice it, or serve it), 20th-century Harrisburg life has had a special piquancy because of the work of three generations of the Shammo family.

PHICO INSURANCE GROUP

The Pennsylvania Hospital Insurance Company (PHICO), flagship of the PHICO Insurance Group, was born in crisis. In October 1975 the insurance company that had been providing malpractice and general liability insurance for most of the state's hospitals announced that it was withdrawing from Pennsylvania. There were, said the company, too many problems at too many hospitals. Exposures it faced as an insurer were too high. Most of the other insurance companies also withdrew from the market.

Nearly 150 hospitals and 2,000 hospital-based physicians faced nonrenewal of their malpractice coverage. Newly passed Pennsylvania law required all hospitals to carry liability insurance, but few companies were willing to insure most institutions.

In response to this crisis, the Hospital Association of Pennsylvania formed a wholly owned but administratively independent "captive" insurance affiliate. With active assistance from the Insurance Department, the company was created and licensed in two months. Its first policy took effect on March 1, 1976.

As demanded by the Insurance Department, the new organization would be a financially sound and responsive insurance company, first, and part of the health care delivery system, second. Its original board of directors included a lawyer, a financial manager, a hospital administrator, and a banker, among others. All were Pennsylvania hospital trustees.

A management team headed by president and chief executive officer Donald G. Steffes was recruited from insurance companies and health care providers throughout the nation. Experts in malpractice, risk management, and other corporate concerns, they were drawn by the prospect of building a new company and resolving a critical insurance need.

PHICO's first priority was reducing and controlling losses by improving hospital practices and procedures through the introduction of risk management. The company has proven itself so successful at this function that commercial insurers have returned to the state, seeking to reestablish the business they abandoned in 1975. This achievement has been noticed. PHICO has received numerous requests for technical

assistance and now markets its hospital risk management expertise and claims services to non-PHICO policyholders through a subsidiary, Pennsylvania Insurance Management Company (PIMCO), formed in 1981.

Another PHICO subsidiary, Pennsylvania Casualty Company, was originally formed in 1978 to provide hospitals with workers' compensation insurance. In 1979 Pennsylvania Casualty began complementing PHICO's hospital malpractice policies by offering malpractice insurance to individual physicians.

The PHICO Insurance Group is licensed in 17 states. It maintains offices in Chevy Chase, Maryland, Indianapolis, and Denver, and is the endorsed carrier of the Indiana Hospital Association, the Medical Society of Delaware, and the Independent Insurance Agents of Colorado. In 1985 the group will open a new national headquarters complex in Silver Spring Township, Cumberland County.

An architect's rendering of the new home office headquarters building of the PHICO Insurance Group, scheduled for completion in 1985.

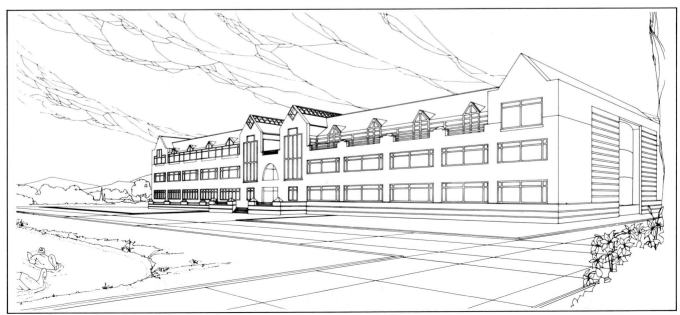

AYCOCK, INC.

An Aycock crew gathers at a 1940s job site.

If you think moving a piano or a refrigerator is touchy, take a look at the jobs regularly handled by Aycock, Inc. The Camp Hill contractor specializes in moving and installing industrial machinery—equipment like giant electrical turbine generators, condensers, and nuclear reactors. Its 144-wheel modular trailer hauls loads weighing over 720 tons. Other tools of this unusual trade include a 700-ton-capacity traveling crane, jacking towers, stator elevators, hoists, and other heavy equipment.

Aycock crews were responsible for erecting such well-known local land-marks as the sooperdooperLooper and Kissing Tower at Hersheypark. They also installed generators at P.P.& L.'s Brunner Island Plant, coating machinery at Appleton Paper, and much of the plant machinery at Quaker Oats and Hershey Foods.

Aycock's affiliated company,

Cumberland Bridge (founded in 1957) is a steel fabricator. Cumberland Bridge fabricated the steel and Aycock handled mechanical erection responsibilities for such projects as Founder's Hall in Hershey and the bridges for the Harrisburg Airport Expressway.

Jesse N. Aycock founded the company in 1946. Born in North Carolina in 1907, Aycock was a student in the School of Fine Arts at the University of North Carolina, but came to Pennsylvania in 1925 to study architecture at the University of Pennsylvania.

During World War II Aycock served with the Army Corps of Engineers in China, Burma, and India. He was construction engineer for the Stilwell cutoff to the Burma Road. After the war Aycock started the company by contracting to clear demobilized defense plants and mothball their

machinery and equipment. Aycock, Inc., remains a closely held corporaton.

A major installation contract may require two or three years to complete. The company is responsible for hiring a local labor force, for receiving, unloading, and storing thousands of parts as they arrive on site, and for precision assembly of the machinery. The project may be massive with the sum of the parts weighing thousands of tons. But assembly often requires precise tolerances to within .001 inch.

So if you need to install a turbine or a rolling mill or erect the steel superstructure for a bridge or a building, call Aycock. But if you built a boat in your basement and can't get it out, even this Camp Hill specialty contractor probably won't be able to help you.

HARRISBURG ACADEMY

The Harrisburg Academy, like the city it serves, was founded by John Harris who granted "the rents, issues, and profits of his Ferry across the river Susquehanna to the endowing of an English and German Academy." The first classes met in 1784, in a room of the Harris home at the corner of Front and Washington streets.

Schoolmaster Samuel Barnes Davis' mission was critical and challenging. Working on the frontier, it was his task to preserve and transmit the ideals, knowledge, and culture of civilization. He faced major obstacles. Books were scarce, and the other teaching tools were few and primitive.

But Davis and Harris persevered. Early in the new century the school was chartered by the Commonwealth as "an academy or public school for education of youth in useful arts, sciences, and literature." The state even appropriated $1,000 to assist the Academy with its purchase of "globes and such other astronomical and mathematical apparatus as may be necessary."

The Academy has educated the children of many families famed in Harrisburg history. And several historic Harrisburg homes sheltered the school. In 1847 it moved to the home of Senator William Maclay at Front and South streets. It stayed at that site through the administration of Headmaster Jacob Frindley Seiler, who led the school from 1860 to 1907.

Early in the 20th century the Academy was a small community school housed on the Maclay property. Under the leadership of headmaster Arthur E. Brown (1912-1940), the Academy expanded to over 200 students at its new campus (now University Center) and enrolled many boarding students. This was one of the most dynamic periods in the school's history. But financial difficulties and falling enrollment came with the Great Depression and World War II. The new campus was sold, and the

Academy moved once again into a local home—the McCormick Mansion at 305 North Front Street.

In 1948 the Academy merged with the Seiler School (founded in 1898 by Miss Sue Seiler and Miss Martha Seiler, daughters of former Academy Headmaster Jacob Seiler). From this merger came a coeducational institution with 233 students. It was housed in the Wallower Mansion at Front and Maclay streets.

The Harrisburg Academy moved to the Wormleysburg campus it presently occupies in 1959; its current headmaster, Ralph E. Gillette, assumed his position in 1978. More than 370 students are enrolled in kindergarten through 12th grade. The academically challenging college preparatory program is still conducted in the Academy's traditional small, highly personalized classes. The school is co-ed; its social, religious, ethnic, and

racial composition is diverse. Scholarships help many Academy students pay for their education. The curriculum includes such contemporary subjects as computer science that would doubtless amaze John Harris. But the mission of the Academy—providing a quality education for Harrisburg area youth—remains unchanged since its earliest days.

Three generations of Harrisburg Academy families review yearbooks and photographs in anticipation of the school's 200th anniversary. Seated (left to right) are George W. Reily III, class of 1926; Barbara Fleming Reily, Seiler School, class of 1935; Ann A. Colvin, grade 2; William A. Pearson, class of 1926. Standing (left to right) are Sarah B. Miles, grade 8; William C. Miles, Jr., grade 10; Helen McVey Colvin, class of 1960; and Richard Pearson Lefever, grade 9. (Courtesy of Katherine Oates Nixon.)

OLEWINE'S INCORPORATED

More than 80 years and four generations of the Olewine family connect the tractor-trailer rigs of today's Olewine's Incorporated with Ben Olewine's corner grocery at Fifth and Dauphin streets. Ben Olewine, Sr., started his corner store in 1900. Today his grandson is president of a family corporation that wholesales institutional foods throughout Pennsylvania, Maryland, New Jersey, Delaware, northern Virginia, and Washington, D.C. And his great-granddaughter is the corporation's vice-president for administration.

Ben Olewine expanded his corner grocery business to include a stall at the Kelker Street Farmers' Market in 1910. When the Kelker Street Farmers' Market closed in the 1920s, Olewine's moved to the Chestnut Street Farmers' Market, and then to the East Harrisburg Farmers' Market.

As the farmers' market side of the business expanded, so did the role of Ben Olewine, Jr. Ben Jr. enjoyed the delicatessen business, especially cheese

The new warehouse, distribution center, and corporate headquarters of Olewine's Incorporated is at 4000 Industrial Road on the north edge of Harrisburg.

marketing. By 1932 the Olewine's markets became known as Olewine's Cheese House. Ben Jr. also began expanding the business in other ways. He bought a warehouse at Cherry Alley in downtown Harrisburg and began wholesale operations with his brother George. In 1942 he started a catering service with his brother Forrest.

Ben Olewine III became an active part of the family business in the 1940s. Ben Olewine, Sr., had been a grocer; Ben Jr. had created Olewine's Cheese House delicatessen; Ben Olewine III was most interested in wholesale activities. Under his father's supervision, Ben III began expanding the wholesale business. Olewine's soon outgrew the Cherry Alley warehouse, and in 1948 the company moved to a larger facility at Fourth and Vaughn streets.

Ben Olewine III took over control of the firm in 1958 and immediately began a series of changes. First, he moved into the institutional foods field. Second, he introduced the Olewine's label, making quality the company trademark.

The new strategy brought a rapid increase in business. By 1965 the

Ben Olewine III, president and chief executive officer of Olewine's Incorporated.

warehouse at Fourth and Vaughn had to be expanded to handle the private-label canned goods and a new line of frozen foods. With the expansion came new company labels—Host Favorite, Host Delight, and Olewine Frozen. Olewine's had now become a full-

Under the management of Ben Olewine, Jr., the company was known as Olewine's Cheese House and operated stores at several area markets as well as a wholesale distributorship.

service institutional food distributor.

These labels are not familiar to most consumers. Don't look for them on the shelves of your grocery store. But professional food service people know them well.

Olewine's is a major supplier of foods for national chain restaurants, schools, hospitals, and other institutions. Those Olewine's trucks that often are seen on Harrisburg highways may be headed for major hospitals, health care facilities, well-known colleges and universities, and large government installations in the metropolitan Philadelphia or Baltimore-Washington markets.

To provide its customers with full-line service, Olewine's now stocks more than 3,000 items including canned goods, meats, dairy products, frozen foods, and disposables. Its new warehouse at 4000 Industrial Road (just north of Harrisburg) provides 60,000 square feet of office and warehouse space including nearly 600,000 cubic feet of frozen storage, 150,000 cubic feet of refrigerated storage, and more than one million

cubic feet of dry storage space. That's a pretty big pantry.

It's a big enough pantry, in fact, to make Olewine's one of the largest institutional foods wholesalers in Pennsylvania, and one of the top 75 in the country. All corporate activities are run from the Harrisburg office. By 1983 Olewine's Incorporated had 93 employees.

Ben Olewine, Sr., started delivering groceries from a horse-drawn wagon. His son organized a fleet of panel trucks. Ben Olewine III has a fleet of refrigerated trucks and tractor-trailers

to deliver his merchandise to customers in five states and the District of Columbia.

The company remains wholly owned by the Olewine family. Ben Olewine III is president and chief executive officer. Son Ben Olewine IV, a marketing consultant based in New York City, is a director of the corporation. Daughter Kris Olewine is vice-president for administration and a director. Marian Olewine, a sister of Ben Jr., was an officer and credit manager for the corporation until she retired in 1980.

Ben Olewine attributes much of his company's success to its extensive reliance on sophisticated data-processing systems. Industry analysts have concurred, and interest in Olewine's expertise with computer systems is spreading. In 1982 Olewine's established a wholly owned subsidiary, Inter-State Management Information Systems, Inc. From its Sixth Street offices, ISMIS offers a full line of data-processing services.

Olewine's became best known throughout greater Harrisburg for its stands at various markets. This photo shows Ben Jr. at the old Chestnut Street Farmers' Market.

KITZMILLER'S, INC.

In June 1948 Clarence Kitzmiller traded his 1938 Chevrolet for a pickup truck and entered the roofing business. Kitzmiller had been working as a roofer for the Elkwood Company for more than a year. He thought that he understood the business and would be better off working for himself. His office and workshop was the garage at his home—421 Market Street in New Cumberland.

Kitzmiller's, Inc., had 75 employees by 1962 and was involved with drywall work, siding, and remodeling, as well as roofing. Much of the residential and commercial development of the West Shore area was roofed by Kitzmiller, including major portions of Highland Park, Hampton Township, and Lower Allen Township. Kitzmiller's, Inc., also has been responsible for post offices in Scranton and Wilkes-Barre, shopping malls in the Poconos, and Bell Telephone buildings throughout central Pennsylvania.

The Kitzmiller family emigrated from Germany in the early 18th century. Johannes Kitzmiller (1669-1745) was an early immigrant, arriving in 1728 aboard the ship *Mortonhouse.* He settled near Schaefferstown, Lebanon County. His son Jonas Kitzmiller (1691-1745) had emigrated separately, arriving in the New World before his father. He first settled along the Little Conestoga Creek west of Lancaster. By the early 1730s he had moved to the banks of the Tulpehocken Creek near Myerstown.

John Jacob Kitzmiller (1744-1812) was an early resident of Schaefferstown who served in the militia during the Revolution. His son John (1781-1852) moved to Shippensburg, where the family has now lived for seven generations and over 180 years. Five generations of the family are buried in Shippensburg's Spring Hill Cemetery.

Clarence Kitzmiller is proud of his

family and of his company. His children, Glenda (Maxton), Marty, Robert, and Richard, all work at Kitzmiller's, Inc. His brother Richard originally had planned to join Clarence when the business first started, but decided at the last minute to keep his job as a security guard at New Cumberland Depot. He later came to work for the enterprise and retired in 1983 as a superintendent.

The company has been located on Bosler Avenue in Lemoyne, Orchard

The Kitzmiller family goes back to the early beginnings of Pennsylvania history. This Revolutionary War officer is buried in Christ Reformed Cemetery in Littlestown.

Kitzmiller's, Inc., located in the Manor section of New Cumberland, is a family-owned and -operated business. Posing with Clarence Kitzmiller (second from left) are (left to right) sons Marty, Bob, and Rick, with Brady Maxton behind his grandfather.

Road in Lower Allen Township, and Bridge Street in New Cumberland. In 1982 Kitzmiller's, Inc., moved to 1605 Elm Street. Kitzmiller bought that facility in 1976 and moved his firm there after extensive remodeling. But he must have been thinking about that move for a long time. It was the site of the old Elkwood Building, where he first went to work as a roofer back in 1947.

G.S. ROCKEY COMPANY, INC.

G.S. Roksandic, founder of the G.S. Rockey Company, was the son of East European immigrants to America. His mother was from Poland, his father from Serbia. The Roksandics settled in Steelton, where their sons (G.S. was one of five children) became well-known basketball players.

During World War II Roksandic served in the Ordnance Corps as a supply sergeant. It proved to be valuable training, and he found that he liked the business. After the war he accepted a job with Harris Company, a local office supply dealer.

The family moved from Steelton to the Swatara Township community of Rutherford in 1960. Roksandic started his own office supply firm in 1963. It was located in the basement of the family's home at 6620 Mifflin Avenue. Roksandic's son, George T. Roksandic, remembers helping move supplies

scheduled for the day's deliveries up from the basement every morning before school. George Sr. was the salesman and buyer for the company. His wife, Catherine, handled the phones and office duties for the first two years. She quit when their son John was born; they hired Helen Brady as bookkeeper and office manager at that time.

G.S. Rockey Company, Inc., moved to its current location at 6340 Derry Street in 1965. It was a small facility, little larger than a two-car garage. Two additions and leased warehouse space have since allowed the firm to expand significantly. That expansion became necessary as the business started working with major clients such as Hershey Foods, Berg Electronics, and United Telephone.

George T. Roksandic, current vice-president of the G.S. Rockey Company,

was an undergraduate microbiology major at the University of Pittsburgh and is a graduate of the University of Pittsburgh School of Dental Medicine. He spent three years as a dentist in the army, and when he says that the office supply business is "much harder than pulling teeth," he speaks from experience. He joined the family business in 1976, shortly after his discharge from the service.

The G.S. Rockey Company now has 21 employees, is expanding its marketing activities to Carlisle and York, and is becoming involved with computer system sales and service. An extensive remodeling and expansion completed in 1983 has made space for the new marketing activities.

From left to right are George T. Roksandic and his father, G.S. Roksandic, founder of the G.S. Rockey Company, Inc.

KINNEY SHOE CORPORATION

Few businesses have made a more lasting impression on Harrisburg than Kinney Shoes, founded by George Romanta Kinney in 1894. Greater Harrisburg has played a central role in the history of Kinney Shoes. And Kinney Shoes has become one of the leading industries of the region.

G.R. Kinney opened his first shoe store in Waverly, New York, and his second in Corning, New York. But he showed early interest in Pennsylvania. His third store was located in Wilkes-Barre and his fifth in Reading. Kinney's first Harrisburg store was one of the first 15 in his nationwide chain.

G.R. Kinney died in 1919. At the time, his chain included 62 stores with an annual sales volume over $14 million. Edwin H. Krom, a boyhood friend of Kinney's and an early associate in the company, became president of the corporation.

Krom decided to expand corporate activities to include manufacturing. He realized that this also would require major new warehousing and distribution facilities. This expansion program brought Kinney Shoes to Harrisburg.

In October 1919 Krom acquired

Kinney's first Harrisburg store, founded in 1909, was at 1200 North Third Street. Today there are seven Kinney stores in the greater Harrisburg area.

George Romanta Kinney (left), founder of the Kinney Shoe Corporation, and Milner Kemp, cobbler (right), pose in front of Kinney's first store in Waverly, New York, for this 1894 photo.

three regional shoe manufacturers and took over their factories. They included Johnson-Baillie Shoe Company in Millersburg, Bedford Shoe in Carlisle, and J.R. Landis Shoe Company in Palmyra. (He also bought a fourth plant in Huntington, West Virginia.)

To support this growing network of plants and stores, Kinney Shoes decided to add a Harrisburg warehouse and distribution center to existing facilities in Boston and Chicago. In 1919 the company leased its first Harrisburg facility at 325 Market Street.

Just two years later Kinney had

outgrown its expanded warehouse and distribution system. The firm decided to close the Boston and Chicago operations and concentrate on Harrisburg. It selected a Second Street site held by the Frank McCormick estate. But purchasing the property proved more difficult than anticipated.

Edgar Dimm, a longtime Kinney executive, remembers hearing that some Harrisburg business leaders objected to the move and tried to stop it. He recalls that Kinney had a reputation of paying wages that were considerably higher than the established local scale. They may also have been responding to the desires of local shoe retailers.

For whatever reason, it is clear that pressures were brought to bear on the trustees, and the sale was almost blocked. Kinney was able to complete the purchase only with the help of Frank Payne, an Elizabethtown shoe manufacturer (and Kinney supplier), who acted as a "straw man" and bought the property on behalf of

Kinney. Payne later became a Kinney executive.

Kinney Shoe Corporation completed its South Second Street warehouse (now owned by Gable Hardware) in June 1921. It completed a major expansion in 1924. By then Kinney Shoes had made a substantial commitment to central Pennsylvania. In addition to the warehouse and distribution center, the corporation had three of its four factories there, and seven stores. (At the time Kinney had 207 stores nationwide, including 32 in Pennsylvania).

But Harrisburg was not yet through making things a little uncomfortable for the shoe company. In 1927 the city undertook a general improvement program, which included construction of the Paxton Street Bridge, regrading Second Street, and relocating all railroad tracks. The new warehouse was threatened. Two years of negotiations and legal proceedings were required before the project went forward and portions of the warehouse center were destroyed. By 1930 a new expansion program was

under way to replace the lost facilities. The remodeled complex was completed in 1940.

Kinney Shoes was a publicly owned corporation until 1956, when it was acquired by the Brown Shoe Company. At the time Brown was the nation's leading shoe manufacturer, and Kinney the leading retailer. An antitrust suit forced dissolution of the partnership, and Kinney was sold to F.W. Woolworth in 1963.

Kinney Shoe Corporation today is an international retail company with extensive operations in Canada and Australia as well as the United States, where it also is one of the largest manufacturers of footwear. Sales for 1982 exceeded $1.1 billion.

The corporation has become involved with extensive public service activities. These include a major program of consumer education, sponsorship of a world-class track meet, and sponsorship of a national competition for high school cross-country runners.

President of Kinney Shoes is Cameron I. Anderson. Anderson is the son of a long-term Kinney store manager, and helped deliver promotional flyers and sell shoes as a young man. He became president in 1979. Harold C. Rowen is senior executive vice-president. Claude

Cameron I. Anderson, president of Kinney Shoe Corporation.

Lewis, Jr., is executive vice-president.

The headquarters of Kinney Shoes is in New York City, but many corporate operations employing more than 2,200 people are located in central Pennsylvania. There are seven Kinney retail stores in the area, along with several of the company's other retail operations. These include a Susie's Casuals store and a Foot Locker store in Harrisburg.

In addition to retail stores, regional corporate activities include factories in Millersburg, Palmyra, and Carlisle. Mechanicsburg is home to distribution facilities for Kinney Shoes, Stylco, Susie's Casuals, Frugal Frank's, and Fredelle divisions, as well as the Quality Control Center. The Kinco (outside sales) distribution center is in Carlisle.

Kinney Shoes' main warehouse and national distribution center is located in Camp Hill. The sprawling, 600,000-square-foot complex also houses the corporate Retail Accounting Center and Management Information Center. Kinney Shoes today is the largest single taxpayer in Cumberland County. Those folks sure sell a lot of shoes.

Kinney Shoe Corporation's Distribution Complex in Camp Hill includes warehousing operations for Kinney Shoes and other retail divisions, and houses the Retail Accounting Center and Management Information Center.

R.T. GRIM COMPANY

When Grim & Company opened for business in September 1928, things couldn't have looked better. C.L. Grim and his two sons, Clair Grim and Russel T. Grim (later joined by brother Raymond L. Grim), were riding the crest of technological revolution. Clair Grim had been experimenting with radio (amateur license 3 BBV) since 1916. The firm had agreements to sell Crosley and Amrad sets, "the best values in the low- and high-priced fields." And the brothers already were experimenting with television.

Then came the Great Depression. Radio had been the glamour industry of the Roaring '20s but was one of the most severely depressed during the decade that followed. The company survived for a while on the repair business, but when Clair Grim quit, it looked like the firm would have to close.

Instead, it was purchased by Evelyn Brunner, an employee of a Harrisburg wholesale radio distributor. She, along with Russel T. Grim, reorganized the business, dropped the sales activities, concentrated on service and repair work, and changed the firm's name to the R.T. Grim Company. She also changed her own name to Mrs. R.T. Grim.

All radio equipment was in scarce supply during World War II. Bob Grim, the current president, remembers hearing his parents talk about the extreme security precautions they took to protect their stock of spare parts.

After the war the R.T. Grim Company became involved with a new national craze—radios installed in automobiles—and the firm has remained active as a car radio repair specialist. Since 1976 it also has been a wholesaler of automobile sound systems.

The original office, shop, and laboratory of the R.T. Grim Company at 1849 Market Street in Camp Hill.

"The service business has become highly specialized," says Bob Grim. "Many small towns have no one who can service car radios. So dealers and radio shops send radios here for the actual work. We never abandoned radio repair."

R.T. Grim died in 1963. His wife Evelyn took over the business, running it with the help of his brother Raymond and one employee. Bob Grim took over in 1969, when he returned from service as an Air Force pilot. Since then, renewed public interest in radio, company contracts for repair of computer components for automobile climate controls and engines, and expanded marketing activities have stimulated growth. The firm now has about 40 employees. In 1982 it repaired 6,100 radios and remanufactured 12,000 engine computer modules and 32,000 electronic climate-control systems.

It also continued the family's traditional repair service (including warranty service for numerous manufacturers). These days, the R.T. Grim Company works on home audio and video systems as well as repairing radios. And one other thing has changed. In 1928 the typical radio repair cost $1.50. These days, the charge is a little higher.

Floral tributes joined the newest and finest radios available on Grim & Company's opening day in September 1928.

HERSHEY CREAMERY COMPANY

Whether you prefer chocolate, vanilla, strawberry, or any other flavor of ice cream, you'll love Hershey Creamery Company. This modern, efficient corporation headquartered in its Cameron Street, Harrisburg, complex, owner of a large fleet of trucks, employer of more than 300 area residents, is the home of Hershey's ice cream. Inside its plant, massive tanks, freezers, and other industrial equipment is dedicated to providing us with that ultimate taste treat—cool, thick, rich, and delicious ice cream.

The four Hershey brothers who started the company at the turn of the century were Lancaster County farmers. For years their homemade ice cream was a community favorite. They started making it in 1894, packing it in their own, specially designed metal-lined wooden containers. Horse-drawn wagons made daily deliveries to markets, ice cream parlors, and private homes.

The salesmen packed each storage cabinet with a fresh supply of ice just before delivery. In those pre-refrigerator days, Hershey's often delivered more ice than ice cream. But the extra care paid off, and demand for Hershey's ice cream grew rapidly. The firm moved to its Cameron Street location to better serve that widening territory.

During the Great Depression Hershey's adopted a new marketing concept, becoming the first ice cream manufacturer to offer its product in prepackaged pints and quarts. It was the start of the "carry-out" era, and it took ice cream out of the luxury category (except in calories), making it a readily available, popular treat.

Fritz Nelson, Hershey vice-president and secretary, has been with the firm for 50 years. He still remembers the pre-electric freezer days when returning drivers had to wash down the brine-packed cans before the day's work was done. (Today Hershey's entire truck fleet is still washed thoroughly, inside and out, after every run.)

After World War II Hershey's added its line of novelty items including Popsicles, ice cream sandwiches, coated ice cream bars, and other favorites. The popularity of ice cream on a stick led to further plant expansion. Today Hershey's specially developed high-speed equipment produces, molds, freezes, wraps, and boxes over 600,000 Popsicles a day during periods of peak demand.

While the technology has come a long way since the hand-cranking of 1894, the quality and care that go into the product remain true to Hershey's heritage. Nuts are still inspected and roasted on the premises. All syrups are made in the plant. The company even supplies dealers with its own cabinets and freezers.

Hershey's is a publicly owned corporation. George H. Holder is chairman of the board and president. George Hugh Holder is vice-president and sales manager. Hershey's ice cream is sold in 15 states through 21 distribution centers. That's a far cry from the Lancaster County, horse-and-wagon days.

HERSHEY ENTERTAINMENT & RESORT COMPANY

This photo, taken in 1933, shows The Hotel Hershey as it neared completion. In its half-century history the hotel has hosted Presidents, celebrities, foreign dignitaries, and countless other honored guests.

The Hershey Entertainment & Resort Company, HERCO Inc., was incorporated in 1927 and originally called Hershey Estates. Its mission was to be responsible for all of the nonchocolate-producing business activities of Milton Hershey's growing empire. HERCO Inc. today is an independent, privately held corporation. It is wholly owned by the Hershey Trust Company, trustee in trust for Milton Hershey School.

The oldest HERCO property is Hersheypark, first opened in 1907. One of America's finest theme parks, Hersheypark is the home of an operating antique Carrousel, a 330-foot Kissing Tower, the sooperdooper-Looper (the first loop coaster in the East), and several other famed rides.

Hersheypark's ZooAmerica_{sm}, a 10-acre environmental zoo, features animals and plants in their natural habitats.

Hersheypark Arena has been the home of the American Hockey League Hershey Bears and major ice shows

and concerts since the 1930s. Other sports and entertainment facilities include Hersheypark Stadium, Hershey Gardens, and enough golf courses to make Hershey the golf capital of Pennsylvania. Hershey Country Club's West Course is the site of the annual LPGA Lady Keystone Open tournament. Ben Hogan was golf pro for 10 years at Hershey Country Club.

The Hotel Hershey is the crown jewel of HERCO Inc.'s hotel and resort properties. Opened in 1933, The Hotel Hershey has been a favorite resort for President and Mrs. Eisenhower, John F. Kennedy, and explorer/writer Lowell Thomas. In its dining room Metropolitan Opera diva Frieda Hempel once entertained a group of soldiers with an impromptu concert of "Dixie" and "Home Sweet Home."

Other HERCO Inc. properties include The Hershey Lodge & Convention Center (opened 1967), The Pocono Hershey Resort (1976), The Hershey Philadelphia Hotel (1983), and The Hershey Corpus Christi Hotel (1984). The corporation also owns and operates Hershey Highmeadow Campground, Hershey Drug Store, Hershey Meats &

Commissary, Hershey Nursery, and other commercial operations.

Chairman of the board and chief executive officer of HERCO Inc. is Edward R. Book; president and chief operating officer is Kenneth V. Hatt; executive vice-president and chief financial officer is Robert A. Houck; senior vice-president is J. Bruce McKinney.

In its earlier days, just as it has today, Hersheypark had a special section for younger visitors. This 1940s photo shows the children's Ferris wheel.

ESHENAURS INC.

The Roaring '20s were going all out back in 1928 when Walter C. Eshenaur, Sr., established his new plumbing, heating, and air conditioning business. He set up his one-man operation in his parents' home at 1626 North Street. Later, as the business started to expand, he moved to his own home at 1915 North Street and ran the company from his garage.

The Great Depression slowed things briefly, but W.C. Eshenaurs continued to grow. In 1938 the firm moved to 2838 Booser Avenue in Harrisburg. In 1951 it added fuel oil deliveries to its other services.

In 1955 Walter C. Eshenaur, Sr., formally incorporated W.C. Eshenaurs Inc. in order to continue handling residential and small commercial accounts, as well as fuel oil sales. At this time he also created Eshenaurs Inc. as a company that would specialize in industrial and large commercial mechanical contracting.

Eshenaurs Fuels, Inc., was formed in 1962 as the direct heir to W.C. Eshenaurs Inc. The new company continued to perform residential and light commercial work in addition to

Eshenaurs Inc. used this truck to make service calls in 1939.

fuel oil sales. Thus, Eshenaurs Fuels, Inc., became the firm which had the most direct contact with the general Harrisburg area public. Eshenaurs Inc., on the other hand, became a large and well-known mechanical contractor, working primarily with large commercial and industrial applications.

Eshenaurs Inc., which currently employs about 135 persons, is a closely held corporation. The president is Walter C. Eshenaur, Jr., although Walter C. Eshenaur, Sr., remains active as the chairman of the board of directors. Other corporate officers include vice-president Charles Zogby, secretary Richard Mummert, and treasurer Lori Eshenaur. Eshenaurs Inc. has performed major mechanical contracting work for such clients as Pennsylvania Blue Shield, Harrisburg Hospital, Holy Spirit Hospital, and the Harrisburg School District.

Eshenaurs Fuels, Inc., with a work force of approximately 55 persons, is

also a closely held corporation that has successfully operated as an independent concern since its inception. Although both Walter Sr. and Walter Jr. were officers with Eshenaurs Fuels when it was incorporated in 1962, John Miller is the current president. Other officers include vice-president Robert Stahle and secretary/treasurer Cindy Eshenaur Beck.

While Eshenaurs Fuels primarily handles residential and smaller commercial accounts, it has performed work for Berg Electronics (now part of Du Pont), Nationwide Insurance, and the Blue Ridge Country Club. Eshenaurs Fuels storage tanks hold more than 1.1 million gallons of fuel oil. That capacity enabled the business to service its customers without interruption throughout the oil crisis of the 1970s.

Walter C. Eshenaur, Sr., founder of Eshenaurs Inc.

IBM FIELD ENGINEERING DIVISION

IBM Corporation's Field Engineering Division's distribution center is located in Mechanicsburg. Headquartered in Franklin Lakes, New Jersey, the Field Engineering Division provides maintenance and related services for IBM's intermediate and larger information-processing systems. The critical flow of parts and publications needed to support IBM's products and programs is coordinated at the Field Engineering Division's Mechanicsburg distribution center.

The Harrisburg area's proximity to IBM plants and customers first placed this important operation at Mechanicsburg in 1958. The new distribution center, located at 180 Kost Road, was completed in 1982.

The facility consists of three interconnected sections. An 82,000-square-foot administration building is linked by covered walkway to a 254,000-square-foot operations facility where orders for parts and publications are processed. A third unit, the high-rise 70,000-square-foot unit load building, provides storage for palletized parts and publications.

Moving this critical IBM distribution facility from its Trindle Road location to the new facility in 1982 was a difficult and carefully choreographed operation. Members of the administration team were the first to occupy the new complex, followed by the publications staff. Parts and publications people made a phased transition from the old to the new facility through the spring and summer of 1982. The move involved over 400 people, 90,000 parts, and 41,000 documents. It was completed with no service disruption and no significant delay in the processing of orders.

In a typical 24-hour day at the Mechanicsburg distribution center, approximately 105,000 parts and publications items are processed. The task requires a combination of skilled, dedicated people and a highly

The largest distribution center for IBM Corporation's Field Engineering Division is located in Mechanicsburg at 180 Kost Road. Copyright 1982, Jon Naar.

The critical flow of parts and publications needed to support IBM's products and programs is handled by highly sophisticated equipment. Copyright 1982, Jon Naar.

sophisticated inventory-handling system.

The Mechanicsburg system is controlled by an IBM System/370 Model 158 and two Series 1 Models with full back-up. In the high-rise unit load building, seven 80-foot-high cranes travel along 483-foot tracks. The cranes store and retrieve 37,000 pallet loads of parts and publications, each weighing up to a ton. The system can handle 300 pallet loads an hour.

As the cranes ply the seven aisles in the storage complex, they are serviced

by 13 "robocarriers," signal-controlled pallet-carrying devices that bring loads to and from the high-rise unit load area.

The battery-powered robocarriers travel at 200 feet a minute, controlled by radio frequency signals carried through 2,400 feet of wire recessed in the concrete floor. They transport pallet loads to a platform area where order processors and specialists pull the desired items. The pallets are returned via robocarrier to the storage building where a crane automatically

places them in the most efficient locations.

The facility also features a 21-aisle mini-load area which stocks 95 percent of Mechanicsburg's parts items. Parts are stored from the floor level and picked from a mezzanine level. The two levels provide a total of 42 work stations, serviced by 21 cranes traveling on 78-foot tracks. They are capable of processing 1,300 line items an hour from the area's 23,000 storage bins. Each crane can carry a 500-pound load.

In the publications department, orders are entered via terminals at IBM branch offices worldwide. The

The skilled, dedicated employees enjoy many benefits at the IBM facility, such as a modern cafeteria and recreational facilities. Copyright 1982, Jon Naar.

information is transmitted to Tampa, Florida, to initiate transactions, then relayed to Mechanicsburg for fulfillment. Publications employees work with an inventory of 35,000 different hard copy publications and 6,000 microfiche items.

A fleet of 43 mobile publications tuggers is utilized to accomplish the three-shift publications mission. An IBM computer organizes the work by determining the physical size of each

document stored in the data base. With this information, the system optimizes the available space on each publications-processing module and sequences the orders by picking location. This processing method permits the filling of up to 192 orders during one trip by a tugger through the storage area. The computer also adds up the weight of each document and automatically displays the most economical method of shipment. The system then applies appropriate postage for shipment.

Such functions as accounting, personnel, purchasing, and planning are carried out by Mechanicsburg people working with five functions—Personnel and Administration, Field Parts Support, Parts Planning and Inventory Control, Plans and Controls, and Field Distribution Operations—in the administration building.

IBM traces its history to the 1911 merger of three companies—Computing Scale of Dayton, Ohio, Tabulating Machine Company of Washington, D.C., and International Time Recording of Endicott, New York. The new venture, Computing-Tabulating-Recording Company, adopted a new name, International Business Machines Corporation, in 1924.

In 1914 the firm had 770 stockholders, 1,346 employees, and a gross income of $4 million. In 1957 IBM's gross income first topped one billion dollars. One year later the Electric Typewriter Division produced its millionth typewriter. By 1969 IBM had more than 549,000 stockholders and 258,000 employees. By 1980 the company had a worldwide total of approximately 340,000 employees and a consolidated gross income of $26.2 billion.

Greater Harrisburg can take great pride in IBM's Mechanicsburg Field Engineering distribution center and in being part of this great international corporation.

INDEPENDENT BANKERS OF PENNSYLVANIA

In 1973 the state legislature was considering a new law that would allow banks and savings and loan associations to establish branches throughout the Commonwealth. The law was actively supported by some of the state's largest and most powerful banks—especially those based in Pittsburgh and Philadelphia.

Statewide banking was opposed by Pennsylvania's community banks. These locally owned banks are operated by people who know and are concerned primarily about meeting the financial needs of their own communities. They were concerned that statewide branching would bring powerful new banks into their communities—banks that could not respond to local issues and requirements.

The statewide banking question split and neutralized the Pennsylvania Bankers Association. The way seemed clear for the impersonal banking corporations to carry the issue through the state legislature. But the community bankers decided to form their own organization to make a goal line stand on statewide banking.

The Independent Bankers Association of America sent an organizer who met with 37 community bankers at Harrisburg's Host Inn. Among the founders were James Taylor and Reed Albig of McKeesport, Harold Bossard of Bernville, and Congressman D. Emmert Brumbaugh of Claysburg. The Harrisburg area was represented by William L. Shoap of Hummelstown.

On the day of the senate vote, hundreds of community bankers came to Harrisburg to speak to their representatives. The crucial vote was a tie; statewide branching was defeated.

Independent Bankers of Pennsylvania's victory provided a 10-year respite. A similar measure became law in 1982, and competition for banking services has also come to many communities from such nontraditional sources as brokerage houses, insurance companies, and Sears, Roebuck & Co. During that period, Independent Bankers grew into a full-service professional trade association.

Independent Bankers still is actively involved with legislation, but now it is moving to provide new educational and other support services for its member institutions. It has just chartered its own bankers' bank, the Pennsylvania Independent Bank. This new institution will help the bankers keep local control of their own banks while offering customers many of the

C.B. (Lee) Shank, president of Independent Bankers of Pennsylvania.

efficiencies and services previously available only through larger companies.

Harrisburg area members of the Independent Bankers of Pennsylvania include CCNB, N.A. (New Cumberland), Dauphin National Bank, Farmers Bank and Trust Company (Hummelstown), First Bank and Trust Company (Mechanicsburg), and First National Bank of Marysville. The association has more than 160 members. Officers are C.B. (Lee) Shank, president; Leslie D. Eshelman, first vice-president; Ronald H. Frey, second vice-president; Wayne T. Wright, secretary; and William L. Shoap, treasurer. Bruce A. Senft is executive director.

The Pennsylvania Center, at 3425 Simpson Ferry Road, is the headquarters of Independent Bankers of Pennsylvania.

MANPOWER, INC., OF HARRISBURG

The headquarters office of Manpower, Inc., of Harrisburg is at 2929 North Front Street.

What do Mamie Eisenhower, the Notre Dame football team, and a traveling carnival all have in common? Simple. All three have used the temporary employee services of Manpower, Inc., of Harrisburg. Mamie Eisenhower needed an extra driver when she was moving antiques out of the family farm in Gettysburg. Notre Dame needed someone to transport the team uniforms and equipment to State College. The carnival needed people to pack little plastic bags with elephant manure as part of a promotional campaign.

Manpower, Inc., is a temporary-help service that assists companies in meeting temporary employment requirements. Manpower provides temporary help for clerical, labor, light assembly, chauffeur, delivery, or other positions needed by business, industry, or government.

Manpower was founded in 1948 in Milwaukee and Chicago by two lawyers, Elmer Winter and Aaron Schenfeldt. It has more than 700 offices in 32 countries. Since 1976 it has been a wholly owned subsidiary of Parker Pen.

The Harrisburg franchise was founded in May 1964 by Melvin Griffith. Its first offices were at 14 North Fourth Street. John D. Grabau, the current owner and president, bought the company in February 1966. At the time its assets consisted of one full-time employee, two desks, and three file cabinets.

The one employee who was with the company when Grabau acquired it was Carole A. Taylor. She currently is vice-president and general manager; the firm now has 10 full-time employees, 800 client companies, and 1,120 temporary employees. Its main office is at 2929 North Front Street in Harrisburg, with branch offices at 309 South 10th Street in Lemoyne and at 900 Eisenhower Boulevard.

Manpower temporaries have helped keep the work flowing at the Pennsylvania Bureau of Vital Statistics while the office was being moved; they have demonstrated toys for Sears and worked in grocery stores offering samples. One took a note pad and donned boots and overalls to accompany an insurance adjuster through the ruins of a major Harrisburg fire.

Today most of Manpower's temporary employees are young men between regular jobs, and women returning to the job force after several years of working in the home. "It's exciting to watch some of these women," says Taylor. "At first, they have no confidence in their job skills. But after a few months they really become self-assured. Lots of them end up with high-level, permanent jobs."

There are many other unusual fringe benefits for temporary workers. The drivers who took Notre Dame's equipment to University Park were invited to attend the football game. One truck driver got his first plane ride as a result of a Manpower assignment. The crew who worked for the carnival got to keep all the samples they wanted. Oh well, that's show business.

Patrons

The following individuals, companies, and organizations have made a valuable commitment to the quality of this publication. Windsor Publications and the Chamber of Commerce of the Greater Harrisburg Area gratefully acknowledge their participation in *Life by the Moving Road: An Illustrated History of Greater Harrisburg.*

Albert L. Allen Company, Inc.*
AMP Incorporated*
Aycock, Inc.*
Benatec Associates, Inc.*
Berman, Boswell & Tintner*
Judge Genevieve Blatt
Caldwell, Clouser & Kearns
Capital Blue Cross*
Frank M. Caswell, Jr.
Commonwealth National Bank*
E.N. Dunlap, Inc.
Eshenaurs Inc.*
The Farmers Bank and Trust Company of Hummelstown*
Feinerman Insurance
Gable's, Inc.
Gannett Fleming, Inc.*
Jack Gaughen
R.T. Grim Company*

Harrisburg Academy*
Harrisburg Area Community College*
Hershey Creamery Company*
Hershey Entertainment & Resort Company*
Homestead Savings Association
Hood, Light and Geise, Inc.*
Ralph D. Huston
IBM Field Engineering Division*
Iceland Seafood Corporation*
Inclinator Company of America*
Independent Bankers of Pennsylvania*
Kessler's, Inc.*
The Law Firm of Killian & Gephart
Kinney Shoe Corporation*
Kitzmiller's, Inc.*
Earl Latsha Lumber Company*
Paul McConnell, Inc., Electrical Contractor
McNees, Wallace and Nurick*
Manpower, Inc., of Harrisburg*
Merchants and Business Men's Mutual Insurance Company*
Miller Oral Surgery, Inc.
Dr. & Mrs. Benjamin G. Musser
Nationwide Insurance Company*
Novinger's, Inc.*
Olewine's Incorporated*
Patriot-News Publishing Company*

Pennsylvania Blue Shield*
Pennsylvania Credit Union League*
Pennsylvania Medical Society*
Pennsylvania National Mutual Casualty Insurance Company*
PHICO Insurance Group*
The Quaker Oats Company*
Reynolds, Bihl & Schaffner
Rite Aid Corporation*
G.S. Rockey Company, Inc.*
R.J. Romberger & Sons*
Shammo's Quality Foods*
Shamrock Rapid Delivery Service, Inc.
Sherman Associates
Shumaker and Williams
Chas. D. Snyder & Son, Inc.
A.B. Springer
Stephenson's Flower Shops*
TRW, Inc.*
United Republic Life Insurance Company*
Wert Bookbinding, Inc.*

*Partners in Progress of *Life by the Moving Road: An Illustrated History of Greater Harrisburg.* The histories of these companies and organizations appear in Chapter 17, beginning on page 151.

BIBLIOGRAPHY

Published Sources

Allen, Jean Gray. "One Hundred Stepping Stones, 1860-1960, Harrisburg Centennial." In *Harrisburg Centennial Celebration, 1860-1960* (Official Program). Harrisburg, Pa.: n.p., 1960, pp. 15-35.

Ayres, George Bucher. "The Burning of John Harris. Reeder's Painting." *Papers of the Historical Society of Dauphin County*, vol. 1, n.d., pp. 37-41.

Beers, Paul. *Profiles from the Susquehanna Valley*. Harrisburg, Pa.: Stackpole Books, 1973.

_____ . *Pennsylvania Politics, Today and Yesterday; The Tolerable Accommodation*. University Park, Pa.: Pennsylvania State University Press, 1980.

Bell, Margaret Van Horn (Dwight). *A Journey to Ohio in 1810 as Recorded in the Journal of Margaret Van Horn Dwight*. Ed. Max Farrand. New Haven: Yale University Press, 1912.

Bigart, Homer. "A Quiet Setting for a Big Trial; Harrisburg Awaits Opening Today of Berrigan Case." *New York Times*, January 24, 1972, p. 12, col. 3.

Bodnar, John. "The Formation of Ethnic Consciousness: Slavic Immigrants in Steelton." In *The Ethnic Experience in Pennsylvania*. Ed. Bodnar. Lewisburg, Pa.: Bucknell University Press, 1973, pp. 309-330.

_____ . *Immigration and Industrialization: Ethnicity in an American Mill Town, 1870-1940*. Pittsburgh: University of Pittsburgh Press, 1977.

Book, Janet Mae. *Northern Rendezvous*. Harrisburg, Pa.: Telegraph Press, 1951.

Boyer, Richard, and David Savageau. *Places Rated Almanac*. Chicago: Rand McNally, 1981

Cochran, Thomas C. *Pennsylvania; A Bicentennial History*. New York: W.W. Norton, 1978.

Coleman, Michael B. *The Jews of Harrisburg, An Informal History by a Native Son*. Harrisburg, Pa.: privately published, 1978.

Constitution, By-Laws, and Rules of Order, of Central Division, No. 10, of the Sons of Temperance, of the State of Pennsylvania. Harrisburg, Pa.: J.A. Spofford, 1845.

Dauphin County Historical Review. Vol. 1, 1952-Vol. 14, 1966.

Davis, Amelia, Carl Oblinger, and David McBride, eds. *Glimpses into Our Lives: Memories of Harrisburg's Black Senior Citizens*. Harrisburg, Pa.: Pennsylvania Historical and Museum Commission, 1978.

Day, Dorothy. "Tale of Two Capitals." *Commonweal*, July 14, 1939, pp. 289-290.

Dewitt, William R. *Profanity and Intemperance, Prevailing Evils*. Harrisburg, Pa.: Fenn and Wallace, 1840. Printed for the Young Men's and Young Ladies' Total Abstinence Society of Harrisburg.

Dill, Malcolm H. *Planning for the Future of the Harrisburg Area; Report of the Harrisburg Area Regional Planning Committee of the Municipal League of Harrisburg, Pennsylvania*. Harrisburg, Pa.: Municipal League of Harrisburg, 1940.

Donehoo, George P. *Harrisburg, The City Beautiful, Romantic, and Historic*. Harrisburg, Pa.: Telegraph Press, 1927.

Egle, William Henry. "Old Times and Old People." *Papers of the HSDC*, vol. 2, n.d., pp. 75-103.

_____ . *History of the Counties of Dauphin and Lebanon in the Commonwealth of Pennsylvania: Biographical and Genealogical*. Philadelphia: Everts and Peck, 1883.

_____ , ed. *Centenary Memorial of the Erection of the County of Dauphin and the Founding of the City of Harrisburg*. Harrisburg, Pa.: Telegraph Printing House, 1886.

First Annual Report of the Board of Trustees of the State Lunatic Hospital of the State of Pennsylvania. Harrisburg, Pa.: Theo. Fenn and Co., 1852.

Frew, Ken. "Tales From 'Pancake Row.'" *Harrisburg Heritage; Monthly Newsletter of the Historic Harrisburg Association, Inc*. August, 1978, pp. 1-5.

Garraty, John. *The American Nation*. 2 vols., 3rd ed. New York: Harper and Row, 1975

Harrisburg; A Walk Through History. Harrisburg, Pa.: Harrisburg Branch, American Association of University Women, and Historic Harrisburg Association, 1981.

Harrisburg, Pennsylvania, As Seen by the Carrier Boys of Harrisburg's Greatest Home Newspaper, the Daily Telegraph. Harrisburg, Pa.: Telegraph Press, 1904.

Harrisburg, Pennsylvania Industrial Survey, Harrisburg Chamber of Commerce, 1928.

Hiler, Jean. "Dr. John Curwen and Victorian Psychiatry in Pennsylvania." M.A. Thesis, Pennsylvania State University, Capitol Campus, 1981.

Huston, Ralph D. *No—Back and Over*. Privately published, 1975.

Inglewood, Marian. *Then and Now in Harrisburg*. Harrisburg, Pa.: n.p., 1925.

Keefer, Horace Andrew. "Early Iron Industries in Dauphin County." *Publications of the Dauphin County Historical Society, 1927*

Kelker, Luther Reily. *History of Dauphin County*. 3 vols. New York: Lewis Pub. Co., 1907.

Klein, Philip S., and Ari Hoogenboom. *A History of Pennsylvania*. 2nd ed. University Park, Pa.: Pennsylvania

State University Press, 1980.

Klein, Theodore. "Hot Times in Harrisburg; The Fire Boys from 1837-1871." *Papers of the Historical Society of Dauphin County*, vol. 1, n.d., pp. 61-71.

_____ . "East Market Street When I Was a Boy." *Papers of the Historical Society of Dauphin County*, vol. 1, n.d., pp. 23-33.

Laverty, George Lauman. *History of Medicine in Dauphin County Pennsylvania*.

Lewis, C. *Temperance. Lecture Delivered in the Lochiel Church, Saturday, February 6, 1869*. Harrisburg, Pa.: Sieg, pr. State Guard, 1869.

Maclay, William. *The Journal of William Maclay*. 1890; rpt. New York: Albert and Charles Boni, 1927.

Milspaw, Yvonne J. "Folklore and the Nuclear Age: The Harrisburg Disaster at Three Mile Island." *International Folklore Review*, 1 (1981), pp. 57-65.

Morgan, George H. *Annals of Harrisburg*. rev. ed. by L. Frances Morgan Black. n.p. 1906.

Myers, Richmond E. *The Long Crooked River*. Boston: Christopher Publishing House, 1949.

Orwig, J.R. *The Harrisburg Visitors' Guide, 1876, for the Use of Strangers Visiting the City*. Harrisburg, Pa.: Patriot Publishing Co., 1876.

Pardoe, Hiles C. *Up the Susquehanna*. New York: Hunt and Eaton, 1895.

Patriot, The (Harrisburg)

Polk's Greater Harrisburg City Directory. Vol. 70. Boston: R.L. Polk, 1946.

Prolix, Peregrine. (pseud.) *Journey Through Pennsylvania—1835—By Canal, Rail and Stage Coach*. Intro. William H. Shank. 1836; rpt. York, Pa.: American Canal and Transportation Center, 1975.

Proposed Municipal Improvements for Harrisburg, Pa.; Report of the Executive Committee to Subscribers to Fund for Investigating Municipal Improvements, Nov. 21, 1901. n.p.

Report of the Trustees and Superintendent of the State Lunatic Hospital of Pennsylvania, 1858. Harrisburg, Pa.: A. Boyd Hamilton, 1859.

Rupp, I. Daniel. *The History and Topography of Dauphin, Cumberland, Franklin, Bedford, Adams, and Perry Counties*. Lancaster, Pa.: Gilbert Hills, 1846.

Schulman, Jay, Phillip Shaver, Robert Colman, Barbara Emrich, and Richard Christie. "Recipe For a Jury." *Psychology Today*, May 1973, pp. 37-44, 77-84.

Snavely, Joseph Richard. *The Story of Hershey, The Chocolate Town*. Hershey, Pa.: n.p., 1953

J.A. Spofford's Harrisburg Directory for 1843. Harrisburg, Pa.: J.A. Spofford, 1843.

Stamm, A.C. "The Progress of Harrisburg." *Publications of the Historical Society of Dauphin County*. April 15, 1935.

Steinmetz, G.M., and Robert Hammond Murray. *Twenty-five Years of Service; The Penn Harris Hotel*. Harrisburg, Pa.: Telegraph Press, 1943.

Steinmetz, Richard, Sr., and Robert Hoffsommer. *This Was Harrisburg*. Harrisburg, Pa.: Stackpole Books, 1976.

Stevens, Sylvester K. *Pennsylvania, Birthplace of a Nation*. New York: Random House, 1964.

Sunday Patriot-News (Harrisburg), "'82 Newcomers Guide," September 19, 1982.

Tocqueville, Alexis de. *Democracy in America*. Ed. Phillips Bradley. New York: Vintage Books, 1945.

Trautmann, Frederick, ed. "Pennsylvania Through a German's Eyes: The Travels of Ludwig Gall, 1819-1820." *Pennsylvania Magazine of History and Biography*, 105 (January 1981), pp. 35-65.

U.S. Immigration Commission. *Reports of the U.S.I.C.: Immigrants in Industries, Part 2: Iron and Steel*, 2 vols. S. Doc. 633, 61st Cong. 2nd Sess. Serial 5669 (1911), pp. 630-659.

Urdang, Laurence. Ed. *The Timetables of American History*. New York: Simon and Schuster, 1981.

Wilson, William H. "'More Almost Than the Men': Mira Lloyd Dock and the Beautification of Harrisburg." *Pennsylvania Magazine of History and Biography*, 99 (October 1975), pp. 490-499.

_____ . "Harrisburg's Successful City Beautiful Movement, 1900-1915." *Pennsylvania History*, 47 (July 1980), pp. 213-233.

Woodside, Robert E. *My Life and Town*. Millersburg, Pa.: n.p., 1979.

Unpublished Sources

Africa, Mrs. Benjamin F. "A Century Ago—Harrisburg and its Residents, As Described by Anne Royall." Lecture, Historical Society of Dauphin County (hereafter HSDC), December 19, 1932. TS.

Allen, Jean Gray. Scrapbooks of Harrisburg newspaper clippings, 1957-59, 1961. HSDC.

Bowman, A.M., comp. "Narratives Regarding the Northern March of the Confederates During the War of the Rebellion." Folder No. 2, TI-7. Dull Collection. HSDC. TS.

"Constitution of the Anti-Slavery Society of Harrisburg, 1836." HSDC. MS.

Crist, R.W. "Harrisburg and the War Effort." Lecture, HSDC, September 20, 1943. TS.

Demming, Col. Henry C. "Reminiscences of Harrisburg During the 60's." Lecture, HSDC, December 14, 1922. TS.

_____ . Letter to Casper Dull, October 15, 1900. Folder No. 4, TI-9. Dull Collection. HSDC. TS.

Detweiler, Bertha Hoffer, comp. Scrapbooks of Harrisburg Newspaper Clippings, 1926-1945. Nos. 1, 5, 9, 11, 15, 28. HSDC.

Drawbaugh, Allen. (sic) Scrapbooks of Notes on Steelton. HSDC. TS.

"For 'Tippecanoe and Tyler Too': The Whig National Convention at Harrisburg." Lecture, HSDC, n.d. TS.

Gorgas, William L. Statement on Confederate Invasion of Pennsylvania. Folder No. 3, TI-8. Dull Collection. HSDC. TS.

Gross, Col. Henry. "Reminiscences of Early Harrisburg." Lecture, HSDC, June 16, 1958. TS.

Hamilton, A. Boyd. Scrapbooks of Harrisburg Newspaper Clippings, 1912, 1935-1938. HSDC.

"The Harrisburg Anti-Slavery Society." Lecture, HSDC, December 1911. MS.

Harrisburg League for Municipal Improvements. Scrapbook, 1902. HSDC.

Keller, J.P. "Personal Recollections. A Few Leading Events in Harrisburg 50 Years Ago." Lecture, HSDC, c1896. MS.

_____ . "Personal Recollections of Earlier Days in Harrisburg." Lecture, HSDC, May 9, 1901. MS.

_____ . "As Others See Us." Lecture, HSDC, June 14, 1906. TS.

Kunkle, Dr. Beverly Waugh. "Genetic (sic) and Geneology of Front Street." Lecture, HSDC, October 1967. TS.

Liebman, Caroline, comp. Data From Patient Records, State Lunatic Hospital of Pennsylvania, Harrisburg,

Pa., 1851-1874. MS in author's possession.

Malmsheimer, Lonna. "And You Were Worried About the Bomb? Image, Fiction, and Frame in the Three-Mile Island Emergency." TS in author's possession.

Miller, Evan J. "When the Circus Came to Harrisburg." Lecture, HSDC, May 18, 1981. TS.

Miller, Herman P. "Early Recollections." Lecture, HSDC, n.d. TS.

Milspaw, Yvonne, and Julius Kassovic. "A Folklorist Perspective on the Three Mile Island Accident." TS in author's possession.

Pearson, William, Sr. "My Early Recollections of Front Street Between Mulberry and Walnut Streets." Lecture, HSDC, n.d. TS.

Rutherford, D.I. "Reminiscences of the War: Capt. James Elder's Company in the Emergency of 1862." Lecture, HSDC, n.d. TS.

Settino, David Lee. "Steelton's Cultural Development." TS in author's possession.

Simonton, Mrs. John (Sallie). Diary, March 16-18, 1865. HSDC. MS.

Simonton, William. "Notes on My Recollections of Country Life in West Hanover Township, Dauphin County, Pennsylvania, in the Thirties of the Nineteenth Century, 1904." HSDC. MS.

Stoner, Carl B., Sr. "Between Shipoke and Goat Town." Lecture, HSDC, March 14, 1966. TS.

Swallow, Rev. Silas C. "The Susquehanna—Navigable Yet Unnavigable." Lecture, HSDC, March 11, 1915. MS.

Wallower, E.Z. "Reminiscences of Old Harrisburg." Lecture, HSDC, November 1930. TS.

Warfel, Stephen G. "The Prehistory of Dauphin County, Pennsylvania." Lecture, HSDC, October 20, 1980. TS.

Weitzel, Walter M. "Some History and Use of the Susquehanna." Lecture, HSDC, June 15, 1931. TS.

Young, R.I. Diary, June 22-July 5, 1863. HSDC. MS.

WAKE UP! THEY'RE LOOKING AT YOU

Index

Italicized numbers indicate illustrations.

Partners in Progress

Allen Company, Inc., Albert L., 181
AMP Incorporated, 184-187
Aycock, Inc., 200
Benatec Associates, Inc., 180
Berman, Boswell & Tintner, 195
Capital Blue Cross, 174-175
Chamber of Commerce of the Greater
  Harrisburg Area, 152
Commonwealth National Bank, 162-163
Eshenaur's Inc., 211
Farmers Bank and Trust Company of
  Hummelstown, The, 193
Gannett Fleming, Inc., 156
Grim Company, R.T,, 208
Harrisburg Academy, 201
Harrisburg Area Community College,
  179
Hershey Creamery Company, 209
Hershey Entertainment & Resort
  Company, 210
Hood, Light and Geise, Inc., 166
IBM Field Engineering Division, 212-213
Iceland Seafood Corporation, 164
Inclinator Company of America, 191
Independent Bankers of Pennsylvania,
  214
Kessler's, Inc., 165
Kinney Shoe Corporation, 206-207
Kitzmiller's, Inc., 204
Latsha Lumber Company, Earl, 153
McNees, Wallace and Nurick, 167
Manpower, Inc., of Harrisburg, 215
Merchants and Business Men's Mutual
  Insurance Company, 154-155
Nationwide Insurance Company, 176-178
Novinger's, Inc., 190
Olewine's Incorporated, 202-203
Patriot-News Publishing Company, 157
Pennsylvania Blue Shield, 172-173
Pennsylvania Credit Union League,
  170-171
Pennsylvania Medical Society, 196-197
Pennsylvania National Mutual Casualty
  Insurance Company, 158-159
PHICO Insurance Group, 199
Quaker Oats Company, The, 182-183
Rite Aid Corporation, 160-161
Rockey Company, Inc., G.S., 205
Romberger & Sons, R.J., 194
Shammo's Quality Foods, 198
Stephenson's Flower Shops, 169
TRW, Inc., 188-189
United Republic Life Insurance
  Company, 168
Wert Bookbinding, Inc., 192

A

Adams, John, 41
American Anti-Slavery Society, 41
American Society for the Promotion of
  Temperance, 41
AMP Incorporated, 127, 128
Annals of Harrisburg (book), 26, 29
Anti-slavery movement, 41, 42, 45
Appalachian Mountains, 18

B

Baldwin, 147
Battle of Gettysburg, 57, 58, 60, 65, 150
Beers, Paul, 22, 123
Bellevue Park, 88
Beth-El Temple, *112*
Bettman, Otto, 67
Black Horse Cavalry, 62
Black residents, 69, 94, 96, 107, 108, 112,
  118, 119, 123, 124
Blessed Martin Home, 118
Blue Ridge Country Club, 122
Board of Trade, 85
Bodnar, John, 93, 94, 96
Boehm, Henry, *45*
Bolton Hotel, *73*
Bowman, A.M., 58
Bowman, Z., 58
Boyer, Charles, 70, 72
Boyer, "Pappy," 66
Breck, Samuel, 29
Brinton, Martin, 58
British residents, 77, 108, 112
Brown, John W., 72
Bruner, James, 108
Bulgarian immigrants, 92, 94
Burd home, James, *32*
"Busy Bee, The" (advertisement), *110*

C

Caldarelli, Carrie, 122
Caldarelli, Dom, 122
Caldarelli, Joe, 122
Caldarelli, Vince, 122
Calder Street School, 78
Camelback Bridge, *18, 19, 131,* 150
Cameron, Donald, 65
Cameron, Mrs. James, *118*
Cameron, Simon, *43,* 55, 65, 67, 80
Campbelltown, 148
Camp Boas, *14*
Camp Curtin, 62, 63, 70; military
  hospital of, *56*
Camp Hill, 57, 58, 60, 65, 149, 150
Capitol Campus, Pennsylvania State
  University, *127*
Capitol Park Extension, 72
Carlisle, 36, *65,* 147, 151
Catholics, 107, 112, 118, 119
Catholic Workers, 118, 119

Cemetery Ridge, 58
Central Division of the Sons of
  Temperance, 43, 44; constitution of,
  43, 44
Chartier, Martin, 150
Chartier, Peter, 150
Chesapeake Bay, 18
"City Beautiful" movement, 83, 84, 85,
  86, 87, 88, 89, 116
City Island, 21
"City Practical" movement, 116, 117,
  118, 119
Civic Club, 87
Civil War, 47, 57, 58, 59, 60, 62, 63, 65,
  67, 70, 99, 150
Claster Wholesale Notion Store, Jos., *80*
Commonweal, 118
Commonwealth Hotel, *39*
Conestoga Indians, 146, 149. *See also*
  Susquehannock Indians
Cook, Harry, 67, 68, 69, 72; funeral of,
  67, 68
Cook, Hattie, 68, 70
Coolidge, Calvin, 111
Cox, John B., 76
Crist, Robert, 150
Croatian immigrants, 92, 94
Cross, Samuel, 42
Cumberland County, 151
Cumberland Valley Railroad Bridge,
  131
Curwen, John, 48, *49,* 50, 51
Cutler, Manasseh, 37

D

Daugherty, Eli, 76
Dauphin County, 111, 147, 148
Dauphin County Centennial
  Celebration of 1885, 75, 76, 77, 78, 79,
  80, 81; Children's Day, 75, 76, 77, 78,
  79, 80; Firemen's Day, 76; Industrial
  Display Day, 76; Military and Civic
  Day, 76; welcoming arch of, *81*
Dauphin County Court House, 42, 80,
  81
Dauphin Narrows, *22*
Day, Dorothy, 117, 118, 119
Delaware Indians, 149. *See also* Lenape
  Indians
Demming, Henry, 60, 62, 63
Depression, Great, 113, 115, 148
Derry Church, 148
Derry Township, 146, 148
Dewees, Samuel, 37
Dewitt, William R., 43
Dill, Malcolm, 116
Dix, Dorothea, *49*
Dock, Mira Lloyd, *85,* 86, 89
Dock Street Dam, 23
Donehoo, George P., 33
Douglass, Frederick, *42*
Draper, E.S., 116

Drawbaugh, Daniel, 150
Dull, Casper, 58, 60, 62
Dwight, Margaret, 37

E
Early, D.S., 76
East Pennsboro Township, 149
Eberly Mills, 150
Egle, William Henry, 30, 31, 47, *76*
Eighth Ward, 68, *69,* 70, 72, *73*
Elder house, John, *45*
Enola, 149
Entertainment, 75, 76, 83, 85, 88, *104,*
  112. *See also* Sports and recreation
Evening News, 122
Ewington, 147
Eysler's Drug Store, *79*

F
Fairview Township, 149
Farm Show Arena, *142*
Federal Building, *144*
Find Brewing Company
  (advertisement), *113*
First National Bank (poster), *64*
Fleming, Charles, 58
Fleming Mansion, *131*
Flooding, 18, *19,* 20, 115, 125, 148;
  Agnes flood, *124*
Forrer, Junior, *107*
Fort Couch, 150
Fort Delaware, 62
Fort Washington, *60*
Franklin, Nibs, 123
French residents, 77
Fuertes, James, 86
Furness, Frank, 67

G
Gall, Ludwig, 37, 39
Garrison, William Lloyd, 41, *42*
Geety, W. Wallace, 76
German residents, 37, 77, 94, 108, 112,
  150; taufshein of, *14*
Gettysburg, 57, 58, 65, *94*
Gettysburg College, 149
Gilbert, Lyman D., 108
Gilbert, Mrs. Lyman D., 108
Golden Sheaf (hotel), *37*
Gottschalk, Louis Moreau, *38*
Governor's Mansion, 123
Grand Opera House, 67, 125
Grant, Ulysses S., *38,* 75
Greater Harrisburg Chamber of
  Commerce's Industrial Survey of
  1928, 111, 112, 113

H
Hamilton, A. Boyd, 36
Hampden Township, 149
Harder, Warren, 150
Harris, George W., 26

Harris, John, *6-7,* 18, 25, 26, 29, 30, 31,
  33, 62, 67, 149, 150; attempted
  burning of, *24,* 25-26, *28, 29,* 30, 31, 33,
  79, *130;* home of, *32, 36, 139*
Harris, Robert, 29
Harris, William, 81
Harrisburg, population of: (1915), 88;
  (1928), 112; (1950), 121, 122; (1957),
  122; (1980), 122
*Harrisburg, The City Beautiful, Romantic,
  and Historic* (book), 33
Harrisburg Academy, 123
Harrisburg Anti-Slavery Society, 42;
  constitution of, 42
Harrisburg Area Chamber of
  Commerce, *136*
Harrisburg City Hospital, *135*
Harrisburg *Daily Telegraph,* 60, 62, 83,
  84, 85, 86
Harrisburg Fire Department, *77*
Harrisburg Hospital, 33
Harrisburg Housing Authority, 117
Harrisburg League for Municipal
  Improvement, 86, 87, 88, 116, 119
Harrisburg Nail Works, *97*
Harrisburg Post Office, *72*
Harrisburg Public Library, *136;*
  bookmobile of, *101*
Harrisburg Tech, 111; football team of,
  113
Harrisburg Telegraph, 72
Harrisburg Transfer Company, 90;
  "Morton Truck," *90*
Harrisburg Wheel Club, *74*
Harris' Ferry, *36,* 150
Harris High School, John, 111
Harris Park, 62, 77, 78
Harris Park School, *78*
Hart, Mary, 122
Hart, Ross, 122
Hay, Charles A., *59*
Hercules, *29, 30,* 31, 33
Hershey, Milton S., 125, 148
Hershey, 146, 147, 148, 149
Hershey Foods, 148
Hershey Medical Center, Milton S., *142*
Hersheypark, 124
Highspire, 146
Historical Society of Dauphin County,
  21, 26, 27, 43, 58, 76
Hockersville, 148
Hoffsommer, Robert, 33
Hoover Jewelry Store, E.G., *87*
Hotel Hershey, 148
Houser, Mary, 122
Houser, Roy, 122
Houston, Ralph "Cub," *98,* 99, 100, *105,
  107, 109;* memories of ragtime, 100-
  104, 106-108
Howe, Lyman, 106
Hummelstown, 146, 149
Hummelstown Homecoming Parade, *118*

Hungarian residents, 112

I
Immigration Act of 1924, 93
Independence Rope Island Ferry, *36*
Indians, 25, 26, 29, 30, 33, 146, 149, 151
Indian Wars, 146
Inglewood, Marian, 30, 31, 33
Irish residents, 37, 42, 77, 94, 108, 112,
  146
Iroquois Nation, 149
Irving College, *106*
Island Park, 84, 88
Italian residents, 77, 108, 112

J
Jackson, Andrew, 41
Jefferson, Thomas, 41
Jewish Community Center, 122
Jewish residents, 69, 92, 94, 107, 108,
  122
Johnson, T.B., *106,* 107, 108
Jones House, 36

K
Keefer, Norman, 150
Kelker, Luther Reily, 30, 31
Keller, J.P., 20, 37
Kelso Ferry House, *20*
Kelso Tavern, William, 150
Klink, Verna, 111
Knipe, Joseph, 60, *61*

L
Lafayette Hall, 68, 69, 70
Lancaster, 146, 147
Lancaster Caramel Company, 148
Lancaster County, 146
Layton, W.H., 78
Lee, Robert E., 57, 58
Lemoyne, 149, 150
Lenape Indians, 149. *See also* Delaware
  Indians
Levittown, 116
Lewis, C., 42-43
Liberator, The, 41
Lincoln, Abraham, *38,* 68, 124
Lincoln School, 78
Lind, Jenny, *38*
Lochiel Church, 43
Lochiel Train Wreck, 125, 148
Londonderry Township, 146
Louther Manor, 149, 150
Lower Allen Township, 149
Lower Paxton Township, 146, 147, 149,
  150
Lower Swatara Township, 146
Lutherans, 107, 112
Lyceum, 85

M
McCormick, Vance, 86, 116

McCormick, Mrs. Vance, *118*
McFarland, J. Horace, 86, 88, 89, *96*, 116
McKinley, William, *38*
McKinney, Mordecai, 42
McPherson, John Bayard, 80, 81
Magyar immigrants, 92, 94
Manning, Warren, 86
Market Square, 36
Marysville, 149
Masonic Temple, 84
Mater, John, 59-60
Meade, George, 57, 58
Mechanicsburg, 58, 149, 150, 151
Methodists, 39, 107, 112
Middle Paxton Township, 146
Middletown, 57, 63, 65, 146, 147
Millen, Harry O., 79
Miller, Herman, 88
Miller, Kate, 78
Millersburg Ferry, 21
Mitchell, "General," *40*
Morgan, George, 26, 29, 30, 31
Mumma, Elsie, 149
Mumma, Isaac, *71*

N
National Geographic, 106
New Cumberland, 58, 149, 150
Nixon, Richard M., 124

O
O'Hara, John, 122
Old Home Week Parade of 1905, *82*
Order of United American Mechanics'
  Steelton Chapter, 96
Orpheum Hall, 106
Oyster's Point, 58, 150

P
Pancake Row, 122
Park Commission, 89
Parkland, 88
Pastor's Aid Society of the Pine Street
  Church, *118*
Patriot, 30, 149
Paxtang, 146
Paxtang church, 30, 31
Paxtang school, 78
Paxton Boys, *31*, 146, 147
Paxton Church, 146
Paxton Creek, 87
Paxton Furnaces, *97*
Paxton Park, *135*
Paxton Rolling Mills, *97*
Peace Church, 150
Pearson, John, *71*
Penn, John, 37
Penn, William, 25, 37, 148
Pennbrook, 146
Penn family, 149, 150
Penn Harris Hotel, *125*
Penn Museum, William, *139*

Pennsylvania Canal and Towpath, *22, 23*, 147
*Pennsylvania Magazine of History and
  Biography*, 37
Pennsylvania National Horse Show, *142*
Pennsylvania Railroad, 70, 72; GG-1
  electric locomotive, *117*
Pennsylvania State Capitol, 68, *84*, 125,
  129, 137; dedication souvenirs, *134*;
  dome of, *27*
Pennsylvania State Lunatic Hospital, *46,
  47, 48, 49, 50, 51, 52, 53, 55*; entrance to
  48
Pennsylvania Steel Company, 86, 147
Perry County, 150
Planning Commission, 89
Polish residents, 92
Poor Man's Fishing Club, *87*
Presbyterians, 43, 107, 112
Profiles from the Susquehanna Valley
  (book), 33

R
A Rage to Live (book), 122
Reading Railroad Bridge, *19*
Reeder, William S., 29
Reist's Dance Bowl, George, 111
Religion, 49, 96, 112, 113, 146, 147, 150
Rescue Mission, 72
Reservoir Park, 88, *133*
Revolution, American, 35, 147
Reynders, John, 86
Riverfront Park, 33
Rockville Bridge, *71, 77, 137*
Roosevelt, Theodore, *38*, 83
Rowhouses, 100, 113, 116
Royal Canadian Mounted Police
  Musical Drill Team, *142*
Royalton, 146
Rudy, Jonas K., *70*
Rupp, I. Daniel, 26, 29, 31
Russian residents, 69, 112
Rutherford, William, 42

S
St. Patrick's Cathedral, 107, 118, *134*
St. Peters Kirk (church), 147
St. Stephen's Episcopal Church, 42
Sayford, Samuel, 70
Schlitzer, Elsie, 122
Schlitzer, Ralph, 122
Schwab, Charles M., *92*
Scottish immigrants, 146
Scranton, William, *120*
Serbian immigrants, 92, 94
Sharfman, Bern, 149
Shawnee Indians, 149
Sherred, M.R., 86
Shipoke, 23, 122, *123*
Shopp, Samuel, 58, 59
Silver Spring, 149
Simonton, Sallie, 18, 23

Simonton, William, 44
Simpson's Ferry, 150, 151
"Sixteen Bleeders," 70
Slovenian immigrants, 92, 94
Snyder, John, *71*
Sports and recreation, 73, 76, 83, 85, 88,
  104, 112. See also Entertainment
State Street Bridge Gang, 70
State Theatre, *123*
Steel industry, 91, 92, 94, 96, *97*, 121,
  147
Steelton, 91, 93, 94, 96, 146, 147, 148
Steinmetz, Sr., Richard, 33
Stem, Nathan, 42
Strawberry Square, *127*
Susquehanna (steamboat), 21
Susquehanna River, 17, 18, *21, 22, 23*,
  25, 26, 36, 62, 70, *88, 127, 128, 143*, 151
Susquehanna Township, 146
Susquehannock Indians, 146, 149. *See
  also* Conestoga Indians
Swallow, Silas, 20-21
Swatara Township, 146
Swedish residents, 77, 108

T
Taylor, M. Harvey, 89
Taylor, Maris Harve, *120*, 121, *122, 127*
Temperance movement, 41, 42, 43, 44,
  45
This Was Harrisburg (book), 33
Thomas, Finley, 76, 78, 81
Three Mile Island Nuclear Power Plant,
  126, 147
Thurston, Howard, 106
Tinian, 32
Trautmann, Frederick, 37
Trinity Evangelical Lutheran Church,
  138
Trundle Springs, 150

U
"Uncle Ben," 23
Underground Railroad, 42
Union Canal, 147
United States Immigration
  Commission, 92, 93, 94, 95; report of
  1911, 93, 94, 95
Upper Paxton Township, 146
USO (United Service Organization)
  Floating Club, *119*

V
Verbeke Street School, 78
Vietnam War, 124
"View of Harrisburg," *10-11*

W
Wallower Mansion, 123
Washington, George, 33, *34*, 36, 37
Weber, Hannah, 55
Weitbrecht, J.H.M., 62

Wert, J. Howard, 72
West Fairview, 149
West Harrisburg Market House
  Company, *102*
Whiskey Rebellion, 36
Whitehall Farm (painting), *131*
White Hill, 58
Whitehill, Robert, 150
WHP (radio station), 111
Wilson, William H., 85, 86, 87, 88, 89
Wilson, Woodrow, 99
Wissel, Peter, 39
Wistar Iron Works, *97*
World War I, 99, 100
World War II, 121

Y
Yellow Breeches, 149, 150
York County, 102, 111, 150
Young, R.I., 63, 65
Young Men's and Young Ladies' Total
  Abstinence Society of Harrisburg, 43
Young Men's Christian Association
  building, 85, 106; Fahnestock Hall,
  106

Z
Zion Lutheran Church, *59*

The Chamber of Commerce-
Greater Harrisburg Area has
sponsored *Life By The Moving
Road* in fondest memory of
John H. Baum.

HISTORY BOOK ADVISORY COMMITTEE

John M. Aichele
Milton Hershey School

William H. Alexander
H.B. Alexander & Son

John F. Banghart
United States Fidelity & Guaranty
Company

Paul B. Beers
The Patriot-News Company

Edward R. Book
Hershey Entertainment and Resort
Company

Joseph K. Goldsmith
Goldsmith/Flanigan

Spencer G. Hall
Commonwealth National Bank

Leonard Kessler
The Book-of-the-Month Club

Wilson D. Lewis
Dauphin Deposit Bank & Trust (retired)

Harold S. Mohler
Hershey Foods Corporation

Gilbert Nurick, Esq.
McNees, Wallace & Nurick

Paul H. Rhoads, Esq.
Rhoads, Sinon & Hendershot

Richard D. Rife
Capital Blue Cross

Morris Schwab
D & H Distributing Company

Joseph T. Simpson
HARSCO Corporation

John C. Tuten
Hamilton Bank